Julian Lindsay
February 8, 1963

4.V.74
6.50
.05
_____
8 5.85

Reason and the Imagination

Reason and the Imagination

Studies in the History of Ideas
1600–1800

Edited by

J. A. MAZZEO

NEW YORK: Columbia University Press
LONDON: Routledge & Kegan Paul
1962

First published 1962
by Columbia University Press
Columbia University, New York
and Routledge & Kegan Paul Ltd
68–74 Carter Lane, London, E.C.4
Made and printed in Great Britain
by William Clowes and Sons, Limited
London and Beccles

Library of Congress
Catalog Card Number: 62–7773

Contents

v

FOREWORD

T HIS volume is designed as a tribute to a distinguished scholar, Marjorie Hope Nicolson, as she moves from a sphere of action bounded by official limits to others not so bounded. Obviously, it could have been much larger or very different. The form it has taken is the result of deliberate policy. The friends, former students, and colleagues who began in 1959 to lay plans for such a book agreed from the start that Marjorie Nicolson would not be best honoured with a collection of essays so miscellaneous in character that they would have to be 'yoked by violence together.' They therefore chose a subject, the history of ideas in the seventeenth and eighteenth centuries, and the editors guided their requests for contributions accordingly. The book is thus intended to honour Miss Nicolson by contributing to the specific field in which she has done her own work—in the very idiom, so to speak, of her own scholarship.

Even for a book so designed, the number of possible contributors was far in excess of the number of contributions for which space was available. Selection had to proceed on rigid principles. The editors decided to seek essays both from Miss Nicolson's distinguished compeers and from her former students. By giving half of the space to contributions from men and women trained under her, we wished to signalize her work as a teacher. These essays, in addition to their public meanings, will carry those private meanings created by the bonds between teacher and student, known only to their authors, with whom she shared her humanity and knowledge. A great teacher is also a great student, and we are delighted to remind her of that by including a contribution from one of her own teachers, A. O. Lovejoy.

To the several authors of this volume, the editors give their heart-felt thanks. A work of this kind requires an unusual degree of self-abnegation on the part of its authors. Its existence is ample witness that the fullest measure of co-operation from all was forthcoming.

The editorial board that assumed responsibility for bringing the book into being consisted of Rosalie Colie, Eleanor Rosenberg, Miriam Starkman, James L. Clifford, William Nelson, and myself. To their number I should add, *honoris causa*, Henry Wiggins of the Columbia University Press, whose office (when our work had sufficiently progressed) became the clearing house for all our transactions, and Vergene F. Leverenz, also of the Press, who gave the manuscripts the final editorial touches that turned them into one book. The hard work, patience, efficiency, and tact of all the editors left me, as chairman of their group, with little to do but enjoy the fruit of their labours.

I think I can speak for all associated with the making of this book when I confess that it will no doubt be found to have its faults of omission and commission. Of the general reader we ask no quarter, but of our teacher and friend we ask to be judged by our intention, expressing our hope that 'though she could not transubstantiate all states to gold, yet' she may have 'gilded every state.'

J. A. MAZZEO

MIRIAM K. STARKMAN

Noble Numbers
and the Poetry of Devotion

To examine Robert Herrick's *Noble Numbers* is to be thrust into arithmetic. Except for some small clusters of poems centred around a common subject, form, or source, the order of the volume appears to be entirely fortuitous. Of the two hundred and seventy-two poems, one hundred and seventeen, or very close to half the total volume, are couplets. They are, variously, proverbial, apophthegmatic, epigrammatic, doctrinal, or gnomic. Their function is clearly and immediately didactic. They are almost always perfectly orthodox in their Anglicanism, except that Herrick is a little liberal with the doctrine of predestination. Their chief sources are Scripture and the Church Fathers, particularly the later ones; some few stem from current exegetical writings, notably John Gregory's *Notes and Observations upon Some Passages of Scripture* of 1646; some depend upon the moral wisdom of the Ancients; some few are directly proverbial in origin.[1] Fully half of these one hundred and seventeen couplets are upon the subject of God specifically, many using the word *God* in their titles.

God cannot be defined; He is an *Ens* as well as a *Supra-*

---

[1] See *Poetical Works of Robert Herrick*, ed. by L. C. Martin (Oxford, 1956), for all references to and quotations from Herrick's text; I have preserved Martin's spellings, punctuation, and italics; my indebtedness to his notes is obvious.

entitie; He requires of us the two spotless lambs, prayers and praise; He loads with blessing and unloads from sin; He is all fore-part; God watches while we sleep, sleeps while we watch; He has whips to punish the bad and amend the good; He is most Holy when He is most one; there is none small among God's blessings; to seek God over-much 'argues a strong distemper of the mind'; God's bounty ebbs as man's thanksgiving wanes; in God all is 'perfect Entitie'; God is called Jehovah, which implies Essence; etc.

The majority of these couplets fall somewhere between the technical doctrine of:

> God (as the learned *Damascen* doth write)
> A *Sea of Substance* is, *Indefinite*.
>
> (*God*, 381)

and the homely wisdom of:

> Honour thy Parents; but good manners call
> Thee to adore thy God, the first of all.
>
> (*God to be first serv'd*, 363)

Although a good many of these couplets have a catechetical concern with the definition of God, most of them are devoted to an emphasis on the one God with the two hands, with the stripes and the balm, the rod and the staff.

Of the other fifty per cent of the single couplets in *Noble Numbers*, that is those that are not specifically on the subject of God, the themes turn on a variety of Christian thought and belief in similar doctrinal and apophthegmatic vein. Some few are on Christ:

> To all our wounds, here, whatsoe're they be,
> *Christ* is the one sufficient *Remedie*.
>
> (*Christ*, 390)

—the emphasis being on the humane concern of the Son of God. For the rest: fear, shame, and guilt are the three fatal sisters; the Devil tempts God's saints most; the thankful receive more of God's gifts; the heart must follow the lips; Sin is most horrible when acted upon; dead faith is like a dead lamp; Satan cannot work upon us without our consent; sinfulness becomes habitual; Sin was expelled from Heaven; Sin is the loss of good; Christians need offensive as well as defensive weapons; man is

2

punished for not using his will; Hell is a bottomless, comfortless pit; and so on.

Looking closely into these fifty or so couplets, one sees a basic antithesis operating between them and the couplets previously mentioned: to be estranged from God is to be embedded in sin; sin will damn us unless God saves us; the Christian must make the choice between good and evil. Together these hundred-odd couplets turn on the fundamental axis of salvation and damnation. These couplets are, indeed, simple, but they are scarcely naïve; they represent, rather, a reduction to, an achieved, simplicity.

The proportion of this kind of didactic verse in *Noble Numbers* rises sharply if we admit to its category those verses which have the same subject, rhetorical and logical pattern, but which, instead of being single, are built on multiples of the couplet; of these most are two couplets, double distichs as it were, and the rest three, four, five, and even six couplets; these bring the total of such didactic verses to roughly two hundred of the two hundred and seventy-two verses that comprise *Noble Numbers*. Except that the effect is cumulative, the subject either more complex or more carefully analysed, these four- to twelve-line verses do not differ in quality from the single couplets. And half of them are, again, on the subject of God:

> God when for sin He makes His Children smart,
> His own He acts not, but another part:
> But when by stripes He saves them, then 'tis known,
> He comes to play the part that is His own.
>
> (*God has a twofold part*, 343)

> These temp'rall goods God (the most Wise) commends
> To th'good and bad, in common, for two ends:
> First, that these goods none here may o're esteem,
> Because the wicked do partake of them:
> Next, that these ills none cowardly may shun;
> Being, oft here, the just man's portion.
>
> (*Temporall goods*, 387)

> God hates the *Duall Number*; being known
> The lucklesse number of division;
> And when He blest each sev'rall Day, whereon
> He did His *curious operation*;

3

'Tis never read there (as the Fathers say,)
God blest His work done on the *second day*:
Wherefore two prayers ought not to be said,
Or by our selves, or from the Pulpit read.

(The number of two, 396)

The other half of these multiple-couplet verses, like the single couplets, go ranging over the field of religious wisdom.

Of these two hundred couplet verses, three-quarters are pentameters, the rest tetrameters. And even within their strict confines, Herrick's metrical skill displays itself in their integrity, flexibility, their varied disposition of pause and cadence, in their fluency, their variety. They suit the didactic intention admirably; where the content is dogmatic, the movement is chiselled, antithetical; where the material is more affective, the movement is less fixed, fluid.

Many streams of influence flow into this couplet wisdom, but it would be superfluous to search too far into Herrick's remote past for their sources, for the age was crowded with *sententiae* and the complex was ready at hand. A rich amalgam of well Christianized distich wisdom, primer and catechism piety, pious epigrams, the proverb and emblem tag, secular epigram, and apophthegm was available to him. Some of Herrick's couplets call to mind the very earliest of propitiatory distichs; the *Disticha Catonis* were still being used in the schools for their exemplary piety and morality, and easy Latin.[1] For the origins of the more specifically doctrinal couplets, one has but to turn to primer and catechism, of which multitudes were available. Proverbs were approved didactic devices, though like Herbert's *Jaculum Prudentum* and *Outlandish Proverbs* they tended to be largely secular in emphasis.[2] As for the sacred epigram, its widespread use in Reformation and Counter-Reformation indicates its utility as a didactic, doctrinal instrument. In Quarles and his followers we may see how the emblem tag became a vehicle for

[1] See *Dicta Catonis*, in *Minor Latin Poems*, ed. and trans. by Arnold M. Duff (Cambridge, 1934; Loeb Classical Library). See also Donald Leman Clark, *John Milton at St. Paul's School* (New York, 1948), pp. 110, 114, 117.

[2] Compare 'He that will enter into Paradise, must have a good key' (*O.P.* 895) and 'The Divell never assailes a man, except he find him either void of knowledge, or of the fear of God' (*J.P.* 1176), in *Works of George Herbert*, ed. by F. E. Hutchinson (Oxford, 1953), pp. 350, 361.

pious sententiousness.[1] And gnomic verse already absorbed into devotional poetry is to be seen clearly in Herbert's 'Church Porch' as it may have stemmed from Southwell and ultimately from the wisdom poetry of collections like Tottle's *Miscellany*.[2]

What constituted the immediate occasion of these verses for Herrick one can only conjecture: were they his commonplace-book gleanings, his parochial primer or catechism, his pious emblems, his *Epigrammata Sacra*, his *Christian Doctrine*, or a combination of several or all of them? This much, however, seems clear: that their mode of discourse is largely plain statement, that they have an immediate didactic, almost dogmatic, intention, and that in large measure they give *Noble Numbers* its characteristic tone.

With some notable exceptions to be discussed later, the remaining third of the volume may be characterized as consisting of prayers and praises, of which the majority, some forty verses, fall into the category of affective prayers. About half of these are built solidly on the pentameter and tetrameter couplet, the rest ranging through a variety of fairly complex stanzaic patternings. Their emotional range is broad, from the utmost certainty of salvation to the most palpable doubt and anguish, the whole range between the extreme 'poles of adoration and penitence.'[3] Most are addressed to God, some few to Christ.

Perhaps the most complex of these affective prayers, *To his sweet Saviour* (358), is notable for its virtuosity of versification, its subtle shifting of pause and cadence in restless movement from detail to detail of the central image of the race of life, all adapted to the delineation of hasting time and the tormented struggle of the suffering soul and body:

> Night hath no wings, to him that cannot sleep;
> And Time seems then, not for to flie, but creep;
> Slowly her chariot drives, as if that she
> Had broke her wheele, or crackt her axeltree.

---

[1] See Rosemary Freeman, *English Emblem Books* (London, 1948), chap. 5. For Herrick's rare emblematic usage, see *Beggars* (383) and *Gods Hands* (380).

[2] Louis Martz, *Poetry of Meditation* (New Haven, 1954), p. 198.

[3] Evelyn Underhill, *Worship* (New York, 1957; Harper Torchbooks), p. 228.

Just so it is with me, who list'ning, pray
The winds, to blow the tedious night away;
That I might see the cheerfull peeping day.
Sick is my heart; O Saviour do thou please
To make my bed soft in my sicknesses:
Lighten my candle, so that I beneath
Sleep not for ever in the vaults of death:
Let me Thy voice betimes i'th morning heare;
Call, and I'le come; say Thou, the when, and where:
Draw me, but first, and after Thee I'le run,
And make no one stop, till my race be done.

Sometimes the movement of these affective prayers is as neatly antithetical as in the didactic couplets:

Here give me thornes; there, in thy Kingdom, set
Upon my head the golden coronet;
There give me day; but here my dreadful night:
My sackcloth here; but there my *Stole* of white.

(To God, 343)

At the other extreme, *Another to God* (351) illustrates Herrick's stanzaic variety, his fondness for feminine rhyme, the irreducible simplicity of diction, syntax, and figure, the artfulness of Herrick's use of childhood to achieve a bedrock emotional honesty:

Lord, do not beat me,
Since I do sob and crie,
And swowne away to die,
Ere Thou dost threat me.

Lord, do not scourge me,
If I by lies and oaths
Have soil'd my selfe, or cloaths,
But rather purge me.

The images in these affective prayers are the conventional images of devotion. The Christian is a sinner wracked by darts and daggers; he is bruised, rent, wounded, tried in the fire, scourged, striped; he sighs and weeps and bleeds. He is a debtor, a prisoner at the bar who cannot repay the awesome debt he owes to Christ; he lays his case before the mercy seat; he is a child who has soiled himself with sin. Christ is the candle in the ark; He has the saving balm and balsam; He is broken and bruised for man; He drinks tears, and vinegar and gall for him; He is the strong tree around which the weak vine, man, clings; Life is a perilous journey, a race beset by obstacles, bars and stiles; it is a pathless, dark sea. Man stumbles, falls, creeps, crawls along the way. Time, the hasting chariot, will not wait for him. The sinner offers up sacrifices of lambs, ewes, rams, and bullocks; he decks the altar with flowers and jewels; he brings gold, and frankincense and myrrh. He pines to see the throne of God, the palms and stoles of white, to hear the harps and viols, the angels sing.

These images, then, are conventional in so far as they stem, ultimately, from Scripture, from liturgy, and from the literature of devotion. But it is to be noted that, in contrast to a usage like Herbert's, for example, Herrick's figures are symbolic only in the sense of a received rather than an exploited symbolism. Even his metaphor is subordinated to plain statement: 'Here give me thorns . . . there . . . the golden coronet.' Deeply felt and intently meant as Herrick's figures are, his devotional metaphorical mode has already travelled far from its allegorical and symbolic base, and like his didactic couplets moved on to a more rationalistic ground. The recognition of this fact, perhaps more than any other, makes for the discernment of the characteristic quality of *Noble Numbers*.

There is, however, another variety of prayer in *Noble Numbers*, the less affective, more intellectual prayers. They are frequently occasional in the sense that they are particular and personal; they are specifically Herrick's in contradistinction to most of the affective prayers, which might be prayed by any Christian. These intellectual prayers, then, are at a minimum, but it is interesting to note that they are the best known and loved, certainly the most reprinted and anthologized poems in *Noble Numbers*, as though we valued the volume for its atypicalities.

Of these poems, perhaps the most revealing are the ones which define Herrick's attitude towards his Sacred Muse, his prayers for his book. Conventionally apologetic for having entertained the secular Muse,[1] and deeply earnest of his whole duty as a Christian, Herrick makes his confession and apologia

[1] Lily B. Campbell, *Divine Poetry and Drama in Sixteenth Century England* (Los Angeles, 1959), *passim.*

7

for his 'unbaptized Rhimes' in the first three verses of *Noble Numbers*, his dedication to his Sacred Muse, which is God: *His Confession* ('our foule Dayes do exceed our faire'; 'Men are prone To do ten Bad, for one good Action'; though actually Herrick's proportion, in terms of *Hesperides* and *Noble Numbers*, is more like five to one); *His Prayer for Absolution*:

> For Those my unbaptized Rhimes,
> Writ in my wild unhallowed Times;
> For every sentence, clause and word,
> That's not inlaid with Thee, (my Lord)
> Forgive me God.

To finde God, the third of these poems, is much like *The Argument of his Book* of *Hesperides*; it is literally a 'finding out of the matter' of his book, as difficult as weighing the fire, measuring out the wind, distinguishing the floods, counting the inhabitants of the deep, and, finally, seeing 'Him / That rides the glorious *Cherubim.*' Elsewhere in the volume he voices his plea for 'one beame of Glory' to shine upon him and his 'Work' (*To God*, 371); his delight in his Book 'that *Thou, my God, art in't*' (*To God*, 355); his faith that his work will be acceptable to God:

> The work is done; now let my *Lawrell* be
> Given by none, but by Thy selfe, to me:
> That done, with Honour Thou dost me create
> Thy *Poet*, and Thy *Prophet Lawreat*.
>
> (*To God*, 398)

The conviction grows as we study these poems that we are by no means in the presence of some merely casual, conventionally struck off pious pieces, but of a seriously intentioned devotional work. But though Herrick, not unlike Milton, bespoke himself as prophet and poet (note too the quotation from Hesiod's *Theogonie* on the title-page of *Noble Numbers*), his characteristic manner is not prophetic; indeed, it stands at the opposite pole to prophecy, at the point of an utter dependence upon and acceptance of God the Father. It is this acceptance that makes for the pervasive image of the poet as child in *Noble Numbers*. But Herrick's use of childhood is not, like Vaughan's or Traherne's, a quest for the longed-for, lost, pristine innocence; it is rather an adult assumption of an *ingenu* role. Its essence is simplicity, and it is achieved without sentimentality

8

or strain. In this *ingenu* role the actual figure of the poet as child is only one aspect. It can be achieved in a variety of ways, as when, for example, the child acts as 'catalytic to adult character,'[1] when the tone is childlike. Devotionally it seems to stem from a great reverence for and identification with the Infant Jesus, the helpless Infant who helps all our woe. This childlike tone ought not to be confused with childishness, as is so often done in Herrick criticism.[2]

Although the childlike tone is often visible in Herrick's didactic couplets and in the affective prayers, it is most clearly manifest in the occasional, personal prayers. Take, for example, Herrick's treatment of the thanksgiving theme. His couplet on the subject is propitiatory:

> Thanksgiving for a former, doth invite
> God to bestow a second benefit.
>
> (*Thanksgiving*, 348)

See then *Another Grace for a Child* (364):

> Here a little child I stand,
> Heaving up my either hand;
> Cold as Paddocks though they be
> Here I lift them up to Thee
> For a Benizon to fall
> On our meat, and on us all. *Amen.*

If the little hands lifted up to God are cold, and the devotion somewhat hasty (note the rapid insistence set up by the trochaic usage), the thanksgiving is by no means cold or quick. Indeed, the more modest God's blessings, the more simple the giver of thanks, the more total is the thanksgiving:

> God! to my little meale and oyle
> Add but a bit of flesh, to boyle
> And thou my Pipkinnet shalt see,
> Give a *wave-offering* to Thee.
>
> (*To God*, 377)

---

[1] Martin Jarrett-Kerr, *Studies in Literature and Belief* (New York, 1954), p. 89.

[2] See F. W. Moorman, *Robert Herrick, A Biographical and Critical Study* (London, 1910), p. 137: 'the truth is that his conception of religion, in spite of his reading of the Fathers, was scarcely more mature than that of a child of eight.'

or:

> As my little Pot doth boyle
> We will keep this *Levell-Coyle*;
> That a Wave, and I will bring
> To my God, a Heave-offering.
>
> (*To God, his gift*, 397)

Herrick's *ingenu* role is most brilliantly exploited in *A Thanks-giving to God, for his House* (349 ff.). Heightened by the use of anticlimactic dimeters to rhyme with the tetrameter first line of each couplet, sustained through twenty-nine couplets in which the rhyme is never repeated, the versification of the piece is the reflection of the central irony that controls the poem. The blessings described are very small, but the thanks-giving is great. The irony is perhaps more involved than appears on the surface. For emerging from the thanksgiving is the most ingenuous questioning of the ways of God to man. See how little I ask, the poet seems to be saying, and how great my thanks-giving for the little I get, for the little house, the low porch, the worn threshold, the single daily egg, the little fire, the worts, the purslain, the water cress, and the beet.

Much the same kind of domestication, the intense and simple naturalizing of prayer, the assumption of a passive role that breeds strong Christian acceptance is to be seen in Herrick's *His Letanie, to the Holy Spirit* (347 f.), stemming from an artful wedding of litany and meditation both.[1] Of the litany only the refrain and methodical reiteration remain—'Sweet Spirit comfort me!' But this refrain achieves much; it provides an urgency and a feeling of complete abnegation to the Holy Spirit that produces the childlike quality of the poem. For the rest, the effect is achieved through a detailed composition of place, Robert Herrick on his death-bed. The details are purely naturalistic: he is 'Sick in heart, and sick in head,' the house sighs and weeps, the doctor's potions and pills fail, the bell tolls, the taper burns low, he can only nod to the priest 'cause my speech is now decayed,' the prospect of hell's flames 'Fright mine eares, and fright mine eyes.' In Herrick's medita-

---

[1] See Robert Parson's meditation on death as quoted partially in Martz, p. 137. Note that Herrick's specifically labelled *His Meditation on Death* (392) is technically more of a Horatian ode than a formal meditation.

tion on death there is no skull in evidence; even Herbert's represents a less comfortable acceptance.

To see all these strains merge, the didactic, the affective, the meditational, the domestic or naturalized, one has to look at the last nine poems of *Noble Numbers*, a kind of Holy Week sequence. Probably because of their subject matter, they avail themselves too of an earlier, a symbolic, usage that makes them comparable to certain of Herbert's poems. They have, further, a dramatic immediacy that, beyond their reliance upon the meditational composition of place, makes them perhaps the most interesting of the poems in *Noble Numbers*. They deserve to be better known.

A pageant-like quality informs them; they read almost like poems meant to be publicly performed, as though the priest and his congregation were engaged in pious mumming, in latter-day *ludi theatrales*. Stage directions are explicit; provision is made for recitation, song, and movement. But whether this illusion of lived experience is the result of the literal meditational manner, a *prosopopoeia*, an artful merging of past and present tenses, or a liturgical experience relived with more than usual ingenuousness, taken together these nine poems have an enormous effectiveness bred of a three-fold signification: the historical Crucifixion and the Resurrection; their liturgical re-creation in the events of Holy Week; and their real, or imagined, re-enactment in Devon. The effect of this sequence, thus, is simultaneously domestic and incarnational.

In the first of the series, *Good Friday: Rex Tragicus, or Christ going to His Crosse* (398 f.), the central image is a theatrical one. The poem begins:

> Put off Thy Robe of *Purple*, then go on
> To the sad place of execution:

and continues:

> The Crosse shall be Thy Stage; and Thou shalt there
> The spacious field have for Thy *Theater*.

Christ is depicted as the player king:

> Thou art that *Roscius*, and that markt-out man
> That must this day act the Tragedian,
> To wonder and affrightment: Thou art He,
> Whom all the flux of Nations comes to see;
> Not those poor Theeves that act their parts with Thee.

11

This 'scene' takes 'life and sense' from Christ. The robe is put off; the tormentor stands ready to 'pierce thy tender Feet and hands'; the sinful multitude stands by; the soldier is ready with his spear; the vinegar is prepared; the thieves stand by; Christ, the king, is ready to ascend the cross which is his throne, and proceeds to 'act' his Passion 'As Hell, and Earth and Heav'n may stand amaz'd.'

Two short colloquies follow: *His words to Christ, going to the Crosse* (399), and *Another, to his Saviour* (399). The fourth poem of the sequence is a simple *improperia*, *His Saviours words, going to the Crosse* (400). This is followed by *His Anthem to Christ on the Crosse* (400), scored for Verse and Chorus. Even the 'Crosse-Tree' poem following, that by reason of being a shape poem[1] might seem intended for reading rather than recitation, has the stage quality of the others:

> *This Crosse-Tree here*
> *Doth* Jesus *beare*
> *Who sweet'ned first,*
> *The Death accurs't.*
> Here all things ready are, make hast, make hast away;
> For, long this work wil be, & very short this Day.
> Why then, go on to act: Here's wonders to be done.

The proceedings begin to draw to a close with *To his Saviours Sepulcher: his Devotion* as the speaker approaches the tomb with flowers. It ends with an 'Extasie' of feeling:

> Ravish't I am; and down I lie
> Confus'd, in this brave Extasie.
> Here let me rest; and let me have
> This for my *Heav'n*, that was Thy *Grave*:
> And, coveting no higher sphere,
> I'le my Eternitie spend here.

The immediacy of effect is sustained through the last poem of the series, *His coming to the Sepulcher*:

> Hence they have born my Lord: Behold! the Stone
> Is rowl'd away; and my sweet Saviour's gone!

[1] Herrick's *To Heaven* (106) may also be construed as a shape poem, an altar from which the speaker longs for a glimpse of Heaven, of the chaste souls in white stoles in a ring before God.

> Tell me, white Angell; what is now become
> Of Him, we lately seal'd up in this Tombe?
> Is He, from hence, gone to the shades beneath,
> To vanquish Hell, as here He conquer'd Death?
> If so; I'le thither follow, without feare;
> And live in Hell, if that my *Christ* stayes there.

A glance at parallel poems in Herbert's *Temple* indicates both
the particular and the traditional quality of Herrick's usage.
Herbert's *Good Friday* needs no Roscius to play the drama;
nevertheless the sinner plays out the conflict within his own
breast, and faces, if not the vinegar and gall, his conviction of
sin. The complex, subtle *improperia* of Herbert's *Sacrifice*
becomes in Herrick's *His Saviours words, going to the Crosse* a
simple witness of one 'Who suffers not here for mine own, /
But for my friends *transgression*'; of a recognition of 'What bitter
cups, had been your due, / Had He not drank them up for *you*'.
Only the listing of the cross, the cords, the nails, the myrrh, the
gall, and vinegar remains, rather than their rhetorical exploita-
tion in symbol. Even the 'shape' poems preserve the contrast
between the inner and outer enactment, the symbolic in
contrast to the loosely figurative mode, for Herrick's 'Crosse-
Tree' poem in contrast to Herbert's *Altar* is primarily a shape
to be worshipped, a shape recalling the cross that Christ bore.
For all that, some of the traditional, liturgical irony remains in
Herrick's poem: the cross tree bore Jesus as He bore it; on it he
suffered the death accurst for our accursed death; his blood is
our healthful balm; our wine and oil are to cure the sore made
by our sin; the tree of death is our tree of life. In Herbert's
Sepulcher man's stone heart is the inadequate sepulchre of
Christ's love for man; Herrick's *To his Saviours Sepulcher: his
Devotion* visualizes the sepulchre, adorns it, and adores at it.
Certainly the religious experience of the two poets differed, but,
more to the point, their poetry, moving on a common ground of
a received tradition and a common matter, illustrates the broad
range and history of the devotional kind.

Herrick's two dirges in *Noble Numbers—The Dirge of
Jephthahs Daughter: sung by the Virgins* (359 ff.) and *The
Widdowes teares: or, Dirge of Dorcas* (373 ff.)—help us to gauge
the range of his devotional art. *Dorcas* is still conventional of
Herrick's typical usage. All but a pastiche of lines from the

13

Psalms and the Song of Solomon, it begins with an echo from
the Psalms:

> Come pitie us, all ye, who see
> Our Harps, hung on the Willow-tree

and ends with an echo from Luke:

> *Chor.* And after us (distressed)
> Sho'd fame be dumb;
> Thy very Tomb
> Would cry out, *Thou art blessed.*

The poem centres on the period before the raising of Dorcas by
Peter, as reported in Acts 9.36, while the widows are bewailing
the death of Dorcas, her comeliness and good works. It is not
her resurrection that has captured Herrick's imagination, but
the humane quality of Dorcas during her lifetime. The argument
of the poem centres around the image of Dorcas's acts, the
garments she made for the poor:

> There were thy Acts, and thou shalt have
> These hung, as honours o're thy Grave.

It is difficult, however, to ascertain how much actual symbolic
intention is subsumed in the poem. One wonders whether in
Dorcas's comeliness and good works there is not more than a
hint of Christ's *laetitia* and *caritas*; whether her garments are
to be understood as reminiscent of Christ's garments as a type
of love;[1] whether in 'Come pitie us, ye Passers by' there is the
remote echo of an *improperia.* Certainly the sixth stanza seems
to support a symbolic reading:

> But, ah, alas; the Almond Bough
> And Olive Branch is wither'd now.
> The Wine Presse now is ta'ne from us
> The saffron and the Calamus.
> The Spice and Spiknard hence is gone,
> The Storax and the Cynamon.
> *Chor.* The Caroll of our gladnesse
> Ha's taken wing,
> And our late spring
> Of mirth is turn'd to sadnesse.

[1] See Rosamond Tuve, *A Reading of George Herbert* (Chicago, 1952),
p. 130.

More clear in its intention, *The Dirge of Jephthahs Daughter* is also more diverse in its origins; as lyrical and pastoral as *Corinna's going a Maying*, it is devotional to the core in its combination of dirge and lamentation, and simultaneously elegiac and reminiscent of the classical epithalamium[1] all at once. The maidens move in processional, bring flowers, lay down their maiden filletings, and, in good Virgilian fashion, burn male incense; but they bring their offerings to the tomb of a virgin martyr, vow an everlasting chastity and lent, leave 'Christall Vialls fil'd / With teares, distil'd / From teeming Eyes'; and, incidentally, in good English country fashion they enjoin screech owls and wolves away from the tomb. Primarily, however, Jephthah's Daughter emerges as a type of the virgin martyr:[2]

> O Thou, the wonder of all dayes:
> O Paragon, and Pearle of praise:
> O Virgin-martyr, ever blest
>   Above the rest
> Of all the Maiden-Traine: We come
> And bring fresh strewings to thy Tombe.

Of what remains in *Noble Numbers*, one may mention the four musical pieces written to be performed by King Charles's choir at the chapel in Whitehall, two of which were scored by Henry Lawes: *To God: an Anthem, sung in the Chapell at White-Hall, before the King* (342); *A Christmas Caroll, sung to the King in the Presence at White-Hall* (364); *The New-yeeres Gift, or Circumcisions Song, sung to the King in the Presence at White-Hall* (365); *The Star-Song: A Caroll to the King; sung at White-Hall* (367). A fifth, not specifically noted as intended to be sung at Whitehall, *Another New-Yeeres Gift, or Song for the Circumcision* (366), also belongs to this same group of praises to Christ and the King: 'Let's blesse the Babe: And as we sing / His

---

[1] See Catullus 61 in *Catullus, Tibullus, and Pervigilium Veneris*, ed. and trans. by F. W. Cornish (London, 1950; Loeb Classical Library), pp. 70 ff.

[2] Usually it was Jephtha rather than his daughter who commanded the interest of the divine poets; from Chaucer and Gower on through Du Bartas he figured as a type of rashness. Most similar to Herrick's conception of the story is George Buchanan's *Jephthah*. See *Sacred Dramas of George Buchanan*, trans. by Archibald Brown (Edinburgh, 1906).

praise; so let us blesse the King.' But though Christ and Charles are praised together, the crown in Herrick's songs is no longer functioning as a religious symbol; it is temporal, personal, and even political adulation that we see and hear.[1]

In addition to their scoring, furthermore, these lyrics bear the closest relationship to devotional music; musically these few pieces span the whole range from public to private devotion. In the baroque period, the anthem (one of the chief types of sacred, Anglican music), partially under the influence of the Lawes brothers, developed into the verse anthem, in contradistinction to the full anthem.[2] Thus, in Herrick's *To God: An Anthem* the dialogue between Verse and Verse Chorus is worked out in perfect rhetorical antithesis.[3] Nor should one be surprised by Herrick's stanzaic and thematic sophistication in *A Christmas Carol* and *The Star Song: A Caroll*, for the carol, though less formally ecclesiastical than the anthem, often 'overlapped with the hymn'[4] in church usage and was a more serious devotional form than it is usually taken to be, ' "popular by destination" rather than "popular by origin"—a statement that applies to lyric as well as music.'[5] Furthermore, the close relationship between musical and poetic devotion was supported by a close kinship between musical and poetical rhetoric, by the whole baroque musical doctrine of affections and figures, through a whole *ars inveniendi*, the invention and development of musical topics.[6] Generally Herrick's musical pieces in *Noble Numbers*, both the scored and the unscored, are enriched by

[1] Malcolm Mackenzie Ross, *Poetry and Dogma* (New Brunswick, 1954), p. 127.

[2] Manfred F. Bukofzer, *Music in the Baroque Era* (New York, 1937), pp. 198 ff.

[3] See also Herrick's *His Anthem, to Christ on the Crosse* (400).

[4] *Oxford Book of Carols*, ed. by Percy Dearmer, R. Vaughan Williams, and Martin Shaw (Oxford, 1931), p. xxiii.

[5] Manfred F. Bukofzer, *Studies in Medieval Music* (New York, 1950), p. 169 (quoting Richard L. Greene).

[6] Bukofzer, *Music in the Baroque Era*, pp. 388 ff. See also Ernst Robert Curtius, *European Literature and the Latin Middle Ages*, trans. by W. R. Trask (New York, 1953), p. 78. Ruth Wallerstein notes that the chorales written for King Charles's choir by Herrick and others were influenced by religious music in a variety of subtle ways, 'and these elements are not present in their other verse.' *Richard Crashaw* (Madison, Wis., 1959) p. 49.

being read against the background of musical devotion, of sacred music with freely invented rather than Scriptural words.

An *Ode of the Birth of our Saviour* (345) achieves its song-like quality through a complex stanzaic pattern of short lines of feminine and identical rhymes and experimental rhythms.[1] The Babe is decked with silks and jewels and 'Lilly-work'; the chamber with Ivorie and Amber. It is a purely lyrical, English domestic celebration that takes place. Just so it is a purely domestic gift song, a *dona*, that he presents in *To his Saviour a Child, a Present by a child* (354) in which a flower is sent to the Babe to be pinned on his 'Bibb, or Stomacher,' a whistle to calm his cries, but, alas, no coral because the giver is 'monilesse.' Another circumcision song, much like the one to King Charles, plays with the typical conceits of that theme:

> That little prettie bleeding part
> Of Foreskin send to me:
> And I'le returne a bleeding Heart,
> For New-yeeres gift to thee.
>
> (*To his Saviour: The New yeers gift*, 376)

Tulips and roses will grow from the child's blood, the Babe '(Like a *Bride*) / Will blush to death' unless all's purified. The themes, like the images, are familiar, but to them Herrick has brought a childlike acceptance, an innocence, a lyrical purity that naturalizes and domesticates them.

As we sum up our examination of some of the mainstreams of Herrick's *Noble Numbers*, we find that we are in the presence of a large, metrical prayer book: creeds and graces, confessions and thanksgivings, litanies and dirges, nativity and circumcision songs, anthems and carols, plus a large body of near-catechetical wisdom.[2] As we compare Herrick's with the body of major seventeenth-century devotional poetry, of John Donne, George Herbert, Richard Crashaw, Henry Vaughan, we find that the difference between Herrick and the others is not primarily a

---

[1] See also Herrick's *An Ode, or Psalme, to God* (363).

[2] It is perhaps significant to note that in 1645 *The Book of Common Prayer* was abolished and *The Directory of the Public Worship of God in the Three Kingdoms* was substituted. See Stanley Morison, *English Prayer Books: an Introduction to the Literature of Christian Public Worship* (Cambridge, 1943); Charles C. Butterworth, *English Primers (1529–1545)* (Pennsylvania, 1953), p. 3.

difference in the religious experience that begot the poetry, that is of intensity and complexity (heretofore the only ground on which Herrick's religious verse has been approached), but a difference in mode. That difference in mode is determined not by difference in form, theme, and matter, but in symbolic usage, which, in turn, is determined, at least partially, by the dogmatic situation. The dogmatic situation in the Caroline period was a movement away from 'sacrament to ornament, [a] declension of symbol to metaphor'; it accompanied 'the distortion and eventual destruction of central Eucharistic dogma'; in contrast, the 'spiritual Anglicans,' like Herbert, represented a counter-movement towards a healing of the breach.[1] Largely didactic and affective in intention, Herrick's poetry is thin in symbolic and allegorical usage; his figures may be called 'received'— inherited and complete; the effect of the poem rarely depends upon their working through in emblematic or meditational development. His figurative usage is passive rather than active, conceptual rather than formal. The devotional points are made explicitly and didactically. What is distinctive about *Noble Numbers* is the way in which worship is domesticated and re-enacted in personal and humanistic terms, acclimated to the local situation and scene. If this analysis be just, we find ourselves in *Noble Numbers* in the presence of a body of devotional poetry considerably different in tone from what we have taken to be characteristic of Herrick's time.

From these poems Herrick emerges as a most pious Christian. If ever a norm of spiritual modesty and acceptance were available, it is here in *Noble Numbers*. God dwells in Devon and is praised by Scripture and liturgy, with daffodils and roses. A truly homely odour of sanctity pervades *Noble Numbers*; and if the odour seems as often to come from the kitchen-garden as from the altar, the piety is not reduced. If this is paganism, Christian devotion ought to make the most of it.

For all his difference from the more familiar 'spiritual Anglicans,' for all that Herrick's universe is no longer infinitely correspondent, it is no more perverse to define devotional poetry by Robert Herrick than it is to define Herrick by his devotional poetry. Just as we have been thrown off balance by the anomaly of the singer of silken petticoats turned priest, and

[1] Ross, p. 64.

18

have artificially resolved the anomaly by the cliché of Herrick the 'pagan-priest,'[1] so we have been confused by generalizations about the religious poetry of the seventeenth century as generically anguished, metaphysical, rigorously meditational, or mystical, or symbolical and witty, and Donne has become the norm. Of late grave metaphysical beauties have been read into *Hesperides*,[2] but the approach, fortunately, has stopped short of turning *Noble Numbers* into another *Temple*. The most sympathetic approach has been that of Douglas Bush, who finds that 'the simple beauties and pieties of *Noble Numbers*' have been drowned out by the 'deeper and more personal note of the greater souls of Herrick's time.'[3] This is undoubtedly true; the point at issue, however, seems to me to be more a matter of mode than of greatness, of Herrick's particular functioning within a literary kind.

That kind I should like to distinguish more strictly and systematically than is customarily done as 'the poetry of devotion.'[4]

The literature that is conventionally called *devotional* has been distinguished by Helen White as that which 'takes the hand of the believer and leads him into the presence of the God he has been seeking.'[5] Concerned with prayer and other exercises

---

[1] See *Oxford Book of Christian Verse*, ed. by Lord David Cecil (Oxford, 1940), p. xx, describing Herrick as 'essentially not a Christian but a latter day pagan.'

[2] See Cleanth Brooks, *Well Wrought Urn* (New York, 1947; Harvest Books), pp. 69 ff; S. Musgrove, *Universe of Robert Herrick*, in *Auckland University College Bulletin*, No. 38, English Series, No. 4, 1950, *passim*.

[3] *English Literature in the Earlier Seventeenth Century* (Oxford, 1946), p. 116.

[4] As a general descriptive adjective the word devotional is used frequently enough, but seldom in a generic sense. A marked exception is Sir Henry Newbolt, ed., *Devotional Poets of the Seventeenth Century* (London, 1929), who includes a substantial number of poems from *Noble Numbers*. Newbolt's criterion for inclusion in his volume is 'verse upon religious themes, so charged with sincere religious emotion as to be essentially independent of religious dogma' (p. xii). The relationship among the poets he includes, however, he sees only as that which stems from a 'common purity of temperament.'

[5] *English Devotional Literature (Prose) 1600–1640* (Madison, Wis., 1931), pp. 9, 12.

promoting piety, the literature of devotion is as technical and specialized as the literature of science or technology, its subject, however, being worship. As related to worship, technical devotion is related to the totality of man's 'adoring response' to the divine. It is to be thought of in terms of a 'willed response to God's inciting action.' Undoubtedly worship has its humane as well as its divine components, but it takes care not to allow the humane to usurp the total attention. Even the use of art in worship 'is not a mere imitation of the creative work of God, nor is it only a homage rendered to Christ; by giving an embodiment to invisible realities, it continues the Incarnation of the Word.' And even where the worship is more protestant and less incarnational, when 'adoration of the Logos' is not emphasized and moral self-fulfilment is, the natural movement of worship is still a theocentric, 'God-ward' one, towards an other-wordly consummation.[1] And one of the means to achieve this consummation is through the varieties of technical devotion.

Another and a more humanistic way is through devotional art as distinct from the devotional technology just mentioned; i.e., for the poet the fusion of the ways and means of *belles lettres* with the materials and ends of devotion. Immediately, however, a problem of the relationship between the humanistic and the devotional obtrudes itself, to which the much relied upon concept of Christian Humanism is not an entirely happy solution. Though the doctrine of Christian Humanism may spell out some major relationships between Christianity and humanism in the Renaissance, it does not spell out the relationship between the secular and the religious except, in effect, to insist upon the identity of the two. By the very definition of Christian Humanism, the whole culture was substantially religious, Shakespeare as well as Milton, *Hesperides* as well as *Noble Numbers*. Nor is the relationship clarified so much as insisted upon through the equation of 'theocentric' humanism with the true humanism, as exemplified by the religious poets of the seventeenth century, and of 'anthropocentric' humanism with false humanism, with 'Jacobean pessimism in literature and Mannerist frigidity in art.'[2] In any case, the term Christian Humanism is severely

[1] Underhill, pp. 61, 177, 71, 81, 340.
[2] M. M. Mahood, *Poetry and Humanism* (New Haven, 1950), pp. 18–20, citing Jacques Maritain.

limited by history; our modern quest for it is in effect a kind of neo-medievalism, a 'Noble anachronism.'[1]

The problem of the relationship between humanism and religion in 'religious' poetry is much better served by a recognition of a specific category of devotional poetry, by a study of its theory, practice, and history. However, to speak of 'religious' poetry at all is to court confusion at the very beginning, to extend a hospitality that far outreaches the devotional, that at one extreme includes the ecclesiastical and at the other as secular a piece as *Hamlet*. It is to be hospitable to the metaphysical, the transcendental, the mystical, the occult, at times even to the sociological, psychological, or scientific. Or, as Hoxie Neale Fairchild has it: 'Any idea or sentiment which the poet happens to regard as religious is grist for my mill, and I shall include poetic responses to philosophic and scientific trends which have significant religious implications.'[2] Such hospitality is generous, but it does not go far to helping us to isolate the particular qualities of *Noble Numbers*,[3] which though certainly religious is not religious in the sense of Shelley's *Prometheus*, for example.

The designation we have been availing ourselves for the significant religious poetry of the seventeenth century is, of course, the 'religious metaphysical,' for the poetry of Donne, Herbert, Crashaw, and Vaughan. But though we know their poetry is not of a piece (and the more we learn about them the more the differences emerge), we continue to use the term. Furthermore, the term metaphysical, even secular metaphysical, soon proves to be simultaneously too loose and too restrictive for comfort. The 'metaphysical' has been used variously to denote a school, a style, a genre, a philosophical system, a habit of mind, a sensibility, a metaphorical system. Very often (and most correctly) it means little more than John Donne. As a metaphorical system, the metaphysical has been proved to be no discrete phenomenon, however; in logic and rhetoric it is

---

[1] Douglas Bush, *Renaissance and English Humanism* (Toronto, 1956), p. 104.

[2] *Religious Trends in English Poetry* (New York, 1939), Vol. I (1700–1740), p. vii.

[3] I believe five poems in *Noble Numbers* may be said to be religious rather than devotional: *Upon Time* (346), *Eternitie* (354), *To His Conscience* (357), *The Bell-man* (372), *The White Island: or place of the Blest* (376 f.).

exactly of a piece throughout the Renaissance and deeply imbedded in the Middle Ages.[1] Modern formalist criticism, on the other hand, has given a kind of autonomy to metaphysical wit and set it up as the poetic norm. Very recently the formal emphasis has been supplanted by a philosophical one which takes the metaphysical back into the Middle Ages and defines it as 'medieval theological wit,' or the relationship 'of the one and the many.'[2] Now uncertain as all this secular metaphysic is, the definition of the metaphysical that is also primarily religious, in contrast to the metaphysical which even at its most secular is religious, becomes even more elusive and complex. Nor do the complexities eventually lead far beyond a subtle appreciationism, or into generic or historical definitions.

Some attempts to get beyond loose subjectivisms about the 'religious metaphysical' have, on the other hand, proved most fruitful. A most rewarding concept suggested as helping to define the main body of seventeenth-century religious poetry, brilliantly conceived and defended by Louis Martz,[3] has opened up vast areas of understanding and insight to us in individual poems and characteristic modes of thought. Professor Martz's concept, however, is in some danger of outstripping itself in its very youth. The poetry of meditation is suggested as a genre, even like the epic, though we find it functioning happily as a sub-genre within conventional genres like the sonnet. It is proposed as stemming from and dependent upon the formal meditation, though contemplation and prayer are somehow untidily tucked within its limits. Much is said of its logic and rhetoric, and yet they seem to be no more than conventional Renaissance logic and rhetoric after all. It is defined as a genre which deals with serious and important themes providing it set a stage upon which 'the actor may enact the process' of his 'finding';[4] it allows room for Wallace Stevens as well as Donne,

---

[1] Rosamond Tuve, *Elizabethan and Metaphysical Imagery* (Chicago, 1947).

[2] Walter J. Ong, 'Wit and Mystery: A Revaluation in Medieval Latin Hymnody,' *Speculum*, XXIII (1947), 310–41; James Smith, 'On Metaphysical Poetry', *Determinations*, ed. by F. R. Leavis (London, 1934), 24.

[3] Martz, *passim.*

[4] Louis Martz, 'Wallace Stevens: The World as Meditation,' in *Literature and Belief: English Institute Essays, 1957*, ed. by M. H. Abrams New York, 1958), p. 155.

Herbert, and Crashaw, but not, we are told, for Wordsworth, or, for Browning. It is given much weight as apparent source for certain poems, and yet when the modelling is too close, the poem being modelled seems to lack a certain broad, humane relevance, and remains, after all, like Donne's *First Anniversary* imperfectly realized as a poem, however excellent it may be as a spiritual exercise.

And beyond the meditation, and including it, as Rosamund Tuve proves, stands a primary mode of thinking and writing, a mode growing out of a deeply felt, symbolic inheritance stemming from liturgy, dogma, art, indeed from the whole complex of religious thought and belief which does avail itself of the meditation, but only as it avails itself of the whole vast body of liturgical, ecclesiastical, and iconographical materials.

It seems useful then to find a term to replace the elusive 'religious metaphysical,' a term that should be hospitable to the symbolic, the meditational, the emblematic, where they occur; a term that should allow for the various figurative modes that were actually employed, for genres from the couplet to the epic; a term that should allow room for the didactic couplet as well as the affective prayer; a designation that is susceptible of being used with historical as well as intrinsic signification.

That term suggested here is 'the poetry of devotion,' and its values are suggested as follows. It implies a specifically Christian *donnée*. It supposes the matter of the poetry to be more or less orthodox, inclusive of the incarnational as well as the humane, in relative proportions, but always of a final intention of worship. Thus it immediately suggests a differentiation between the secular, the generally 'religious' (that is the Bible and general aspects of Christian life as incidental reference rather than primary matter),[1] and the intentionally devotional. It recalls a body of technical devotion, the devotional handbooks as well as ecclesiastical dogma, as source and inspiration. It encourages an examination of the precise relationship between

[1] Miss Campbell appears to differentiate 'divine' poetry from the devotional; divine poetry she sees as 'based directly on the Bible' (p. 4). With her contention that it is this divine poetry 'which resulted in the poetry of Donne and Herbert and those others in the seventeenth century who praised God in nobler words and sounder rhythms' (p. 33) I find myself in substantial disagreement.

the poetic mode and the dogmatic history, particularly where the symbol is concerned.[1] It invites reference to related arts, to devotional painting and music. It carries with it connotations of piety and concern. As poetry, the poetry of devotion suggests a humanistic rhetoric and logic, though the relative weights of the Christian and the humanistic components will vary from period to period according to history and according to the religious experience of the poet and his characteristic usage. In differentiating from the ecclesiastical and dogmatic on the one hand and the loosely religious generality on the other, 'the poetry of devotion' allows room in between for all varieties of devotional matter and manner. Formally it allows room for any poetical genre.

It is also useful to be able to characterize the range of devotional poetry from the extreme of 'common' prayer (that is 'public' as the word is used in *The Book of Common Prayer*) to the extreme of 'private' devotion, from poetry as it is germane to and might be prayed by almost any Christian, like some of Herrick's affective prayers, to that which is peculiarly the poet's, like Herrick's *Thanksgiving to God for his House*.[2] Or, put in another way, the range extends from that which is almost entirely dependent on Christian dogma for its meaning to that which means 'something even outside the domain of believed Christian dogma.'[3] It is not surprising, in view of this range, that Herrick's *Thanksgiving* is one of the few widely known and reprinted poems of *Noble Numbers*, just as it is not surprising that *Paradise Regained* has a fairly limited appeal. The more dogmatic the devotional locus, the more nearly ecclesiastical it is, the less humanistic the appeal. Just so Milton's poems help us to see not only the range of devotional poetry, but the difference between the religious and the devotional. *Comus* and *Lycidas* are both deeply religious poems; *Paradise Lost* is a devotional one.

[1] Ross, *passim*.

[2] For a distinction between public and private prayer, see the following: G. W. O. Addleshaw, *High Church Tradition, a Study in the Liturgical Thought of the Seventeenth Century* (London, 1941), pp. 38, 39, 59; Butterworth, p. 274; Helen C. White, *Tudor Books of Private Devotion* (Madison, Wis., 1951), pp. 4–6.

[3] Tuve, *A Reading of George Herbert*, p. 128.

Of some considerable consequence to the nature of devotional poetry is the relationship implicit between religious and poetic belief, for the poetry of devotion makes demands upon both. The relationship between the two, in general, is complex, ranging as it may from an identification of poetry and prayer to poetry as serving a religious function even when it most dissociates itself from 'a decadent or coercive religious tradition'; from a vision of the poet as seer and prophet to poetry as a distraction from prayer; from poetry as 'secular revelation' to a complete secularist dissociation of the two.[1] Thus, to say that one understands *Paradise Lost* better because he believes it[2] is to simplify matters unduly. Nevertheless those stretches of didactic revelation in *Paradise Lost* which make demands on the reader's dogmatic belief come close to the ecclesiastical limit of devotion, and, standing at the farthest remove from the humanistic, breed dissatisfaction. It is the dissatisfaction of the reader who in the midst of the humanistic devotion of the total context is suddenly being asked to exert an act of dogmatic rather than poetic belief. To say that one understands Herrick's affective prayers better because he believes in Jesus Christ is probably true enough. On the other hand, one might well not be committed to the resurrection of Dorcas and still be in substantial possession of the poem.

Where poetic and religious belief have been made generally equivalent, a pervasive antihumanism has often resulted. In our time poetic and religious belief have been seen as identical, or consubstantial; or poetry has been seen as promoting belief in others, as unconsummated mystical experience, as secular or latent revelation, as purifier of dogma, and generally in the name of some variety of Christian Humanism. Even so temperate a Christian Humanist as Douglas Bush arrives, somewhat sadly, at the conclusion that it is necessary to temper humanism 'with a sobering faith in something like original sin.'[3] If one sees modern nostalgia for the Christian Humanism of the seventeenth century as related principally to the devotional art of the seventeenth century, however, one is put to no great historical

[1] Amos N. Wilder, *Modern Poetry and the Christian Tradition* (New York, 1952), pp. 18, 9 ff., 38.

[2] C. S. Lewis, *Preface to Paradise Lost* (London, 1952), p. 64.

[3] Bush, *Renaissance and English Humanism*, p. 100.

confusions. Devotion to the poetry of devotion is any *dévot's* privilege.

It is no cause for wonder, then, that Herrick's *Noble Numbers* has not been more cherished even in the midst of our own neo-classical worship of our seventeenth-century Ancients. In terms of his spiritual experience he stands greatly removed from our Homer, John Donne. Nor is his manner sufficiently complex, like Crashaw's, for example, to serve our interests. Approaching neoclassicism, particularly in his didactic couplets and in his plain statement mode of discourse, he has not, in *Noble Numbers*, paralleled our quest. And yet, in another sense, perhaps one might wonder that *Noble Numbers* has not been exploited, as in a sense Milton has been exploited, for his sheer devotional matter, of whatever stripe.

Noble Numbers is certainly not 'religious metaphysical' nor except in some isolated instances meditational; rarely is it emblematic. Still less does it support the cliché of Herrick the pagan-priest, for what is classical in *Noble Numbers* had long since been acclimatized and enfranchised. Such symbolism as it employs is of the most deeply absorbed and received kind; its figurative mode is essentially metaphorical. It can only be described generically as the 'poetry of devotion' and it is very inclusive of its kind. It happens to be largely didactic and affect-ive, approaching 'common devotion.' It grows more distinctive, humanistically, on the comparatively few occasions when the devotions grow more 'private,' and when they grow more symbolic. It grows most original when Herrick's peculiar quality, the *ingenu* quality, grows marked, and when Herrick's devotional muse follows in the path of his secular one. By its inclusiveness it catches us up to the recognition of the existence of much seventeenth-century devotional poetry that, failing our exigencies, has been politely ignored, poetry even of Herbert, *The Church Porch*, even of Donne, *The Lamentations of Jeremy*.

Nor, finally, should one be unrespectful of the particular power of *Noble Numbers*, a power that has gone completely unrecognized. Conventional as much of it is, much has under-gone a sea change into something particularly immediate, personal, local, simple, and humane. But to speak of Herrick's simplicities is never to suggest naïveté. Herrick's is an achieved simplicity, a certitude of matter and manner both. Nor is it suggested when one says that Herrick humanized devotion that he minimized the incarnational beyond the characteristic habits of his time. Indeed, one of his distinguishing qualities is that, even at his most incarnational, he succeeds at many points, in his intention to humanize it. He domesticates the mystery.

Herrick thus may serve us to good purpose. By nature of the didactic and affective quality in *Noble Numbers* we are enabled to see the less spectacular actualities of devotional poetry in a way which a more complex and dramatic synthesis of humanism and devotion like Donne's or Herbert's do not easily allow. By the distance between *Hesperides* and *Noble Numbers* we are able to find out differences between devotional and nondevotional poetry that stepping between Donne's secular and holy sonnets does not so easily permit. In Herrick's didacticism we see the ecclesiastical foundations of the devotional poet more easily than an involved symbolism, like Crashaw's, easily allows. In Herrick's prayers and praises we may mark the close relationship of religious and poetic belief that informs devotional poetry. In his occasional sorties into private devotional poetry, Herrick shows us the close boundaries between the devotional and the humanistic, the point at which the art, ceasing to remain entirely integral, becomes absorbed into the devotional intention.

Besides serving a historical, descriptive function, *Noble Numbers* helps us to clarify our modern, neo-classical use of the devotional tradition, a use that has not always been entirely knowing, complete, or even disingenuous, a use that makes one suspect we have kidnapped a devotional tradition and tried to enlarge it to a humanistic one. *Hesperides* tells us a good deal about Herrick's Ancients; *Noble Numbers* tells us as much about our own.

J. A. MAZZEO

Cromwell as Davidic King

B EFORE we can fully understand Marvell's transformation of Cromwell from a kind of Machiavellian prince in the *Horatian Ode* into a Davidic king in the later poems we must first consider some aspects of traditional biblical exegesis and the philosophy of history to which it gave rise.[1]

The allegorical interpretation of Scripture antedates Philo Judaeus, although he was the major influence on Origen and other Eastern Fathers who preferred his abstract, moral, and philosophical reading of Scripture to a more literal one. In the West, the work, first of Tertullian, and then of Augustine signalized the triumph of a more concrete and historical way of interpreting Scripture which has since come to be known as typological allegory or, as Erich Auerbach called it, 'figuralism.'[2]

This is the method of interpreting Scripture whereby the

[1] See my article 'Cromwell as Machiavellian Prince in Marvell's "An Horatian Ode," ' *Journal of the History of Ideas*, XXI (1960), 1–17.

[2] See H. A. Wolfson, *The Philosophy of the Church Fathers*, I (Cambridge, Mass., 1956), 24 ff., for a study of rabbinical, Philonic and patristic allegory, and Beryl Smalley, *The Study of the Bible in the Middle Ages* (2d ed.; Oxford, 1952), for later developments. Auerbach's thesis is presented in 'Figura,' *Archivum Romanicum*, XXII (1938), 436–89. Reprinted with minor changes in *Neue Dantestudien* (Istanbul, 1944). See also his 'Typological Symbolism in Medieval Literature,' *Yale French Studies*, IX (1952), 3–10, and, more extensively, *Typologische Motive in der Mittelalterlichen Literatur* (Krefeld, 1953).

persons and events of the Old Testament are seen as 'figures,' realities which are also simultaneously prophetic signs of the drama of salvation unfolded in the New Testament. The New Testament in turn is prophetic of the events and realities of the Last Judgment, not only when it is obviously prophetic, but even through the events and personages it describes. The latter, when properly understood, point to further future events of which they are the paradigms.

While the Eastern tradition of allegorical interpretation tended to weaken the literal and historical veracity of the Old Testament, the figural method was based on the literal and historical value of the events recorded in Scripture. It is unlike ordinary allegory or symbolism in that both terms in the analogy are literally and historically true. They are realities and not merely signs. Thus Moses, Adam, Joshua are types of Christ, but they are also Adam, Moses, and Joshua. The Deluge is a type of baptism, but there was a real deluge. The sacrifice of Isaac was a type of the sacrifice of Christ, but there was a real Isaac and a real Abraham. In short, the relationship between the terms of a figural analogy is not that of sign to reality signified, but that of shadow (*umbra*) or *imago* to its fulfilled truth. Both terms are concrete, real and historical realities, and only the link between them is abstract.[1]

This method of interpretation, in the Christian tradition, begins as early as Paul. Thus the Jews in the wilderness are types of the present human situation (I Cor. 10.6,11). The Jewish law is a shadow of what is to come (Col. 2.16 ff.), and Adam is both the type and the antitype of Christ (Rom. 5.12 ff.; I Cor. 15.21). The relations between the law and grace, bondage and freedom are prefigured in the relationship of Hagar and Ishmael or Sarah and Isaac (Gal. 4.21–31). The Pauline method of interpretation was rooted in rabbinical allegorical exegesis, the *Midrash*, but Paul modified it and turned it into a weapon for his attack on the judaizing Christians. His main intention was to deprive Judaism of its normative character because of his profound convictions on the paradoxical and anti-thetical character of the relations which obtain between law and grace, or between justification by faith and by works. In effect, he tried to reduce the Old Testament to a prediction even in

[1] Auerbach, 'Figura,' pp. 454 ff.

those many parts which were not prophetic in character. In so doing, he made the unfamiliar history and mythology of a particular people accessible—in an enormously altered way, to be sure—to gentiles, but his transformation of Scripture also contained the seeds of a new philosophy of history and a new way of interpreting contemporary events.[1]

Augustine, as in other important matters in the Western Christian tradition, gave definitive shape to figural interpretation and to other exegetical techniques as well.[2] Along with rather abstract moral and philosophical allegories of a more familiar sort we also discover in his writings many typological allegories. Thus Noah's ark is a figure of the Church, Moses of Christ: the priesthood of Aaron is a shadow and figure of the eternal priesthood, Hagar is a figure of the earthly Jerusalem or the Old Testament, while Sarah is a figure of the New Testament, the heavenly Jerusalem, or of the City of God; Jacob and Esau are figures of Jews and Christians, and so on.[3] Such figuralizations do not serve merely to moralize those parts of Scripture repugnant to a later moral consciousness and reduce them to mere allegory. Indeed, even where the Bible reports immoral acts Augustine insists that they are to be taken literally and historically. However, they are also, like the more edifying episodes, to be taken figuratively as well, although the interpreter should here use the figurative interpretation alone.[4] This is not as arbitrary a procedure as it may seem. The actual polygamy to be found in the Old Testament, for example, is to be understood as a special divine dispensation appropriate to a special time in the historical drama of salvation. Nevertheless, even though such practices are no longer permissible, the now immoral events that Scripture records have an eternal reference, a figurative and moral meaning which is always applicable, and a prophetic meaning which will last until the end of history. This is why the Bible must be read both literally and historically

[1] Cf. *ibid.*, pp. 466–68, and Rudolf Bultmann, *History and Eschatology* (Edinburgh, 1957). These brilliant Gifford Lectures survey the field of Christian historiography briefly and lucidly.

[2] For a brief survey of kinds of scriptural and secular medieval allegory see my *Structure and Thought in the Paradiso* (Ithaca, N.Y., 1958), chap. 2.

[3] *De civitate Dei*, XV.27, X.6, XVIII.11, XVII.6, XVI.31, XVII.3, in Migne, *PL*, Vol. XLI. Cf. Auerbach, 'Figura,' pp. 456 ff.

[4] *De doctrina Christiana*, III.12, 20, in Migne, *PL*, Vol. XXXIV, col. 73.

on the one hand, and figuratively and prophetically on the other.[1]

We can easily grasp here one of the ideas which, especially after it was secularized and applied to lay figures and the history of 'secular' peoples, could easily lead to the possibility of countenancing apparently or actually immoral actions on the grounds that they were providentially ordered. In its barest form and stripped of some of its complexity, the conception underlies a good deal of Marvell's apologia for Cromwell.

The nature of figural interpretation and its historiographical implications might be further clarified if we compare it to modern historical interpretation. The latter places events in a sequence moving, so to speak, horizontally toward an ever receding horizon. The meaning of any single event is given in a development to a further event which defines what came before. Hence each generation must write its own history anew, for each event alters the significance of the past. On the other hand, in figuralism, the meaning comes from above. It is given by a vertical dimension, by the operation of divine grace and judgment. The pattern of events is not a uniform series. There are breaks, mistakes, miracles, moral incongruities, and conversions, and this is particularly true of sacred history.[2]

II

The figure of David passed into medieval history and imagination in two modes, as the type of biblical king, anointed of God and an instrument of Providence, and as the moral type who combines the antithetical attributes of humility and sublimity. The first is more strictly the political tradition of David symbolism, the latter was bound to a moral ideal pre-eminently found in moral interpretations of Christ and Francis of Assisi. However, these two modes were closely bound to one another in view of the fact that, until Machiavelli, the ideal ethical man and the ideal ruler were generally assumed to be synonymous, and that all the attributes of the good man were believed to be indispensable to the good ruler.

Let us turn first to the earliest medieval version of the figure

[1] *Ibid.*: 'non solum historice et proprie, sed figurate et prophetice.'
[2] Cf. Bultmann, *History and Eschatology*, p. 148.

of the Davidic king before discussing the 'humble psalmist' and Marvell's effort to place Cromwell in the framework of these traditions.

The crowning of Pepin saw the introduction of the Biblical rite of royal unctions into European history so that, according to the theories of the Franks, his coronation marked a revival of the kingship of David. This revival is simply one symptom of the growth of the use of liturgical formulas and techniques in the secular sphere, in turn a result of the strong tendency to employ theocratic techniques in the political realm. By the time of Charlemagne, it is clearly established that the ruler of the Franks was simply continuing the tradition of Davidic kingship.

Ever since the time of their victory over the Arabs, the Franks had come to consider themselves as a new chosen people, and this they did with full papal approval. They chose to identify themselves with a 'new Israel' which carried on from biblical and ecclesiastical history rather than with a 'new Rome,' although they also claimed descent from the same Trojan stock which founded Rome. Nevertheless, they did not think of their armies as reconstituted Roman legions, but as armies that might have fought under the leadership of David or Gideon.

'Like other nations in revolutionary times, like the English people under Cromwell, the Franks believed themselves to be God's chosen people destined to execute the plans of Divine Providence.' The Frankish kingdom was a *regnum Davidicum*, its king a *novus Moysus* or *novus David*. He was also a priest, a *christus Domini*, anointed of God and the ruler of a new Jerusalem. As Kantorowicz points out, Pepin's anointment as if he were a king of Israel was of great importance for the political evolution of Europe, for it is 'the keystone of this evolution and at the same time the cornerstone of medieval divine right and *Dei gratia* kingship.'[1] Not only were the Franks a chosen people and their king a new David, but they were at the centre of the universal *populus christianus* and their king was *Rex Christianissimus*. Indeed, this conviction led them to feel superior to the

---

[1] *Laudes regiae, a Study in Liturgical Acclamations and Medieval Worship* (Berkeley and Los Angeles, 1946), pp. 56, 57. See also Kantorowicz' references there, and cf. his latest book, *The King's Two Bodies: A Study in Medieval Political Theology* (Princeton, 1957), pp. 77, 81, 83.

ancient Romans, for the latter were pagans while the Frankish dominion was Christian.[1]

The liturgical acclamations of the time not only link the king to biblical traditions of kingship, but also to angelic intercessors who constitute, as it were, a continuation of the hierarchy of which he is the temporal pinnacle and which reflects the hierarchical order of the unseen world. Thus the political as well as the ecclesiastical order is conceived as a temporal imitation of the unseen superhuman order of saints and intelligences, made a part of that 'ladder cosmos' up which men climb to God and down which all divine gifts descend. The political and the secular sphere thus have a likeness to the structure of the City of God and these formulas are among the earliest attempts to posit such a structure.[2] The surrounding of the ceremony of crowning with biblical concepts and ecclesiastical legitimation, with a sacramental and liturgical character, simply reflected this continuity and fundamental unity of the *scala Dei*. What is most important here for our purposes is that the sanction for all this and the type of the inauguration was the anointing of David by Samuel.[3]

This tradition of Davidic kingship as model kingship which started with Pepin persisted through the Middle Ages into the Renaissance. Thomas Aquinas, for example, in *De regimine principium* (chap. 8) gives David as an example of the ideal ruler, one who does what every ruler should and places his reward in God. A good example from the Renaissance is offered by Erasmus, who advances David as certainly one of the best models of kingship, although with the proviso that not even the best are perfect, so that the ideal Christian prince should try to imitate the best actions of all the best princes.[4] The uses of David as a political type were varied, as we can see, although it is a little startling to find Grotius arguing that contemporary rulers could use as a precedent the fact that David rightfully took

[1] Kantorowicz, *Laudes regiae*, p. 58.

[2] *Ibid.*, p. 62. Although in Frankish theory there was a sharp cleavage between the *regnum Davidicum* and *Imperium Romanum*, events and the politics of the Holy See turned the Franks into the heirs of Rome (*ibid.*, pp. 62–63).

[3] *Ibid.*, p. 78.

[4] *The Education of a Christian Prince*, trans. with an intro. by L. K. Born (New York, 1936), pp. 202, 255.

the spoils of the Amelekites which they had previously taken from others.[1]

The interpretation of David as a 'humble psalmist' which, along with the conception of kingship attached to his name, had such a profound effect on the medieval understanding of the figure of David does not derive from the general delineation of David in Scripture, from David in his providential and historically important role, but from a specific text in II Samuel. This is the source for Dante's use of him as an example of humility in the *Purgatorio* on the ledge of pride (x.55–69), in harmony with the moral interpretation of David as a symbol of *humilitas*. [2] The biblical text in question is worth citing at length because of the importance of its details in creating this conception of David, details which do not appear in another report of the same incident in I Chronicles 15.16–28.

So David went and brought up the ark of God from the house of Obededom into the city of David with gladness. And it was so that when they that bare the ark of the Lord had gone six paces, he sacrificed oxen and fatlings. And David danced before the Lord with all his might: and David was girded with a linen ephod. So David and all the house of Israel brought up the ark of the Lord with shouting, and with the sound of the trumpet. And as the ark of the Lord came into the city of David, Michal Saul's daughter looked through a window, and saw king David leaping and dancing before the Lord; and she despised him in her heart. . . . And Michal the daughter of Saul came out to meet David, and said, How glorious was the king of Israel to day, who uncovered himself to day in the eyes of the handmaidens of his servants, as one of the vain fellows shamelessly uncovereth himself! And David said unto Michal, It was before the Lord, which chose me before thy father, and before all his house, to appoint me ruler over the people of the Lord, over Israel: therefore will I play before the Lord. And I will yet be

---

[1] *De iure belli ac pacis*, III.vi.vii.1, ed. by P. C. Molhuysen (Leyden, 1919). This work is rich in the use of biblical precedents and should be very useful in elucidating politico-literary allusions in Renaissance culture.

[2] See Erich Auerbach, 'Figurative Texts Illustrating Certain Passages of Dante's *Commedia*,' *Speculum*, XXI (1946), 474–89), 476–77, section II on David as *humilis psalmista*.

more vile than thus, and will be base in mine own sight: and of the maidservants which thou hast spoken of, of them shall I be had in honour. Therefore Michal the daughter of Saul had no child unto the day of her death.[1]

The version of this story in Chronicles (*Vulg. Paralipomenon*) places considerable emphasis on the choice of musicians and singers to accompany the ark into the tent David pitched for it in Jerusalem. However, there is no singling out of David as dancing and leaping before the ark. Nor does Michal accuse David directly of disgracing himself and there is no explanation on David's part of his unkingly behaviour. The emphasis on humility is completely missing. Michal simply looks out of the window to see David dancing and leaping 'and she despised him in her heart.'

Dante uses the version from Samuel:

There, carved in the same marble, were the cart and oxen drawing the sacred ark on account of which men fear an office not committed to them. In front people appeared and the whole company, divided into seven choirs, made two of my senses say, the one: 'No,' the other: 'Yes, they sing'; in the same way, at the smoke of the incense that was imaged there, eyes and nose were in contradiction, with *yes* and *no*. There the humble psalmist went before the blessed vessel girt up and dancing, and at that time he was both more and less than king; opposite, figured at the window of a great palace, Michal looked on, like a woman vexed and scornful.

> Era intagliato lì nel marmo stesso
> lo carro e' buoi traendo l'arca santa,
> per che si teme officio non commesso.
> Dinanzi parea gente; e tutta quanta,
> partita in sette cori, a' due mie' sensi
> faceva dir l'un 'No', l'altro 'Sì, canta.'
> Similemente al fummo delli 'ncensi
> che v'era imaginato, li occhi e 'l naso
> e al sì e al no discordi fensi.
> Lì precedeva al benedetto vaso,
> trescando alzato, l'umile salmista,
> e più e men che re era in quel caso.

[1] II Sam. 6.12–16, 20–23.

Di contra, effigiata ad una vista
d'un gran palazzo, Micòl ammirava
sì come donna dispettosa e trista.[1]

Dante, after indirectly referring to Uzzah's presumption in touching the ark, focuses his narrative on the paradoxical self-abasement of the mighty king who, by his self-imposed humility before the Lord became less a king to such as Michal but more in the eyes of his Creator. This is a perfect *exemplum* of the favourite Christian paradox of *humilitas-sublimitas*, supremely manifested in the life of Christ, the God-man who voluntarily humiliated himself even though he was simultaneously Lord of the universe. Thus David is a type of Christ, a *figura Christi*, while the ark itself is a figure of the Church, the fortunes of which during its persecutions were prefigured in the removals of the ark from one place to another.[2]

There is a third strain in the typological tradition of David, although it is intrinsically related to the theme of the humble psalmist and perhaps ought to be treated as identical with it. In this tradition the stress is on 'psalmist' rather than on 'humble,' for David was famous as a great musician, the composer of the Psalms. Although this talent may appear to be a possible source of sinful pride, we must recall that he manifested his humility precisely in the great gesture of singing and dancing 'psalms' themselves before the ark.

This tradition, as we shall see, came to be related to the political one and to various classical notions concerning music, although the musical reputation of David was quite important in the early Church, even before its philosophical elaboration, as authority for the use of music in religious rituals.[3] A passage

---

[1] I cite the translation of J. D. Sinclair (Oxford, 1948) and the text of the Società Dantesca Italiana (Florence, 1921).

[2] Auerbach, 'Figurative Texts,' p. 477, cites Gregory the Great, *Moralia*, in Migne, *PL*, LXXV, col. 444, for the example of David as *humilis psalmista* and *figura Christi*, and Honorius of Autun, in Migne, *PL*, CLXXIII, col. 369, for the significance of the ark as a type of the persecutions of the Church. For this theme as applied to St. Francis, see Auerbach, 'St. Francis of Assisi in Dante's "Commedia" *Italica*,' XXII (1945), 166–79, and 'Rising to Christ on the Cross (*Paradiso* XI, 70–72),' *MLN*, LXIV (1949), 166–68.

[3] Leo Spitzer, 'Classical and Christian Ideas of World Harmony,' *Traditio*, II (1944), 409–64; II (1945), 307–64, 432.

from Augustine's *City of God* reveals both a puritanical ambivalence about the pleasures of music and the application to David of a well-developed conception of music as the art of cosmic harmony. Augustine felt that it was necessary to apologize for a strong interest in music on the part of this ancestor and *figura* of Christ, and explains that David loved his music mystically, as an image of that unity in variety which is the essence of a well-ordered city. In this way Augustine makes David's musicianship an intrinsic part of his role as a ruler. As we shall see, Marvell makes exactly the same kind of use of Cromwell's fondness of music, a trait of his character which attracted a certain amount of comment.

In the progress of the city of God through the ages, therefore, David first reigned in the earthly Jerusalem as a shadow of that which was to come. Now David was a man skilled in songs, who dearly loved musical harmony, not with a vulgar delight, but with a believing disposition, and by it served his God, who is the true God, by the mystical representation of a great thing. For the rational and well-ordered concord of diverse sounds in harmonious variety suggests the compact unity of a well-ordered city.[1]

Such conceptions of music as Augustine applied to David were by no means new. Greek speculation, beginning in pre-Socratic times, had worked out a complete cosmogony of music based on the notion of cosmic harmony in the world-soul, a harmony reflected in the movements of the heavenly bodies, in the individual soul where it was achieved through musical education, and in the body-politic where it was established through the rule of a good king. The first and most famous

[1] *De civitate Dei*, XVII. 14, in Migne, *PL*, XLI, col. 547: I cite the new text of the *Corpus Christianorum, Series Latina*, XLVIII (Turnholti, 1955) with 'v' for consonantal 'u.' The translation is by Marcus Dodd, in *A Select Library of the Nicene and Post-Nicene Fathers of the Christian Church*, Vol. II (Buffalo, 1887): Procurrente igitur per tempora civitate Dei, primo in umbra futuri, in terrena scilicet Hierusalem, regnavit David. Erat autem David vir in canticis eruditis, qui harmoniam musicam non vulgari voluptate, sed fideli voluntate dilexerit eaque Deo suo, qui verus est Deus, mystica rei magnae figuratione servierit. Diversorum enim sonorum rationalibus moderatusque concentus concordi varietate compactam bene ordinate civitatis insinuat unitatem.

synthesis of such ideas of universal harmony is Plato's *Timaeus*, a work which in turn was the source of Cicero's conception of a 'musical' world-soul and of his conception of the music of the spheres as a cosmic analogue of the order of the state. Boethius, of course, was for the Middle Ages the most important source of the medieval preoccupation with music as the symbol of world harmony, and the references to him in this connection are abundant in this period. Later references to him would indicate that the influence of *De musica* extended well into the seventeenth century.[1]

For our purposes, we need to stress the political aspect of these traditions of cosmic harmony to which the figure of David was assimilated and to which, in turn, Marvell assimilated Cromwell through David. Indeed, politics is the essential link between the 'humble psalmist-cosmic musician' on the one hand and the 'sublime,' divinely anointed king, on the other. The Davidic archetype we discern in the *First Anniversary of the Government* and the *Poem on the Death of O.C.* is a model political figure who is, as it were, our focus for Cromwell. Around the *figura* and its fulfilment cluster many of these ideas of divine election, humility-sublimity, and charismatic mystical insight into those universal principles of order which were presumed to underlie all great statecraft.

III

The first correspondence which Marvell establishes for Cromwell in *The First Anniversary of the Government under O.C.* is with the sun, the ruler of the cosmos. As the king of celestial bodies moves with greatest rapidity through the signs of the Zodiac exceeding the other planets, so Cromwell exceeds all other princes in his efficiency and ability. The lesser princes, indeed, do not even approximate the speed of the next most swift

[1] For a masterly survey of these concepts see Spitzer's work already cited, and cf. G. L. Finney, 'A World of Instruments,' *ELH*, XX (1953), 87–120. On the analogies between human organism, state, and universe see Rudolf Allers, 'Microcosmus,' *Traditio*, II (1944), 319–407. esp. 368 ff., and on the musical terminology for these same analogies see pp. 375 ff.

heavenly bodies but function in analogy with Saturn, the slowest and most malignant planet.

> *Cromwell* alone with greater Vigour runs,
> (Sun-like) the stages of succeeding Suns:
> And still the Day which he doth next restore,
> Is the just Wonder of the Day before.
> Cromwell alone doth with new Lustre spring,
> And shines the Jewel of the yearly Ring.
> 'Tis he the force of scattered Time contracts,
> And in one Year the work of Ages acts:
> While heavy Monarchs make a wide Return,
> Longer, and more Malignant than *Saturn*:
> And though they all *Platonique* years should raign
> In the same Posture would be found again.[1]

(7–18)

Not only can Cromwell accomplish more than other rulers, but he does the right things. He is, indeed, of the type of Solomon, a ruler who will actually 'build the Temple in their days.' Thus Marvell begins to interweave the 'astronomical' with the biblical conceptions of the ruler and prepares us for the assimilation of Cromwell to David by the allusion of Solomon. While lesser rulers passively consult astrologers to learn how much time Fate has decreed in which they can remain free of their deserved punishment, Cromwell is himself, as sun or 'star,' a maker of destiny, or like any star, an instrument of Destiny in the sense of divine providence. The stars or planets, from antiquity believed to be the instruments of necessity or fate (with some allowance for free-will on the part of the orthodox), do not control Cromwell. Like a true man of *virtù* he is himself the fate of others and we can assume that his only overlord is Providence itself. In his freedom from blind astrological necessity and his rapid effective action we discover that Cromwell is also a Machiavellian ruler, the new ruler of sure ability who will also build the Temple of the state in his own time, a true master architect of the nation.

[1] I cite the edition of Hugh MacDonald, *The Poems of Andrew Marvell* (Cambridge, Mass., 1952), since it reproduces the unique copy of Marvell's Miscellaneous Poems (1681) containing the Cromwell poems. I have, of course, had continual recourse to the standard edition of H. M. Margoliouth, *The Poems and Letters of Andrew Marvell* (Oxford, 1952; 2 vols. 2d ed.).

No other care they [i.e. heavy Monarchs] bear of things above,
But with Astrologers, divine, and *Jove*
To know how long their Planet yet Reprives
From the deserved Fate their guilty lives:
Thus (Image-like) an useless time they tell,
And with vain Scepter strike the hourly Bell;
Nor more contribute to the state of Things,
Then wooden Heads unto the Viols strings.
  While indefatigable *Cromwell* hyes,
And cuts his way still nearer to the Skyes,
Learning, a Musique in that Region clear,
To tune this lower to that higher sphere.

(37–84)

Cromwell, the 'sun,' rises to the skies, where he learns the music of cosmic order, the music of the spheres, an order which he will transmit to the microcosm below, imposing thereon the political form of universal harmony. In effect, these lines tell us that Cromwell fulfils the function of a truly providential ruler, one who can attune the microcosm of the state to the orderly motion of the heavenly bodies and the harmonic proportions between them which is their music.

This identification of Cromwell as a political and cosmic 'musician' leads immediately to a further identification with him as Amphion, the artist who built the walls of Thebes by playing on his lute, the heavenly gift of Hermes, with such skill that the stones moved of their own accord to form a wall. Cromwell is thus not only a musician but by virtue of being the kind of musician he is, also an architect. Marvell develops this notion by describing the miraculous building of the walls of Thebes in terms of the variations of Amphion's music:

So when *Amphion* did the Lute command,
Which the God gave him; with his gentle hand,
The rougher Stones, unto his Measures hew'd,
Dans'd up in order from the Quarreys rude;
This took a Lower, that an Higher place,
As he the Treble alter'd, or the Base:
No note he struck, but a new Story lay'd,
And the great Work ascended while he play'd.

(49–56)

The order of music is here transformed into the hierarchical order of architecture, levels of the building of the state corresponding to the various notes, high and low, of a musical structure, making a kind of 'Harmonious City of the seven Gates' (66):

> Such was that wondrous Order and Consent,
> When *Cromwell* tun'd the ruling Instrument;
> While tedious Statesmen many years did hack,
> Framing a Liberty that still went back;
> Whose num'rous Gorge could swallow in an hour
> That Island, which the Sea cannot devour:
> Then our *Amphion* issues out and sings,
> And once he struck, and twice, the pow'rful Strings.
>
> (67–74)

Cromwell thus is transformed into the ruler as artist, the man who by his *virtù* constructs that supreme work of art which is the state. His 'instrument' is both the apparatus of state and the famous Instrument of Government of 1653 which regulated the position of Cromwell as Protector. From one point of view, we discover here the traditional Machiavellian conception of the successful new ruler, the man with great ability but with no hereditary authority or traditional supports of his rule, a prince who must create his own 'legitimacy.' For Machiavelli, of course, success and efficiency are the only warrants the new ruler needs. If he can gain and hold power, order the state, and win the support of his subjects, he is as 'legitimate' as he needs to be. There was nevertheless a strong impulse on the part of the new rulers and their supporters—one shared by Marvell as well—to legitimize their rules. In the Italian city states the new rulers attempted to substitute the fresh symbols of art and culture for the old traditional symbols of authority to which they had no right. The positive revaluation of the arts and artists which is so important a motif in Renaissance culture in part rests on this phenomenon, although of course legitimate hereditary monarchs also employed the arts as extensions of their power and glory.

But Cromwell does not need these trappings. He is not simply a successful ruler in the strictly secular sense, but a divinely chosen ruler who has been given insight into the workings of the order of the macrocosm, whose love of music implies that he possesses that order in the microcosm of his soul, and who knows how to impose it on the microcosm of the state with speed, unlike 'heavy Monarchs' for whom a platonic year would not suffice, or 'tedious Statesman' who hack away in vain to shape the building blocks of the state.

> The Commonwealth then first together came,
> And each one enter'd in the willing Frame;
> All other Matter yields, and may be rul'd;
> But who the Minds of stubborn Men can build?
> No Quarry bears a stone so hardly wrought,
> Nor with such labor from its Center brought;
> None to be sunk in the foundation bends,
> Each in the house the highest Place contends
> And each the Hand that lays him will direct,
> And some fall back upon the Architect;
> Yet all compos'd by this attractive Song,
> Into the Animated City throng.
>
> (75–86)

Not only does Cromwell place all the units of the state in their proper places, but his architectural skill is so great that the opposition, like the counter-thrusts in a properly constructed building, only serve to strengthen the whole edifice. It is obvious that Cromwell, in Marvell's eyes, created a mixed constitution on the model suggested by Polybius' analysis of Roman institutions and strongly advocated by Renaissance political theorists such as Machiavelli and Guicciardini. In a famous chapter of the *Discorsi* (I,2) Machiavelli adopts Polybius' version of ancient political theories concerning the cycle of the state and maintains that the three forms of government, monarchy, aristocracy, and commonwealth, run through a cycle of decay passing over into their bad counterparts, tyranny, oligarchy, and 'licentiousness.' The only way to interrupt this cycle is to establish a mixed form of government in which the same constitution combines a prince, a nobility, and the power of the people. The three powers would then be able to keep watch on one another and to keep each other in check. In such a government a tyrant could not rise, and both nobles and people would have liberty. In addition, disputes would become a source of strength, since they would lead to a readjustment of the internal balance of stresses and not to revolution:

> The Common-wealth does through their Centers all
> Draw the Circumf'rence of the publique Wall;

> The crossest Spirits here do take their part,
> Fast'ning the Contignation which they thwart;
> And they, whose Nature leads them to divide,
> Uphold, this one, and that the other Side;
> But the most Equal still sustein the Height,
> And they as Pillars keep the Work upright;
> While the resistance of opposed Minds,
> The Fabrick of the Arches stronger binds,
> Which on the Basis of a Senate free,
> Knit by the Roofs Protecting weight agree.
>
> (87–98)

Marvell then returns to the conception of Cromwell as a 'star' and makes more explicit the theme of his leadership. He, like a heavenly body, influences others and, like the pole star, helps others to steer their course.

> When for his Foot he thus a place had found,
> He hurles e'er since the World about him round;
> And in his sev'ral Aspects, like a Star,
> Here shines in Peace, and thither shoots a War.
> While by his Beams, observing Princes steer,
> And wisely court the Influence they fear.
>
> (99–104)

Note too that he has both benign and malignant aspects as the heavenly bodies do for astrologers, the first hint of a new antithesis, 'creation-destruction' which, as we shall see, is developed later in the poem.

The return to the theme of Cromwell as 'star,' destiny, or fate, is followed by a long attack on the other, so to speak, 'non-observing' princes of Europe who do not 'humbly tread / The path where holy Oracles do lead' (107–8). It is such who delay the unfolding on earth of Providence's 'great Designes kept for the latter Dayes' (110). Such rulers, Marvell tells us, are 'mad with Reason, so miscall'd of State. / They know not and what they know not hate' (111–12). The historical reference here would seem to be to the failure of Cromwell's attempt to include the Dutch and the Swedes in a general Protestant alliance. The latter, although quite as protestant as Cromwell, found it politically expedient to stay out. There were evidently two kinds of 'reason of state' for Marvell: the kind which appears to be so but is really to be subsumed into the mysterious workings of Providence, and the kind which is not merely apparently unprincipled but actually is. Perhaps a cynic would say that the two kinds are the kind practised by Cromwell and the kind practised by others who should have agreed with him and didn't.

After the outright political realism of the *Horatian Ode* and similar elements in the *First Anniversary* it is a little odd to follow Marvell through a prophetic interpretation of Cromwell in the apocalyptic mode (105–58) where his rule is seen as a preparation for the fulfilment of biblical prophecy. The passage is complete with a coming reign of saints, the destruction of the Great Whore and the Beast, and an ingathering of peoples, especially of the Jews. Cromwell alone chases the Roman 'monster through every Throne' (128), a certain sign of his election for the providential task of reforming the political structure of the world in preparation for the last days and the end of history. The signs would all appear to be actual and Marvell dares to hope:

> Hence oft I think, if in some happy Hour
> High Grace should meet in one with highest Pow'r,
> And then a seasonable People still
> Should bend to his, as he to Heavens will,
> What might we hope, what wonderful Effect
> From such a wish'd Conjuncture might reflect,
> Sure, the mysterious Work, where none withstand,
> Would forthwith finish under such a Hand:
> Fore-shortned Time its useless Course would stay,
> And soon precipitate the latest Day.
> But a thick Cloud about that Morning lyes,
> And intercepts the Beams of Mortal eyes,
> That 'tis the most which we determine can,
> If these the Times, then this must be the Man.

$$(131–44)$$

If this seems incompatible with the political realism of Marvell, it may not prove so on further reflection. The truly Machiavellian view of political activity involves the isolation of that aspect of political behaviour which lies on the other side of customary moral norms and which cannot be understood in terms of an ethic of good intentions regardless of achieved results. What is apparently evil may then from this perspective possibly be good, and vice versa. But this perspective is quite close to the human view of the workings of Providence. If all that happens in history has a providential meaning—i.e., will work out for the best—even though many of these events are ethically incongruous, then those ethically ambiguous phenomena and actions which relate to the arrival of a new ruler on the stage of history—and these are the concern of Machiavelli in *The Prince*—are as capable as any other activity of being subsumed into a prophetic interpretation of history. After all, the moral character of Augustine's *terrena civitas* is not very different from that of the state of Machiavelli. For the former, of course, there is a world of true justice and righteousness outside of space and time, a world where intention and result are harmoniously unified and there is no difference between being and seeming. But for political theory this is of little moment, since such a world will continue to remain outside of space and time.

We should not, however, push these resemblances between Machiavelli and Marvell too far. Marvell, like Malvolio, read many 'politick authors' and accepts the Augustinian and Machiavellian view of the problematic character of action, the inevitable mixture of good and evil in it, the way the results of action change their ethical character depending on the 'time' in which they come to pass and the 'time' from which we view them, the gulf which obtains between what the agent of action seems to be doing and what he actually does. However, he does not believe that God or fortune gives dominion to the good and bad alike. Cromwell is good. We have all sorts of divine warrants for that conviction, and any acts which do not seem good, such as regicide, are a result of the fact that he lives on another plane, the plane of destiny, or as Machiavelli would say, the plane of *necessità*. It is also clear that Marvell theologizes *necessità*. Cromwell, the 'star,' the man of destiny and instrument of Providence, simply cannot be completely judged by customary ethical norms. There was ample precedent for this view in biblical exegesis as well as in Machiavellian political theory. Solomon's harem, Samson's suicide, these and many more ethically dubious episodes of Scripture were seen as divinely ordained dispensations for the 'times,' and, 'if these the Times, then this must be the man' (144).

46

And well he therefore does, and well has guest,
Who in his Age has always forward prest:
And knowing not where Heaven's choice may light,
Girds yet his Sword, and ready stands to fight.

(145–48)

There is no doubt that, for Marvell, Cromwell is the man for
the times, but it is interesting to observe that the prophetic
mode the poet has adopted for this passage closely imitates the
'obscure' mode of biblical apocalyptic prophecy. The times are
troubled ones, and it is difficult to trace out the designs of
Providence in a very real chaos which only the eyes of faith can
see as a mere appearance. Marvell then continues by furnishing
even more evidence of Cromwell's special destiny. His saintly
mother lived to be so old 'That she might seem, could we the
Fall dispute / T'have smelt the Blossome, and not eat the Fruit'
(163–64). This brief and witty allusion to the fall becomes a
very important motif of the rest of the poems in terms of the
antithesis 'Fall-Rise,' 'humiliation-exaltation,' 'humility-sublimity.' The point of departure for Marvell's development of
this theme is a reference to a very literal fall for Cromwell
when, on September 29, 1654, his coach drawn by six German
horses was overturned in Hyde Park while he was at the reins
himself.

How near they fail'd, and in the sudden Fall
At once assay'd to overturn us all.
Our brutish fury struggling to be Free,
Hurry'd thy Horses while they hurry'd thee.
When thou hadst almost quit thy Mortal cares,
And soyl'd in Dust thy Crown of silver Hairs.

(175–80)

This fall becomes the Fall. Nature groans, the cosmic order
is disrupted, and the edifice of the state cracks.

Thou *Cromwell* falling, not a stupid Tree,
Or Rock so savage, but it mourn'd for thee:
And all about was heard a Panique grown,
As if that Nature's self were overthrown.
It seemed the Earth did from the Center tear;
It seemed the Sun was faln out of the Sphere:

Justice obstructed lay, and Reason fool'd;
Courage disheartened, and Religion cool'd
A dismal Silence through the Palace went,
And then loud Shreeks the vaulted Marbles rent.

(201–10)

But Cromwell swiftly and gloriously rises, an ascent described with allusion to the ascent of Elijah and to the progress of the sun:

But thee triumphant hence the firy Carr,
And firy Steeds had born out of the Warr,
From the low World, and thankless Men above,
Unto the Kingdom blest of Peace and Love:
We only mourn'd our selves, in thine Ascent,
Whom thou hadst left beneath with Mantle rent.

(215–21)

Cromwell's physical fall and rise not only has a typological significance in biblical history and a contemporary reference to his indispensable position in the state, but it is in turn the physical analogue of his moral character. He literally fell and rose again and the political world fell and rose with him. But in the moral sphere Cromwell, so to speak, rises and falls all the time simultaneously, for he is at once lowly and exalted:

For all delight of Life thou then didst lose,
When to Command, thou didst thy self Depose;
Resigning up thy Privacy so dear,
To turn the headstrong Peoples Charioteer;
For to be Cromwell was a greater thing,
Then ought below, or yet above a King:
Therefore thou rather didst thy Self depress,
Yielding to Rule, because it made thee Less.

(221–28)

If Cromwell was first Elijah in his translation to the heavens, he next descends as the cloud of rain which broke the three years' drought Israel suffered under the reign of Ahab. This cloud, which Elijah's servant saw only the seventh time he went to look for it, marked both Jehovah's favour and the destruction of the priests of Baal whose cult had been fostered by Jezebel, Ahab's Phœnecian wife (I Kings 17 ff., esp. 17.42–46). It is clear that Marvell here alludes to the political and religious evils of Charles's rule, evils which Cromwell swept away.

Hence Cromwell, like the biblical cloud, is both beneficial and destructive, good for the 'dry land' but murderous to the king:

> For, neither didst thou from the first apply
> Thy sober Spirit unto things too High,
> But in thine own Fields exercisedst long,
> An healthful Mind within a Body strong;
> Till at the Seventh time thou in the Skyes,
> As a small Cloud, like a Mans hand didst rise;
> Then did thick Mists and Winds the air deform,
> And down at last thou pow'rdst the fertile Storm;
> Which to the thirsty Land did plenty bring,
> But though forewarn'd, o'r-took and wet the King.[1]
>
> (229–38)

Marvell is careful again to accentuate the moral balance in Cromwell, who was not over-ambitious and who possessed the classical perfection of *mens sana in corpore sano*. He thus prepares us to accept Cromwell's destructive aspect as supernaturally ordained, not as flowing directly and solely from his own person. Like nature and many of the providential instruments of Scripture, he rewards and punishes, creates and destroys in fulfilment of designs which are in part beyond human comprehension. The force of all the astrological allusions and the references, direct and oblique, to biblical events, converge finally on a justification of the regicide. Cromwell was the instrument of Divine Providence, a divinely ordained architect of the state who must be judged by his magnificent results (a real as against a seeming king), his unfailing prudence, his ability to destroy only in the interest of greater creation. We begin to glimpse that there is a further, divinely sanctioned, antithesis in Cromwell and that is of destruction and creation.

> What since he did, an higher Force him push'd
> Still from behind, and it before him rush'd,
> Though undiscern'd among the tumult blind,
> Who think those high Decrees by Man design'd
> 'Twas Heav'n would not that his Pow'r should cease,
> But walk still middle betwixt War and Peace;

[1] James F. Carens, 'Andrew Marvell's Cromwell Poems,' *Bucknell Review*, VII (1957), 41–70, 69, points out that the imagery of water, storm, and shipwreck which begins in this section of the poem is derived from a speech Cromwell delivered before Parliament in September 1654.

Choosing each Stone, and poysing every weight,
Trying the Measures of the Bredth and Height;
Here pulling down, and there erecting New,
Founding a firm State by Proportions true.

(239–48)

Like Gideon, Cromwell knew how to conquer 'Zeba and Zalmunna' and punish 'Succoths elders,' but he is even more like this *figura* in refusing the headship of state for himself and his sons (249–56; cf. Judges 8–9). And if the 'olive' refused to reign over the other trees, should the bramble be anointed with the oil that belongs to the olive? (257–60). Without wishing to stretch Marvell's analogies even further, it would not be irrelevant to suggest that Cromwell has something better than royal blood in his veins. He has the very oil of unction which makes kings into kings. In so far as Cromwell is thus both more and less than a king, he is assimilated to the figure of David, and in reference to his refusal to accept kingship he is of the type of Gideon. Indeed, he is both more and less than an anointed king; he is a *christus Domini* who, possessing the internal spiritual unction, refuses the external chrisma. In the last analysis he is *sui generis*, a ruler as unique as David, the singular king of Israel.

Whose climbing Flame, without a timely stop,
Had quickly Levell'd every Cedar's top.
Therefore first growing to thyself a Law,
Th'ambitious Shrubs thou in just time didst aw.

(261–64)

Cromwell, to human eyes, seems like a true Machiavellian ruler: a law unto himself, a man with a miraculous sense of the appropriate time and conditions for action, prudent and swift, thoughtful and impetuous at the same time, qualities he demonstrated in his suppression of the Levellers. But Marvell continually reminds us through image and type that from another perspective, rationally irreducible to this one, Cromwell is a divinely endowed and divinely directed instrument.

Political architect, cosmic musician, instrument of destiny, Cromwell is the saviour of the ship of state, not like the helmsman who should have saved it but like 'some lusty Mate, who with more careful Eye / Counted the Hours, and ev'ry Star did

spy, / The Helm does from the artless Steersman strain'
(273–75). From this point of view he is the true man of ability,
of *virtù*, who can count the hours to know the right 'time' and
who in reading every star shows his awareness of that cosmic
order by which we determine our 'place.' He derives his right
to take the helm of state from his artless predecessors because
he has true *virtù*, but we are also reminded that it is a *virtù* in
harmony with the order of things. If Cromwell's achievement
was the imposition of order, the fruit of that order is liberty:

> 'Tis not a Freedome, that where All command:
> Nor Tyranny, where One does them withstand:
> But who of both the Bounders knows to lay
> Him as their Father must the State obey.
>
> (279–82)

> And only didst for others plant the Vine
> Of Liberty, not drunken with its Wine.
> That sober Liberty which men may have,
> That they enjoy, but more they vainly crave.
>
> (287–90)

After a section concerned with the various internal enemies of
the state (291–324), Marvell takes up again the analogy of
Cromwell to the sun, comparing the fear that he would be only
temporarily successful to the fear of the first man that the sun
might not return after its first setting (325–42):

> So while our Star that gives us Light and Heat,
> Seem'd now a long and gloomy Night to threat,
> Up from the other World his Flame he darts,
> And Princes shining through their windows starts;
> And credulous Ambassadors accuse.
>
> (343–48)

These foreigners express amazement that the Protectorate
could create a navy and rebuild itself as rapidly as it did
(349–52), and equal amazement at Cromwell's skill in the
arts of statecraft. They are puzzled by the sublime ability
which in their eyes should mark him as the peer of a legitimate
monarch although he is a usurper, and also by his humble
refusal to 'legitimize' himself by becoming a king.

'Where did he learn those Arts that cost us dear?
Where below Earth, or where above the Sphere?
He seems a King by long Succession born,
And yet the same to be a King does scorn.
Abroad a King he seems, and something more,
At home a Subject on the equal Floor.'

(385–90)

Cromwell is here presented by his own enemies as the truly successful Machiavellian prince who, through the arts of statesmanship, the arts apparently learned 'below earth,' becomes the equal of a hereditary monarch. It is precisely for such that *Il principe* is a handbook, and Cromwell learned his lesson well. Simultaneously he carries the stamp of the Davidic king, whose statesmanship comes from 'above the Sphere' and whose moral nature is a paradoxically harmonious fusion of the antithesis *humilitas-sublimitas*.

Let us now turn briefly to *A Poem on the Death of O.C.*, in which some of the themes we have been considering, particularly the Davidic archetype, become more explicit.

It is in great part a conventional eulogy and, for the purposes of this essay, we need not consider it in as much detail as the *First Anniversary*. The very opening of the poem calls our attention to the providential character of Cromwell's rule.

> THAT Providence which had so long the care
> Of *Cromwell's* head, and numbred ev'ry hair,
> Now in its self (the Glass where all appears)
> Had seen the period of his golden years.

(1–4)

This theme is emphasized later in the poem when Marvell alludes to the great efficacy Cromwell's prayers had in inclining the God of battles to his side.[1] Astonished armies fled before Cromwell, and no man had been more obeyed in heaven since the time of Gideon for whom God stayed the sun in its path. This, of course, is the same Gideon who, in the *First Anniversary*, was the prototype of Cromwell in his refusal to be king.

In this last poem on Cromwell, the 'humility-sublimity' antithesis is first suggested in the form of 'valour-clemency' or

---

[1] Cf. C. H. Firth, *The Last Years of the Protectorate* (2 vols.; London, 1909), II, 205, on the presumed power of Cromwell's prayers.

'force-mercy'. In the *First Anniversary*, let us recall, Cromwell had been interpreted as a synthesis of various antithetical though generally positive values: a Machiavellian 'prince' and a biblical king, an apparently illegitimate usurper who has a higher form of legitimacy than any so-called legitimate monarch, a man with so much energy and freedom of action that he is as fate to others, but who is nevertheless completely an instrument of the Providence whose service is perfect freedom, a sublime and humble man all at once. Now, on the occasion of his death, Marvell largely emphasizes the moral antitheses in Cromwell, and they were of such a unique blend that, unlike a stage ruler, Cromwell was able to die in bed.

> The People, which what most they fear esteem,
> Death when more horrid so more noble deem;
> And blame the last *Act*, like *Spectators* vain,
> Unless the *Prince* whom they applaud be slain.
> Nor fate indeed can well refuse that right
> To those that liv'd in War, to dye in Fight.
> But long his *Valour* none had left that could
> Indanger him, or *Clemancy* that would.
> And he whom Nature all for Peace had made,
> But angry Heaven unto War had sway'd,
> And so less useful here he most desir'd,
> For what he least affected was admir'd,
> Deserved yet an End whose ev'ry part
> Should speak the wondrous softness of his Heart.
>
> (7–20)

It is important to observe that 'valour-clemency' stands in direct proportion to 'heaven-nature.' Cromwell's force and courage which enabled him to suppress his enemies were functions of his role as the instrument of an angry heaven. His mercy, a function of his own nature, disarmed those enemies for whom force was not necessary. Like the best sort of Machiavellian ruler Cromwell was both loved and feared, but his exercise of force is 'moralized' by attributing to Providence the fearful elements in Cromwell's character. It is not insignificant that Marvell makes much of this last poem a description of Cromwell as a tender father watching over his dying daughter Eliza.

As with the death of any truly great man, Cromwell's is

preceded by a great storm ('A Secret Cause does sure those Signs ordain / Foreboding Princes falls, and seldom vain,' 101–2). Marvell then continues with a eulogy of his virtues, singling our valour, religion, friendship, and prudence by name, although he possessed all the rest besides (227–28), and with a description of the greatness of his character and of his public achievements as the Great Protector. What is most significant for our theme, however, is an explicit reference to the type of David as the humble monarch, as the archetypal *figura* of which Cromwell was a contemporary fulfilment:

> No more shall heare that powerful language charm,
> Whose force oft spar'd the labour of his arm:
> No more shall follow where he spent the dayes
> In warre, in counsell, or in pray'r, and praise;
> Whose meanest acts he would himself advance,
> As ungirt *David* to the arke did dance.
>
> (237–43)

Earlier in the poem we were prepared for this passage by a *reprise* of the 'sublimity-humility' themes so dominant in the *First Anniversary*, when Marvell says of Cromwell: 'For he no duty by his height excus'd / Not though a *Prince* to be a Man refused' (84–85). What was the implicit type of the *First Anniversary* and of the earlier portions of *A Poem on the Death of O.C.* finally becomes explicit. Any contemporary reader versed in Scripture and the contemporary techniques of exegesis would have recognized the implicit analogies to David in Cromwell's attributes of *sublimitas-humilitas*, his election by heaven for rule by a special covenant like the one God made with David through Nathan the prophet, and, last but not least, his love of music, the art which in a cosmic and mystical sense is necessary to impose order and harmony on the body politic. They expected that in his death Cromwell's soul would go to join other great lawgivers and biblical kings such as Moses (one of Machiavelli's examples of a successful armed prophet, by the way), Joshua and especially '*David*, for the sword and harpe renown'd' (294).

In the *Horatian Ode* Marvell's 'frame,' so to speak, was Machiavellian. Over the years Marvell gradually transformed Cromwell from the 'Machiavellian prince,' in the authentic and not the vulgar sense of that phrase, into a Davidic king, thus moving from a predominantly secular conception of Cromwell to a profoundly religious one. The typological method is apparent in all of the poems, in its secularized form in the *Horatian Ode*, and in an authentically scriptural form in the others. What is also apparent is that Marvell was impelled in the path we have traced by the persistent need to 'legitimize' the man who was, after all, a usurper. After an attempt, filled with tension, to fuse together both conceptions, that of biblical king and Machiavellian 'prince' in the *First Anniversary*, Marvell concludes by settling on the biblical conception, virtually excluding a 'secular' Cromwell, and legitimizes the Great Protector in the only way he could, by canonizing him.

In his treatment of Cromwell, Marvell reveals those same qualities of imagination that we find throughout his poetry, and which derive from the interpretation of experience through a perspective created by the fusion of antitheses. The theme of 'humility-sublimity' so dominant in the Cromwell poems runs through *Upon Appleton House*, where it receives both an aesthetic and a moral application, with all kinds of subtle changes on true and false humility in life and art, and true and false chastity. Similarly, the antithesis 'art-nature' in all of its paradoxical implications, unites *Appleton House* with the Mower poems. From this point of view the Cromwell poems become of a piece with the rest of Marvell's poetry and lose the anomalous character with which much modern criticism seemed to endow them.

DOUGLAS BUSH

The Isolation of the Renaissance Hero

O NE of the clichés of our time is that the common isolation
of the romantic and the modern hero reflects the sense of alienation from society felt by many romantic and modern artists and
intellectuals. (It might be remarked, by the way, that such
aliens appear to be in danger of losing their special standing,
since society itself is now seen as the lonely crowd.) This is of
course a stereotype of the past century and a half, not the norm
of cultural history. It would be hard to think of any ancients who
felt isolated in the modern sense; even Socrates saw himself as a
citizen of Athens. And we might try to imagine the result of
putting the question 'Do you feel isolated?' to Chaucer or
Rabelais or Shakespeare or Cervantes (though Don Quixote is
the supreme example of romantic isolation, seen in a comic
light). If the romantic or modern hero is usually isolated because of rebellious nonconformity or the recoil of a superior
nature from the gross world, such motives do not seem to be
conspicuous in the literature, at any rate the nondramatic
literature, of the Renaissance. Whereas the romantic or modern
outlaw is likely to be the special ideal of a cultural élite, or the
helpless victim of a society that is condemned, I would suggest
three propositions concerning the Renaissance hero: first, if he
is 'good,' he is the magnified projection of an ideal generally
accepted by society; second, if he is not 'good,' the pity and
terror he evokes still leave the audience confirmed in their

57

attachment to traditional values because these are also the values of the author, who is not—as critics so often say of modern writers— 'seeking a new ethic'; and, third, whether he is good or not, and whatever divine or diabolical prompting he may receive, the Renaissance hero makes his own choices and is responsible for what he does. People more modern-minded than I might say that the first two propositions are tame and unexciting and that the third embodies an obsolete fallacy; I would say that all three help largely to explain the strength of Renaissance literature.

In point of time, the English Renaissance is far closer to us than it was to ancient Rome or the still more remote antiquity of Greece, but the Renaissance hero is far closer to Achilles and Agamemnon, Odysseus and Aeneas, Orestes and Oedipus, than he is to Leopold Bloom or Kafka's K or Frederic Henry or Isaac McCaslin or Willy Loman. This obvious fact is too large and vague to be in itself very enlightening, and we might recall some ways in which the classical ideal was assimilated and modified by Renaissance writers. To do so is to run over many commonplaces, but I for one have never been afraid of them, and, what is more important, writers of the Renaissance were not.

In the first place, it is impossible to exaggerate the veneration authors and readers felt for the ancient thinkers, poets, historians, orators, statesmen, and generals as a race of superior beings. Such hero-worship was bred in the bone and no amount of drill in grammar and rhetoric could kill it. Ancient *exempla* and *sententiae*, collected by Erasmus and others, embodied oracular wit and wisdom helpful for every contingency in life. Such anecdotes and aphorisms did not appeal merely to the Poloniuses of the world; they fertilized and sustained so emancipated a moralist as Montaigne, whose chief teachers were Seneca and Plutarch. The name of Plutarch is alone enough to recall this whole way of thought and feeling; and Sir Thomas North, in his racy and eloquent translation of the *Lives*, seems to view the ancient heroes both as remote demigods and as Elizabethans writ large. From Thomas Wilson's *Arte of Rhetorique* to Milton's *Of Education*, Renaissance humanists cherished the faith that boys who learned and recited the utterances of the ancients could not but become like them. Thus the

Renaissance author, brought up to worship and emulate the ancients, became thereby a conscious link in a great tradition, a member of the European community. Of course the universally held doctrine of imitation, itself an inheritance from antiquity, could and did engender a swarm of epics and dramas which, as Porson said of Southey's epics, will be read when Homer and Virgil are forgotten; but we are not concerned with that underworld of the dead.

Secondly, numerous ancients, from Aristophanes and Plato to Plutarch, had affirmed the didactic function of literature, and this principle was reaffirmed by a much fuller chorus of Renaissance poets and critics throughout Europe. What in our time has been labelled 'the didactic heresy' was the basic theory of literature for some twenty-two centuries. Renaissance critics and poets have little to say about self-expression or the agonies of creation, but they are never weary of insisting that literature is philosophy teaching by examples, that it moves men to the love and practice of virtue and the abhorrence of vice. Thus the aim of literature is identical with the aim of education, virtuous action. We think of Sidney's frequent appeal, in his *Defence of Poesy*, to good and bad examples in classical epic and drama; of that epitome of Renaissance doctrine, Spenser's letter to Ralegh about *The Faerie Queene*, which presents a thoroughly didactic view of the famous heroic poems from Homer to Tasso; of Chapman's worship of Homer as the supreme poet and teacher, the creator of Achilles, the man of perturbation and physical courage, and Odysseus, the man of wisdom and unconquerable endurance. As recent interpreters of Chapman's humanism have shown, the principals in his tragedies tend to fall into two types, that of Achilles and that of his ideal hero, Odysseus.

This positive faith in the efficacy of both moral precepts and exemplary heroes must be emphasized because it is so far from anything we are accustomed to nowadays. If in modern novels we come on a character who appears to be 'good,' we are likely to assume that the author's intention is ironical; and we are left uncertain whether the other characters represent depravity or a new and elusively recognizable kind of virtue. Doubtless many persons would say that the difference is between naïveté and sophistication, but even they might hesitate to apply the word 'naïve' to Shakespeare, who never leaves us uncertain about good and evil. And in general the great writing of the Renaissance is the product of educated, disciplined, realistic maturity; its idealism is not naïve or sentimental or spurious. Unlike a number of current writers of fiction, Renaissance authors had not discovered the fountain of perpetual adolescence.

Some other elements in this idealism may be briefly noted. Renaissance heroes, like classical heroes, are eminent in worldly position as well as in character. High birth implies high advantages and imposes high obligations; moral success or failure is so much the more impressive and far-reaching in its effects. Willy Loman cannot declare, 'Ay, every inch a king'; nor can the bedraggled heroine of *A Streetcar Named Desire* proudly say 'I am Duchess of Malfi still,' or

> Give me my robe; put on my crown. I have
> Immortal longings in me.

Pathetic derelicts have only the souls and the language of pathetic derelicts.

The Renaissance hero was not merely of lofty station; his moral stature, his personality, was commonly enlarged to something like superhuman dimensions. We never think of Shakespeare's tragic heroes as being mere men who could mix with the sober or the glamorous members of Elizabeth's or James's court and council. Of the factors that contributed to the creation of heroes beyond life-size one is negative and general: that imaginative writers were not in bondage to actuality, to dogmas about verisimilitude. Such dogmas did develop in the course of the seventeenth century and led into the Augustan age; but the narrative or dramatic poet of the earlier time was free to make his characters larger than life, to involve them with the supernatural, to do anything at all that he could bring off. Such freedom was a heritage from many things, including the heroic poems and romances of antiquity and the Middle Ages and the nonrealistic allegorical tradition. One positive and concrete symptom of Renaissance idealism is the classical mythology that writers used so much, often flatly, but often too with inspired potency. Mythological allusions could be a language of superhuman significance and intensity. The gods and goddesses and heroes represented power, passion, beauty, greatness in good or evil, beyond human limitations. Examples are everywhere from Spenser and Marlowe through Shakespeare to Milton.

Finally, not to prolong these generalities, we may remember that the English Renaissance was, historically, an ideal period for the imaginative writer. The planets, so to speak, were in such a conjunction as could never have occurred before and could never occur again. Writers of that age were not self-consciously agonizing over their alienation from society, over lost sources of power, over the extinction of 'myth.' They had, in abundance, their own problems, universal and particular, but everything they needed, as poets, was there. The texture of everyday life was at once brutally realistic and sublimely miraculous. Christian belief, in its full fundamentalist and anthropomorphic drama, was—except for a very few sceptics—an all-embracing and immediate reality. The great world and the heart of man were alike the battle ground between God and his angels and Satan and his agents of evil. Within the Christian frame, human life was closely interwoven with both the familiar processes and the mysteries of nature, from the influence of the stars and celestial portents of disaster down to such direct acts of God as frost and flood and the recurring plague. Man was not alone in a mechanized and meaningless universe; he was midway between the beasts and the angels, a being of immortal destiny in a divine order. This was, too, an age in which the English language was in its fresh, rich maturity, with none of its infinite capacities blunted and debased. And one might add that writers, even if they did not get beyond school, were well educated.

For the heroic strain in literature, then, it was of prime significance that writers, most of the characters they created, and most of their readers or hearers looked up as a matter of course to persons and conceptions above the common level. The persons they looked up to ranged from God and the angels down to the sovereign and the aristocracy; the conceptions from the Christian view of life and the world down through philosophic ideas to the ordinances of law and the conventions of society. These persons and conceptions, to be sure, were not of equal sanctity, yet in actual life and in literature (apart from comedy and satire) the mass of people, including writers, were respectfully or reverently aware of planes of being above their own. Nowadays, angry young men in England and beatniks in the United States might conceivably be revolted by this picture of 'the Establishment,' of a nation of 'squares,' but it has no small bearing on the nature of the hero in Renaissance literature.

Recalling again the cliché about the alienation of the artist, we might at first thought say that the Renaissance writer was in a partly similar position. In Europe generally, through much of our period, artists of all kinds might be dependent on royal or noble patronage; writers of noble or gentle birth might disdain the degradation of print; more or less learned writers, aristocratic or bourgeois, like Sidney or Chapman or Jonson or Milton, might scorn the profane multitude and might have a scholarly or a religious sense of dedication to the high office of seer and teacher. Thus, as I said, the Renaissance writer might seem to be, and to have a consciousness of being, set apart from and above his fellows.

Yet, in relation to our subject, these facts are much less important than the fact that serious, educated writers, who came mostly from a sober middle class, had, and knew they had, a sympathetic audience; they were not talking to themselves in a great void. The point is that the elements of Renaissance idealism that have been outlined were held in common by writers and readers—held, to be sure, on varying levels of sophistication, but held none the less. Even the so-called aristocratic outlook, the respect for rank and authority, was shared by such middle-class poets as Spenser and Shakespeare and by their middle-class as well as their courtly audience; it was an integral part of the social and religious order and atmosphere. Shakespeare, cut off as a dramatist from direct commentary, can and does rely on the uniform moral sense of his socially heterogeneous public. Spenser does not have to persuade sceptical readers that traditional conceptions of holiness, temperance, and the other virtues are universally valid; his readers, whatever their individual lapses, believe that firmly already and are prepared to see those virtues and their opposites in action.

It is needless to recall the details of Spenser's fables. His heroes—and Britomart—are examples par excellence of the Christian-classical creed which was a general possession. These characters move through what is outwardly the world of romance but essentially the world of everyday experience, a world crowded with persons representing all shades of good and evil. Even Prince Arthur, who stands above other knights, participates in action in accordance with his inclusive virtue of magnificence or magnanimity, or as the agent of grace or providence. *The Faerie Queene*, in addition to being much else, is a conduct book in verse, and Spenser's outlook is thoroughly social and normal. The Red-Cross Knight, sick at heart from former guilt, longs for contemplative seclusion, but, as a good Protestant, he knows that he must return to the life of action and trial. One small item may be cited because we happen to know how two young romantic poets reacted to it. In the second canto of the fifth book, after the destruction of a pair of upper-class extortioners, a giant who is beguiling the mob with specious demands for communistic equality is, after debate, pushed off the cliff by the arm of justice. Shelley and Keats were both admirers of Spenser but both, independently, resented this act as typical of the way in which power deals with those who question economic and social orthodoxy. Such an attitude might be expected from young liberals of the revolutionary age. But Spenser's attitude was that of all sober Elizabethan citizens, who knew the perils to which their small country was exposed from without and within and who prized stable order above all things. Shakespeare, whose contempt for the fickle mob is amply apparent, took the same view of Jack Cade's rebellion.

Of the many affinities between the sage and serious Spenser and Milton the most obvious and central is their Christian faith, their Christian view of life and Christian scale of values, though Spenser reflects more broadly his own and his age's concern with Renaissance ethics and culture, while religion animates and dominates Milton's writing. And while Spenser, in his letter to Ralegh, celebrated the virtues of Agamemnon and Ulysses and the rest, Milton, who owed so much to the classical epics, expressly repudiated their materials and themes and took the bold step of investing his epic villain, God's adversary, with the heroic qualities of the traditional epic hero; he could rely on his early readers' recognizing the inadequacy and the complete corruption of such qualities. In doing so he did not anticipate romantic criticism of the nineteenth century or those modern critics of nineteenth-century vintage (in Miltonic matters) who apparently cannot understand a Christian and mythic poem.

Whereas Spenser's protagonists are immersed in the active world, Milton's are conspicuously isolated, Adam in the nature of the case, Christ and Samson by dramatic design. The Red-Cross Knight and Adam are both Everyman (Eve is not Una but Everywoman), and Adam also has Guyon's right reason, though it is perverted. Unlike Red-Cross and Guyon, Adam cannot mix with mankind, but, along with his higher endowments, he has his full share of human frailty. In the stories of both Red-Cross and Adam there are two heroes, the man who falls into sin and the one greater man who enables the sinner to enter upon the way of salvation—though there is a difference between Prince Arthur and the Son of God. Further, both Red-Cross and Adam, stricken by guilt, would welcome death, but the vision of both is cleared and both are given the strength to renew the life of duty in the world, which for Adam is no longer idyllic Eden but the grim world of history; it is through Michael's presentation that Adam is linked with all human experience and sin. And, to go no further with affinities, both Spenser (in *Mutability*) and Milton (repeatedly in the later books of *Paradise Lost*) themselves turn away from the troubled and sinful life of earth to a heaven of peace and order and innocence —poignant utterances all, and perhaps especially for Milton, who had striven so long for the establishment of Christ's kingdom among men.

If Christian faith and the Christian scheme have not been available to most modern writers, as they were not to the ancient pagans (though there may be partial parallels in both), we might say that pagan, Christian, and modern heroes stand on common ground by virtue of their acquiring a new and profound self-knowledge. Some kinds of self-knowledge, to be sure, do not go much beyond Parolles' 'Simply the thing I am / Shall make me live'; but we are not concerned with these. In one of the greatest scenes in the *Iliad*, and in literature, the callous Achilles learns compassion; Odysseus is a wiser man from the start, yet he grows in wisdom. The *Aeneid* has a more recognizably religious frame and atmosphere and in the fulfilment of his mission Aeneas gains understanding through trial and error and divine guidance. But the heroic knowledge that Red-Cross and Adam learn is the Christian gospel of love and faith, humility and obedience, which alone can overcome evil. Christian self-knowledge and natural self-knowledge can merge, yet they are distinct. Even Satan has a tincture of the former and it deepens his tragic potentialities, since, whatever his public harangues, he has a conscience that tells him, in soliloquies, what he was and is and might have been. Yet, in his imaginative realization of Satan, Milton did not allow those tragic potentialities to develop beyond a strict limit and then extinguished them altogether; if Satan were made a really tragic figure—something that Milton, being Milton, could never have done anyhow—the poem, as he conceived it, would collapse.

In Milton's two last works the isolation of the hero is set in high relief. It could be said, in terms that cover romantic and modern literature, that this is the isolation of a superior being in a corrupt world; but there are of course essential differences. In *Paradise Regained* Christ is presented in his human role, meeting the trials that Everyman meets, but with the invulnerable strength given by virtues that Adam could only hope to attain. Having light from above, Christ needs no other, not even the moral wisdom of Greece—though he possesses and uses it. We increasingly feel his isolation not only from the world of historical actuality and Satan's bribes but from the people about him; his simple-minded disciples expect him to establish an earthly kingdom and even his mother does not understand him. Satan, so often foiled, can exclaim, with a potent mixture of conscious and unconscious irony:

> Since neither wealth, nor honour, arms nor arts,
> Kingdom nor Empire pleases thee, nor aught
> By me propos'd in life contemplative,
> Or active, tended on by glory, or fame,
> What dost thou in this World?

Throughout Christ shows the superhuman perfection of the Renaissance hero; and in answer to the final challenge both he and Satan receive proof of his divinity.

Samson, the purely human sinner, outwardly isolated as a blind, helpless captive, inwardly as estranged from God, moves from lacerated pride, from preoccupation with his misery and shame, through humble contrition to renewed faith; but that bald statement describes a drama that is charged with irony from the title and the first line onward. Our sense of the hero's isolation steadily deepens because neither friends nor enemies understand what is going on in his soul, and even his father and the Chorus do not grasp the full meaning of his final victory. In his early revolutionary prose Milton had been inspired by boundless confidence in men and movements; in his three late poems he takes his stand on the impregnable ledge of rock that experience has left him, faith in God and the integrity or the regenerative strength of the humble individual soul.

One bridge between the heroic poem and the theatre would be Shakespeare's history plays, his epic dramatization of 'the Tudor myth'—in which a king might become isolated by incompetence or evil-doing—but it is the tragedies that concern us, and only a few familiar questions can be asked about the situation of the tragic hero.

Such heroic poems as those of Spenser, Chapman, and Milton are openly and deeply rooted in the Christian humanism of the Renaissance. The world of Elizabethan and Jacobean tragedy is a world of passion, violence, crime, and horror which may appear wholly secular and naturalistic and which, because of dramatic objectivity, may leave us at times uncertain of its author's attitudes. Shakespeare has been viewed as everything from a great heathen and muddled sceptic to an allegorical expounder of the Atonement. But it seems to be agreed that he was in accord with the religious beliefs and general outlook of his fellow citizens, however far his imaginative insight carried him beyond that level; and probably this holds for most of the other serious dramatists. The only one who can be labelled doctrinaire, George Chapman, found dramatic correlatives for his Christian-Platonic-Stoic humanism, and we have observed how his protagonists partake of his Homeric dichotomy: Bussy, a man of 'outward Fortitude,' is isolated by his passion and pride, Clermont by his inward Stoic wisdom.

Some of our earlier generalities about Renaissance writers apply to the dramatists as well as the heroic poets—tragic heroes are likewise of exalted station, and larger than life—but there are divergences and added complexities. The tragic hero, in Shakespeare most of all, is above the common level in imaginative sensibility and the gift of utterance, qualities which bulk large in the total effect. In the sphere of action, tragedy shows what men do, not what they ought to do. The epic hero, while not perfect, must be less imperfect than most tragic heroes; the epic role would hardly fit Tamburlaine or Macbeth or Coriolanus or Antony. The epic hero, whatever his failures, achieves some kind of triumph and remains alive; the tragic hero meets outward and sometimes inward ruin that is completed by death. Here we may remember some historical antecedents of Elizabethan tragedy. It inherited the conception of the fall from high estate, a conception kept gloomily alive by the multiplying tragedies of the very popular *Mirror for Magistrates*. The cause of the fall might be the turn of Fortune's wheel or, as in Shakespeare's first mature tragedy, *Julius Caesar*, a fatal flaw of character. (That brings up Aristotle and the systematic rigour with which some nineteenth-century criticism discerned a tragic flaw in all Shakespeare's heroes; but there may be such a vast disparity between the actual or alleged flaw and the catastrophe that the formula loses its meaning.) Then there was of course the degree to which Seneca and the Machiavellian tyrant shaped the revenge play and tragedy in general.

To quote my favourite Shakespearian critic, Geoffrey Bush, 'The tragic vision concerns itself with different forms of evil: in Shakespeare's exploration of character divided from the world, his concern is with the evil of acting and believing without meaning.' There is no formula that covers the kinds of isolation in which Shakespeare's tragic heroes find or place themselves, unless it is that, in diverse ways and degrees, if only in a momentary flash, they all attain a truer knowledge of themselves and others. Hamlet is alone in his grief, in awareness of his father's murder, in his plans for action—alone, in short, against the evil of the world about him. But Macbeth is left more and more alone in evil, until the righteous world rallies its forces to end his career of outrage. Both Hamlet the avenging protagonist and Malcolm, who leads the avenging army against the protagonist, see themselves as instruments of heaven. On the other hand Othello, a simple, high-minded leader of men in a Christian world, is led into a hideous crime and, having thus lost his noble self, takes his life in a vain show of pagan magnanimity (though some readers would object to this last phrase). The pagan and passionate King Lear, having lost the trappings of royalty and everything but the love of Cordelia and Kent, learns before he dies the Christian virtues of humility, gentleness, and love. And the Roman Coriolanus and Antony are simply broken because they are the men they are.

A concluding word may be said about some contrasts that have been conventionally drawn between Greek and Shakespearian tragedy: that Greek turns on fate, Shakespearian on character; that Greek tragedy vindicates the moral order which an individual's acts and sufferings have appeared to shake or obscure, whereas the Shakespearian catharsis involves no such vindication but comes about through our feeling for a character whose greatness transcends defeat and death. These commonplaces contain as much error as truth. Fate, the incalculable play of event and circumstance, operates in both Greek and Shakespearian tragedy. If in Shakespeare no character is fated to commit the sins of Oedipus, what is it that causes 'the fatal entrance of Duncan' into Macbeth's castle or brings Antony within the orbit of Cleopatra, that confronts Othello with a tale Hamlet would have promptly seen through and Hamlet with the need for an act that Othello would have promptly performed? The essential thing about Oedipus is not his unwitting sins of the past but his determination to find out the truth at whatever cost to himself; and Antigone, with clear knowledge of the consequences, chooses to obey divine rather than human law. As for the moral order, there is in Shakespeare no such religious and metaphysical solution as Aeschylus evidently had for the Promethean trilogy, though the establishment of the Areopagus in the *Oresteia* has a kind of equivalent in the succession of Fortinbras and the overthrow of Macbeth; and the assertion of a moral order in Sophocles is not quite so clear-cut as it is often assumed to be. In Shakespeare, throughout some tragedies runs an explicit or implicit assertion of a moral order in the world, through others, such as *King Lear*, at least an assertion of the traditional moral values of humanity. As Arthur Woodhouse has observed, whereas Macbeth defies the moral order, Hamlet—like Milton's Samson—perishes at last in giving effect to it: 'They are on the side of the power—the overruling power—which destroys them.' In general, we can say that the Greek dramatists and Shakespeare—and the heroic poets—are at one in assuming a moral order, or in showing either isolated human goodness unconquered by evil or the traditional moral sense of mankind rallying to oppose evil. Moreover, all these writers are linked together, and distinguished from many moderns, in that their heroes are not seen as helpless, unresisting victims of either fate or society; they make choices and are responsible for their acts, even though those acts and their consequences leave us facing the insoluble mysteries of life and character and circumstance.

R. F. JONES

The Humanistic Defence of Learning in the Mid-Seventeenth Century

O F the various dissensions and controversies that racked seventeenth-century England, there is one which, perhaps, has hardly secured sufficient attention, namely, that between renaissance humanism and its two arch enemies, science and puritanism. Though these two did not operate independently of each other, it is humanism's defence against puritan attacks with which this study is chiefly concerned. The core of the controversy was the part that humane learning, to use a term of the day, played in preparing a minister to preach.[1] The dispute developed with the growth of puritanism during the first half of the century, and when the puritans were firmly planted in the seats of power, it grew intense indeed. The situation is easily comprehended. In the Renaissance, Christian doctrine and classical wisdom had been sufficiently amalgamated to produce what is now called Christian humanism. But emerging from the Reformation were certain elements among the Protestants who combated this synthesis by drawing a clear line of demarcation between the two elements, and insisting upon not only a difference but a contradiction between them. Human learning was

[1] The problem of a learned ministry has been recently explored by Howard Schultz in *Milton and Forbidden Knowledge* (1955) chap. 5. The author perhaps places too much stress upon the political and economic factors involved, and grants too little sincerity to the Anglican defence of learning.

wordly and carnal and, as animosity to it increased, it was given a definite immoral character. The Bible and Christian faith, on the other hand, were to be spiritually and not rationally interpreted. The Divine Spirit moved a minister both in understanding and in preaching the Bible, and he needed no other assistance. The opposing forces then were the Anglican humanists on the one side and the more ignorant and fanatical puritan sects on the other. As frequently happens in controversies in which the opponents differ greatly in intellectual and educational equipment, the Anglicans are much more widely represented in print than the puritans, who had to depend more on social than on printed media of communication. For this reason, it is necessary to depend in whole or in part for puritan arguments on Anglican answers to them.[1]

Though the place of learning in a minister's training and profession was the centre of the dispute, other issues emerged from it. Since the universities provided the learning in question, they became the object of attack; so much so indeed that there was fear they would be abolished. Anthony à Wood says that feeling against them ran so high in 1653 that Parliament 'considered among themselves the suppressing [them] . . . as heathenish and unnecessary,' and again, he says that in 1657 the anabaptists in Oxford were so insolent in their hostility to the university, Cromwell found it necessary to send soldiers to protect it.[2] This attitude, however, is characteristic of only the less literate puritans. Certainly the published works of those who oppose a learned ministry almost without exception recognize the secular usefulness of universities and insist upon their reformation, not destruction.[3] We must, however, take into account the more ignorant voices raised against the schools

---

[1] In one of his earliest sermons Robert South says he cannot understand how the trade of butcher, scavenger, or any other trade qualifies a man to preach, and it is evidently with such preachers in mind that he goes on to say, 'almost all Sermons [are] full of gibes and scoffs at Humane Learning.' *Sermons Preached upon Several Occasions* (1679), p. 96. Certainly few such sermons were printed.

[2] See R. F. Jones, *Ancients and Moderns*, p. 119.

[3] William Dell, *A Plain and Necessary Confutation* (1654), preface; John Webster, *Academiarum Examen* (1654), preface; Samuel How, *The Sufficiencie of the Spirits Teaching without Humane-Learning* (1640), p. 12.

in conventicles and other meeting places. In fact, the present writer has met with contemporary statements that the hostility was more loudly expressed in conventicles than in print, though specific references have eluded both memory and notes. At any rate, the clamour against the seats of learning was sufficiently threatening to fill some of the Anglicans with fear that learning itself was on the point of being extinguished. So it was easy to pass from the question of an educated ministry to the value of learning itself.

The central issue, though frequently lost sight of, was the employment of learning and reason in the preparation of a preacher and interpretation of the Gospel. The puritans held that religion and humane learning were incompatible, that the pure spiritual nature of the first could only be contaminated by the carnal nature of the second. 'Humane learning,' says Samuel How, the cobbler preacher, 'crosseth and opposeth the simplicity of the Gospel, and spiritual things and carnal things, such as arts and languages, should not be compared.'[1] That the learning which the puritans had in mind was essentially humanistic is made evident by the many references to the philosophers, poets, historians, and especially the rhetoricians of classical antiquity. In true puritan fashion the opponents of learning take their stand squarely upon the Bible, and Paul furnished them plenty of evidence, especially in the second chapter of I Corinthians,[2] which seems to express antihumanistic ideas, and which the Anglicans found it expedient to explain as

[1] *The Sufficiencie of the Spirits Teaching*, preface, Cf. *A Vindication of Learning* (1646), p. 1; Thomas Collier, *The Pulpit-Guard Routed* (1651), pp. 3, 37–38; John Wele's letter in Jeffery Watts, *A Vindication of the Church and Universities* (1657).

[2] Paul says, 'when I came to you, [I] came not with excellency of speech, or of wisdom . . . And my speech and my preaching was not with enticing words of man's wisdom, but in demonstration of the Spirit and power.' In the second chapter of Colossians he cautions his hearers 'lest any man should beguile you with enticing words,' and 'lest any man spoil you through philosophy and vain deceit, after the tradition of men, after the rudiments of the world, and not after Christ.' In the passage referred to in note 2 *supra* South represents the preachers he is describing as saying, 'Away with *vain Philosophy, with the disputer of this world, and the enticing words of mans wisdome*, and set up the foolishness of *Preaching, the simplicity of the Gospel*. Thus Divinity,' South comments, 'has been brought in upon the ruins of Humanity.'

best they could. The contrast there presented between the wisdom of the world, obviously classical wisdom, and the Spirit of the Lord is urged again and again against the university education of ministers, and at times against the universities themselves.

As has been stated, the puritans for the most part condemn those disciplines which humanism emphasized; 'philosophy, poetry, rhetoric, history, and the classical languages, all summed up under the term humane learning, or frequently, humane wisdom. In their calmer moments they grant such learning value in the secular world, but it becomes evil when it passes into the sphere of religion. Samuel How concedes that it is useful for the training of statesmen, lawyers, physicians, and gentlemen, 'but bring it once to be a *help to understand the mind of God in holy Scriptures*, and there it is detestable filth.'[1] Quite frequently, however, the puritans become so incensed against the mingling of philosophy and Biblical teaching, that they lose sight of the distinction made by How and indiscriminately attack learning and the universities. No less a person than the master of a college in Cambridge University, William Dell, would so reform education that a student would have nothing to do with 'the *heathenish Poets*, who were for the most part the *Devils Prophets*, and delivered forth their writings in his *spirit*, and who through the *smoothness*, *quaintness*, and *sweetness* of their language do insensibly instil the poison of *lust* and *wickedness* into the hearts of *youth*.'[2] Classical philosophy fares no better.

But the puritans are especially severe in their attitude toward rhetoric. They never tire of making specific use of Paul's condemnation of 'the excellency of speech' and 'the enticing words of man's wisdom.' Paul's ministry, says Tobias Crisp, 'was exercised in a low plaine dealing way without either humane rethorick or wisdom of man.'[3] Walter Cradock has rhetoric chiefly in mind when he says that 'the use that men make of it [humane learning] to *dress* the simplicity of the *Gospel* with it, makes it abominable,' and he beseeches his audience to 'stick to Christ Crucified, and to the *simplicity* and

---

[1] *The Sufficiencie of the Spirits Teaching*, p. 12.

[2] 'The Right Reformation of Learning,' appended to *A Plain and Necessary Confutation* (1654), pp. 25–30.

[3] *Christ Alone Exalted* (1643), p. 352.

plainness of the *Gospel.*'[1] Thomas Collier speaks scornfully of the rhetoric of 'the learned humanists,' as he consistently designates the Anglicans.[2] Richard Baxter is one with the puritans of this period in his attitude toward style, for he expresses dislike of too much industry about words, and the hope that he might 'speak pertinently, plainly, piercingly and somewhat properly.'[3] The puritan spirit in Henry Wilkinson declares that eloquence renders Christ's sacrifice ineffectual and that some preachers would rather please their auditors' ears than touch their consciences. After questioning what Paul says about God's making foolish the wisdom of the world, he asks, 'Are swelling words suitable to this examination of the Son of God? Is a lofty stile correspondent with this abasement? Is it fit to discourse sweetly and delightfully upon gall and vinegar, and to beset nailes and thornes with flowers of Rhetorick, and to bring our Saviour in pompe of words, and vainglorious pagents of Art unto his crosse?'[4]

The puritan insistence upon simplicity and plainness in the style of religious compositions, based largely upon Paul, and also perhaps upon the necessity of justifying unordained and uneducated ministers, was accompanied by another movement making for a plain style in secular matters, which sprang from Sir Francis Bacon and which reached its climax in the stylistic programme of the Royal Society. This antirhetorical trend had been slowly materializing in the puritan era, especially with those educational reformers who wished to install in the universities Baconian science and professional and technological subjects at the expense of the traditional curriculum.[5] The two movements did not remain independent of each other, even though their reformations looked toward different ends, in

[1] *Divine Drops Distilled from the Fountain of Holy Scriptures* (1650), pp. 225, 228.

[2] *The Pulpit-Guard Routed*, pp. 17, 38. Cf. John Horne, *A Consideration of Infant Baptism* (1654), p. 160.

[3] See the Premonition prefixed to *The Saints Everlasting Rest* (8th ed., 1659; 1st ed., 1650).

[4] *Three Decads of Sermons Lately Preached to the University at St. Mary's Church in Oxford* (1660), pp. 10, 14. The reference to Paul is to I Corinthians 1.20.

[5] See Jones, *Ancients and Moderns*, chap. v, and *The Seventeenth Century*, by R. F. Jones *et al.* (1951), pp. 73–84.

one case, the introduction of experimental science in the university curriculum, in the other, the elimination of divinity from it. William Dell reflects both movements when in his educational proposals he advocates the teaching of arithmetic, geometry, geography and the like because 'they carry no wickedness, so are they besides very useful to *humane* Society and the affairs of this present life.'[1] Scientific utilitarianism and Pauline spirituality join forces in Dell's attack on humanism, so much so that Joseph Sedgwick complains that it is hard to know exactly what Dell had in mind, since he uses interchangeably two quite different terms, 'carnal and fleshly' and 'unuseful.'[2]

We find the two movements closely joined in the work of John Webster, for he is both an ardent advocate of the introduction of experimental science into the universities, and a determined enemy to the teaching of divinity and the training of ministers there. Though not as extreme in his denunciation of rhetoric as those who opposed it from a religious point of view, he shows it as well as poetry scant courtesy. They 'serve only for adornation, and are as it were the outward dress and attire of more solid sciences,' and he laments the amount of time spent on their study.[3] A more striking example of the fusion of the two trends is found in John Wilkin's *Ecclesiastes* (1646). The author insists on plainness in preaching so as to avoid the obscurity that arises from rhetorical expressions. The plainest style manifests the greatest learning and clarity of understanding in the one using it. When an idea is itself good, it is best presented 'in the most obvious plain expression.' We can detect in these

[1] 'The Right Reformation of Learning,' pp. 25–30.

[2] 'Learning's Necessity,' appended to *A Sermon Preached at Cambridge, May 1st* (1653), p. 37. He also suggests that Dell may be advocating the teaching of secular subjects in the universities 'in conformity to the suggestions of that Noble and judicious Advancer of Learning' (*ibid.*, p. 36). Certainly at times Dell writes more like a Baconian educational reformer than an antihumanistic one, as when he says that university students spend all their time reading such books as 'contain wrangling, jangling, foolish, and unprofitable Philosophy,' and are 'in the end fit for no worthy imployment either in the world or among the faithful.' ('The Right Reformation of Learning,' pp. 25–30.) In general, however, the Baconian reformers did not wish to be confused with the reformers of pulpit eloquence. See the dedication to Noah Bigg's *Mataeotechnia Medicinæ Praxeos* (1651), and the preface to John Webster's *Academiarum Examen* (1654).

[3] *Academiarum Examen*, pp. 88–89.

words what the experimental scientists were beginning to think and what they later fully expressed, but Wilkins has chiefly in mind rhetorical preachers, for he goes on to say, 'St. Paul does often glory in this, that his Preaching was not in wisdom of words or excellency of speech, not with enticing words of mans wisdom.' Later he attacks 'empty and needlesse tautologies which are to be avoided in every solid business, much more in sacred.'[1] Wilkins hardly means to suggest that religious matters are not solid. 'Solid business' probably refers to scientific matters, since the adjective is constantly used to distinguish the experimental from traditional science and such an interpretation could well furnish the antithesis which the sentence seems to call for. With the puritans science as well as religion was demanding a simple style.

The Anglican clergy were, if anything, even more passionate in the defence of humane learning than the sectaries were in their attack on it. This was especially true after the king had been beheaded and the puritans were in a position to threaten learning and the universities and to reduce many Anglican clergymen to straitened circumstances. In the writings of men like Edward Waterhouse and John Gauden, self-declared author of *Eikon Basilike*, we detect a definite fear of despotism, fanaticism, and the loss of civilization itself, together with pity for the suffering of those 'who are unfit to labour and ashamed to beg.' These feelings so move Gauden that he becomes savage in his denunciation, while Waterhouse closes his *Apologie* with the fervent prayer that those in power may 'think upon and commiserate the decaying Universities, the ruined Churches, the wandering Flocks, the impoverished Clergie.'[2] Their bitterness reflects their love for humanistic learning, their belief in its transcendent importance, and their firm conviction that the Anglican ministry was its custodian as well as being the support of the universities. Upon 'a true and authoritative ministry' depend 'all learning and civility, all piety and charity, all gracious hopes and comforts, all true Religion and Christianity itself.'[3]

[1] *Ecclesiastes* (1646), p. 72.
[2] *An humble Apologie for Learning and Learned Men* (1653), p. 256.
[3] John Gauden, *Hieraspistes, A Defence of the Ministry and Ministers of the Church of England* (1653), preface. Edward Waterhouse calls the clergy the masters of learning. *An humble Apologie*, p. 140.

But the best way to defend the ministry was to defend the learning which made it what it was.

Humane learning is defended in various ways. A knowledge of Latin, Greek, and Hebrew renders a minister accurate and independent in his understanding of the Scriptures. Learning enables him to understand the laws, customs, and antiquities of countries that appear in the Bible. It is also valuable because Biblical writers were learned and often refer to philosophical matters, as for instance, physics in Genesis, ethics in Proverbs, logic in the disputations of the Prophets and the Apostles, and allusions to the nature of beasts in various books. Without learning, a country would be without doctors, lawyers, and diplomats.[1] The arguments, however, that are presented with the greatest fervour are those which embody some element of Christian humanism.[2] One that received much stress was the dignity of man founded upon his mind or reason. God, says Waterhouse, has given reason 'to no mortal being but Man, who being Lord (next under God) of this world, he hath endowed with a ray of Temporary Divinity, being created after the Image of his Maker ... Crouned with Honour and Dignity.'[3] An anonymous defender of learning declares that 'the rationall soule (the receptacle of sapience)' is the image of God.[4] It is the high function of humane learning to strengthen or 'ripen' reason, and thus prepare man for virtue and religion, for by this learning 'the *mind*, and all *intellectual* faculties of men's souls (which are the *noblest* and *divinest*) are more easily and fully *instructed* ... in all the riches of wisdome and knowledge; which are parts of the *glory* and *image* of *God* on man's nature.'[5] The virtue which is inherent in our natures, says

[1] Edward Reynolds, *A Sermon Touching the Use of Humane Learning* (1658), p. 17; Henry Thurman, *A Defence of Humane Learning* (1660), p. 18; John Gauden, *Hieraspistes*, p. 416.

[2] The bibliography of humanism is large, but the books which in large part furnish the background of this article are: Douglas Bush, *The Renaissance and English Humanism* (1939); M. P. Gilmore, *The World of Humanism, 1453–1517* (1952); and Fritz Caspari, *Humanism and the Social Order* (1954.)

[3] *An humble Apologie*, p. 9.

[4] *A Vindication of Learning from unjust Aspersion* (1646), p. 1. Cf. Thurman, *A Defence of Humane Learning*, p. 30.

[5] Gauden, *Hieraspistes*, p. 398. Contrast this with what Dell says: '... the power and vertue of the *Gospel*, and the wisdom, knowledge, and

Waterhouse, is weak, but it can be strengthened by learning. In fact, he goes so far as to say that 'the Liberal Arts [are] to be attained before we can attain vertue; for indeed they are the way to vertue, and the paths appointed to lead us to those Paradises.'[1] The Anglicans are more clearly and significantly distinguished from the puritans by their educational philosophy than by any other characteristic. The puritan conception of the purpose of education was to a considerable extent dominated by a utilitarian and materialistic spirit which viewed education as a preparation to meet practical and material needs, while moral ideas were dictated by Biblical authority. The humanistic Anglicans, on the other hand, declared virtue to be the purpose of learning.[2] In other words, the function of education was to mould character, a sentiment more frequently heard in the past than at present.

Another humanistic attitude which figures prominently in Anglican apologies is the belief in the civilizing power of the liberal arts. Without learning, says Joseph Sedgwick, 'we may without cost or paine return to an easie and cheap barbarousness.'[3] Waterhouse proposes in his *Apologie* to show that without learning 'a People can expect nothing but Barbarity and Bestial Vulpinariness . . .. The more men are sunk in ignorance, and estranged from Arts and Sciences, the nearer come they to the life of Beasts and Savages; for unless the power of the mind, by which we are distinguished from bruits, be by liberal sciences ordered and modified, all their virtue and nobility will degenerate into not only a likeness to, but into a degree of rudeness beyond beasts.'[4] As usual, Gauden states the case

utterance of Gods Spirit is more gloriously manifested in *plain men* than in *learned men*: For in the *one*, the Grace and Vertues of the *Spirit* are attributed to *Humane Learning*: But in the *other*, to God only,' *A Plain and Necessary Confutation*, p. 20.

[1] *An humble Apologie*, p. 145.

[2] Learning may promote virtue by presenting as inspiring examples the heroes of classical antiquity made famous by their virtues. Waterhouse, *An humble Apologie*, pp. 192–93; Edward Leigh, *A Treatise of Religion and Learning* (1656), p. 33; and William London's catalogue, *The Most Vendible Books in England* (1658), the introduction to which assails the puritans with fervent praise of learning.

[3] 'Learnings Necessity to an Able Minister of the Gospel,' appended to *A Sermon* (1653), p. 34.

[4] *An humble Apologie*, p. 7.

even more vehemently: 'To these *Patrons* and *professours* of learning, *we owe* our ingenuity, our courtesie, our civility. . . . To *them* we owe our gratitude, our humanity, our rational and religious liberties, which redeem us from *being* beasts or *divels*. Their care and labours have absolved us from the chains and bondage of blindnesse, barbarity, atheism, vulgar admiration, sensualitie, and irreligion.' In the state human relations are characterized by humanity, equity, charity, and the bonds of civility. If these virtues, though innate in man, are not culti-vated and fostered by 'good learning' and 'ingenuous education . . . who sees not, by miserable experience, how mankinde runs out to *weeds*? whole nations *degenerate* to brutish bar-barity: as among the *Tartars, Negroes* and *Indians*?'[1]

Though 'good learning' may civilize a man, it cannot bring him to a state of grace. The humanistic Anglicans always fell short of placing salvation in the power of humane learning. They insist, however, that the latter may prepare one for salva-tion, may so condition the soil that the seeds of righteousness will germinate in it.[2] 'This civility,' says Gauden again, 'was, and is the preface and forerunner of Religion, the great pre-parative to piety, the confines of Christianity, which never thrives untill barbarity be rooted up, and some learning with morality be sown and planted among men.'[3] Here and else-where humane learning is the *litterae humaniores* of the human-ists, as is apparent in what Gauden says next: 'Nor did the Christian Religion ever extend its pavilion much further, than the tents of Learning and Civility had been pitched by the

[1] *Hieraspistes*, pp. 427, 400. The expression 'by miserable experience' looks at the puritans. G. N. Clark says that humanists believed that by study of ancient arts and languages they were breaking away from the barbarism of the world into which they were born. *The Seventeenth Century* (1929), p. 270.

[2] 'All the humane learning in the world cannot bring a man to salvation, it may help to curb corruption, civilize a man, and prepare him for better things.' Thomas Hall, *Vindiciae Literarum* (1654), p. 60.

[3] *Hieraspistes*, p. 399. Thomas Hall asserts that humane learning is 'an excellent meanes to prepare us for the true Religion, it helps to civilize us, and to mollifie the harshnesse and mitigate the fiercenesse of our natures, it roots up barbarisme, beastlinesse, . . . it helpes to preserve humane societies in peace; its also a meanes to improve and perfect our naturall gifts and abilities. It fits us for noble atchievements, and excellent imployments, both in Church and State.' *Vindiciae Literarum*, p. 27.

conquests and colonies of the *Greeks* and *Romans.'* The fusion
of Christian faith and classical culture resulted in Christian
humanism, and it has never been better expressed than by
Gauden, whose faith in it was explicit. 'Religion,' he says,
'never so thrived (after *miraculous gifts* were ceased) as when
the forces and *glory of the Gentiles* came in to Christ; when
Christianity was *graffed* on the old stock of heathen *learning*
and *philosophy*; which now brings forth fruit, not after the old
crabbed sowrnesse, but after the sweetness of the new Olivecion
with which it is *headed*; yea we see, when Christian Religion ran
out to much barbarity, illiterate ignorance, and superstition,
for *many centuries*, till the last, (for want of the culture and
manuring of learning) it brought forth little *fair fruits.'* Gauden
is humanistic in his attitude toward the schoolmen, who in his
eyes hewed out rather than polished the pillars of religion by
intricate disputes which entangled both philosophy and religion
and which were wrapped in barbarous and fulsome Latin.[1]

Since the lower classes could not enjoy the educational
privileges which the Anglicans considered essential to civility
and virtue, it is not strange that the latter, like earlier humanists, were not democratic. Their attitude was not mere snob-
bery; it was the result of the application of standards in which
they sincerely believed. Yet one reason for the intensity of the
attack on learning was the provoking aristocratic nature of the
Anglican establishment, fortified with honours and emoluments.
The outspoken resentment of the puritans increased the
severity of Anglican criticism of them. Waterhouse frankly
admits that he does not love the multitude, who are disorderly,
vain, and cruel. Though he stresses the mutual dependence of
rulers and those ruled, he believes the multitude should be
closely held down by the government.[2] When it appeared that

[1] *Hieraspistes*, pp. 401–2. Edward Leigh exclaims, 'what barbarisms do
they [the schoolmen] use in the Latin Tongue.' *A Treatise of Religion and
Learning*, p. 32.

[2] 'Let who will cry up multitudes, I shall not; for I find them disorderly, vain, injudicious, cruel, like Rivers, sinking every thing that is
solid, and bearing up whatever is light . . . and those Governours neglect
themselves and their people who do not answer their mutinies with
punishments, and encourage their obedience with justice, protection and
honest ease and liberty . . . it is more to good mens content to live where
nothing then where every thing is lawful.' *An humble Apologie*, p. 242.

they were in a position to implement their fanatical attacks on learning and the universities with action, this aristocratic spirit became savage in its denunciation of the mob, animated, it may be true, partly by the loss or prospective loss of livelihoods, but more, certainly, by the desecration of what they valued and held sacred. Sedgwick declares that the puritans cannot sit in judgment on learning because they have none, and he heaps scorn on their 'enthusiastic' aberrations. Henry Thurman denounces 'the haters of humane learning' as irrational, brutish, irreligious persons, inspired by ignorance or malice.[1]

It is Gauden, however, who in the rather long preface to *Hieraspistes*, and elsewhere, engages in the most devastating denunciation of the puritans during this period. He stands firmly and sincerely upon the belief that 'The preserving, and encouraging of a *true* and *authoritative ministry* . . . is the great *hinge* on *which all learning* and *civility*, all piety and charity, all gracious hopes and comforts, all true Religion and Christianity it self depends, as much as the light, beauty, regular motion, and safety of the body, doth upon its having eyes to see.' Unfortunately it is not a dumb spirit, he says, 'but a silly, pratling and illiterate one' that possesses 'the despisers of good learning,' who 'are also . . . degraders even of humane nature; whose divine excellencie, *Reason*, no man above the degree of brutish stupidity, Bedlam madnesse, or divellish envy, ever sought to deprave or depresse.' Since the Anglican clergy pass on to the unlatined members of their congregations the benefits of classical culture,[2] the devil would like nothing better than to put out the eyes of the people who would without them 'like Owls and Bats, and Mouls, onely howle, and chatter, and scratch one another in the dark.' Finally, he warns England that the enemies of learning begin 'to shew their teeth, in their grosse

[1] *A Sermon*, preface and p. 35, and *A Defence of Humane Learning*, dedication.

[2] After a particularly violent attack on the 'despisers of Learning.' Gauden hastens to add, 'Not that here I doe any way despise, or degrade those sober *good Christians* of either sex, whose education, parts, and way of life hath and doth deny them the advantages of personall learning.' Anglican ministers, he assures them, can transmit to them the benefits bestowed by classical learning. *Hieraspistes*, p. 430; see also p. 406.

errors, their rude, and savage manners; which are tokens evident and dreadful enough of their brutish soules' and that 'if the wiser, learneder, and powerfuller world among us in England, should, through baseness, cowardice, and negligence, suffer this *illiterate* and *ferine faction* to increase and multiply, they will soon finde, by their violence, craft and cruelty, that these Islands will be more pestered and infamous for wolves, then ever they were in ancient times.'[1]

The defenders of learning are orthodox in their religious views and conservative in their social and political ideas. They believe in a social hierarchy with the lower classes obedient to the higher and a powerful ruler over all.[2] This is especially apparent in Gauden, who viewed with scorn and trepidation the democratic movement toward liberty beginning to stir in his day. Even in countries, he says, and he means to include England among them, where some are civilized by learning and religion, one may find 'by daily experience' that the unlearned sort are gross and indocile or unpolished and insolent, especially where they arrogate to themselves the liberty of doing and speaking what they please, and elsewhere he exclaims, 'There is no *Jewell* which Swine delight more to *weare in their Snouts*, than this of *Liberty*; which however well it becomes such sordid and indocile cattel,' only those excellent Christians who know how to use liberty can tell.[3] This emphasis on the power of a ruler is accompanied by the humanistic insistence that he be properly educated, so that his virtue might match his power. Thomas Hall holds that learning improves and perfects natural gifts and abilities, and thus trains men for noble achievements in church and state. Waterhouse thinks that learning is the most proper virtue and qualification of a ruler, especially since it tends to curb tyranny. Sedgwick is more explicit regarding the benefits learning confers on rulers. It gives them, he says, magnanimity, eloquence, trained judgment, knowledge of men and manners, precedents, ability to meet crises, examples of 'Divine Providence and humane Prudence,' and inexplicable powers.[4] What

---

[1] *Hieraspistes*, preface and pp. 395, 404–5, 409.

[2] Edward Waterhouse, *An humble Apologie*, pp. 11–12, 38, 242.

[3] *Hieraspistes*, pp. 400, 437.

[4] *Vindiciæ Literarum*, p. 27; *An humble Apologie*, pp. 38–39, 119–20; *A Sermon*, p. 34.

is said of importance of learning to rulers is extended to the nobility and gentry in their more restricted spheres.[1]

In view of the quotations given above, it is hardly necessary to identify humane learning as classical learning or culture. And although all the constituent elements of the `latter are noticed, those humanistic arts, which Edward Leigh says are called liberal because they are worthy of fine and ingenuous men,[2] bear all the emphasis: philosophy, ethics, history, rhetoric, and poetry. It is the learning which in Gauden's words clothes religion with the sublimity of Plato, the method and acuteness of Aristotle, the morals of Plutarch, the eloquence of Demosthenes and Cicero, the sober sense of Xenophon, Livy, Tacitus, 'and other excellent historians,' and 'the elegancies of Homer, Virgil . . . and other poets.'[3] The defenders of this learning do not hesitate to call upon Continental humanists of an earlier day. Leigh mentions among those who restored learning Pico della Mirandola, Reuchlin, Erasmus, and Linacre. Thurman calls upon Erasmus and Pico for arguments, and defends his book with the statement that if it is not proper to praise 'Arts and Arts-men' at Oxford, 'for my part, I say with Picus Mirandula, *Si turpe est bonas literas colere, mallem hanc culpam agnoscere, quam deprecari.'*[4]

In the defence of learning none of the humanistic disciplines receives more attention than rhetoric, or eloquence. Paul's abjuration of 'excellency of speech' and 'enticing words of man's wisdom' inspired the puritans to find in the Bible only a plain simple manner of expression and to see in the Apostles only plain ignorant men who could furnish a precedent for their own unordained preachers as well as an argument against liberally educated Anglicans. In reply the latter went to the Scriptures for evidence in favour of rhetoric, and found plenty

---

[1] Waterhouse, *An humble Apologie*, p. 70; Sedgwick, 'Learnings Necessity,' p. 33.

[2] *A Treatise of Religion and Learning*, p. 36

[3] *Hieraspistes*, pp. 401–2. It is the learning which Waterhouse finds in the Scriptures, though better expressed, and which offers classical heroes as models and sources of inspiration. *An humble Apologie*, pp. 118, 192–93, 228.

[4] *A Treatise of Religion and Learning*, p. 30; and *A Defence of Humane Learning*, pp. 31, 51, 64.

of it. 'There is no Art, no Figures, no choice of those Rhetoricall
Flowers, which surprise mortall curiosity into a pleasing
vassellage . . . but is here [in the Bible] amply matched.' The
Bible, says Kendall, glancing at the puritans, furnishes a man
material for his sermons, but does not instruct him in the way
he is to use it; there are many rare patterns of rhetorical figures
in it, but no rhetorical rules. In the book of Job alone, exclaims
one defender of eloquence, 'there are such admirable Expressions, Metaphors, and Rhetoricall figures,' that the rhetoric
of Cicero and Demosthenes is nothing compared with them.[1]
The Anglican apologists are insistent in pointing out that
Paul did not have true rhetoric in mind, but affected, vain,
insincere 'rhetorications.' ' . . . it is the abuse and not the
right use of learning, which *Paul* condemnes. The scripture
it selfe is full of Divine eloquence and Rhetorick, and it
may lawfully be used by a minister of the Gospell, not for
ostentation, but edification.' Though Joseph Sedgwick is
very critical of the type of pulpit oratory that does not observe
a proper decorum but engages in a 'glarous painted and
ranting Rhetorick,' he maintains that 'true raisedness of expression, a majesticall state, and artificiall and genuine insinua-
tions, with most pathetical captivatings of the minde, are
obvious in Scripture.' Thurman likewise objects to rhetoric
that is used affectedly and unseasonably, but he approves of
those who use it 'to inform the understanding, or to worke on
the affections, or to quicken the attention, or to help the
memory, or some other way to please the Auditory for their
good unto edification.' A grave matron, he adds, decent in
her attire may wear costly jewels upon fit occasions.[2] Not
only do the many eloquent passages in the Bible justify
rhetoric, they require a knowledge of it for their proper interpretation. 'The Scripture,' says Leigh, 'is full of Metaphors
and figurative speeches which have profit as well as ornament.
A great part of the whole 6th of John is framed of such
speeches, how shall one understand the meaning of such places
without some skill in Rhetorick?' Thomas Hall believes that

---

[1] Waterhouse, *An humble Apologie*, p. 117; George Kendall, *Sancti
Sanciti*, p. 165; *A Vindication of Learning*, p. 5.

[2] Hall, *Vindiciae Literarum*, pp. 42–43; Sedgwick, *A Sermon*, p. 55;
Thurman, *A Defence of Humane Learning*, pp. 53–54.

a knowledge of rhetoric, as well as of logic and languages, is required to 'analize and open many obscure phrases in Scripture.' and to prove his point he refers to specific passages, an understanding of which in his eyes requires the assistance of rhetoric.[1]

The defenders of the ministerial use of rhetoric all reflect the high estimate placed upon it by the humanists, who considered it the linguistic counterpart of wisdom. Well fared former times, says Waterhouse, when 'eloquence was a ready step to estimation, and . . . fixed a kind of Majesty on all that had it.' Learned men, he boasts, 'can charm venemous beasts by the Magick of . . . Eloquence.' Praise of eloquence reaches a high note in Gauden, who proclaimed that wisdom and eloquence work hand in hand to civilize men, for the truths 'digested' by logic are 'brought forth unfolded and presented to others in that *order* and *beauty* of *eloquence* which Rhetorick teacheth: By which truths have both an edge and luster set on them, doe most *adorn* them, and *enforce* to the *quickest* prevalencies on mens mindes, and the firmest impressions on their passions and affections; that so their rationall vigour may hold out to mens actions; and extend to the ethicks or *morality* of civill conversation, which is the politure of mens hearts and hands; the softner and sweetner of violent passions, and rougher manners to the candor and equity of polity and society.'[2] It seems that eloquence furnishes motive power to wisdom and makes virtue operative. It is not strange that an age which enjoyed the prose of Jeremy Taylor, Sir Thomas Browne, and John Milton should have, in spite of the puritans, esteemed eloquence so highly. 'What an inchanting force hath Rhetorick!' exclaims Edward Leigh, after he has defined it in the usual manner as speech intended to please and persuade. Sedgwick considers the 'great patterns of eloquence and fit expressing our thoughts' one of the chief assets of a liberal education, while Edward Reynolds goes even further and makes 'the sweetnesse of Eloquence' an instrumentality for bringing men 'into Civill society and the practise of Vertue' by painting Vertues and Vices' and thus 'giving unto spiritual things Bodies and Beauties, such as might best

[1] *A Treatise of Religion and Learning*, p. 33; *The Pulpit Guarded*, pp. 19–20.
[2] *An humble Apologie*, pp. 120, 182; *Hieraspistes*, p. 399.

affect the Imagination,'[1] an idea later expressed by Thomas Sprat.[2]

Besides these testimonies to the value of rhetoric to preaching and understanding of the Bible, other evidence of the importance which the Anglicans ascribed to the matter is revealed in rhetorics devised for religious use only. One, written by John Prideaux, bishop of Worcester, not later than 1650, distinguished sacred from literary eloquence by defining the former as 'a Logicall kind of Rhetorick, to be used in Prayer, Preaching, or Conference; to the glory of God, and the convincing, instructing, and strengthening our brethren.' The tropes of such a rhetoric, he says, differ much in weight and majesty from heathen tropes. In his rhetorical discussions he draws heavily upon classical rhetoricians, but he secures his illustrative examples from the Scriptures.[3] Perhaps a more ambitious attempt is found in Thomas Hall's *Rhetorica Sacra*,[4] the preface of which states that the Bible abounds in tropes and figures of all sorts, but it is only by 'digging' into them that the true excellence of the Scriptures can be perceived. He defines and discusses a large number of them with frequent citations to various books of the Bible. Another rhetoric of the period, not exclusively devoted to religion, was issued by John Sergeant under the name of John Smith. As the title suggests, much of it is devoted to the Bible with the idea of showing how necessary a knowledge of rhetoric is to its interpretation.[5] This interest in the religious use of

[1] *A Treatise of Religion and Learning*, p. 39; 'Learnings Necessity,' p. 34; *A Treatise of the Passions and Faculties of the Soule of Man* (1647), pp. 20–21. Though in general Henry Wilkinson was puritan enough to consider eloquence inappropriate to the purity and simplicity of the Gospel, he thinks it may be used as 'a pious kind of fraud' to gain the affections of a congregation. *Three Decads of Sermons* (1660), p. 10.

[2] *History of the Royal-Society*, pp. 111–12.

[3] *Sacred Eloquence; Or, the Art of Rhetorick* (1659), pp. 1, 3.

[4] This is found, with a separate title page but continuous pagination, at the end of *Centuria Sacra* (1654). The subtitle reads: *A Synopsis of the most materiall Tropes and Figures contained in the Sacred Scriptures; by the knowing of which, we may our selves observe many more like them. Many Texts of Scripture are here expounded, many errors confuted, and the Marrow of most Rhetoricians (in reference to Divinity) collected. All the tropes and Figures are set in an Alphabeticall Order . . . and illustrated with variety of instances. . . .'

[5] *The Mysterie of Rhetorique Unveil'd wherein above 130 . . . Tropes and Figures are severally derived from the Greek into English, together with*

rhetoric, which is also apparent in other works of a rhetorical nature,[1] reached a higher pitch during these years than in any other period of English literary history. In the next decade we find the reverse situation.

The puritans' insistence on a plain style of preaching, and their hostility to the rhetorical preaching attributed to the Anglicans, furnished little assistance to the stylistic movement that reached its fulfilment in the simplification of English prose characteristic of the Restoration. Unlike the trend toward stylistic simplicity fostered by the growing scientific movement, which was an authentic expression of the true character and need of that movement, the stylistic attitude of the puritans was at odds with both their character and their practice. Since, as they never tire of telling us, they trusted in their sermons to the Spirit's moving them, and not to their minds, it was inevitable that their imaginations, being freed from rational restraint, should find expression in a 'natural rhetoric'[2] far removed from clarity and simplicity, as their opponents of this period observe, and as their critics of the next decade point out abundantly.[3] Sedgwick accuses them of walking in the clouds and speaking 'above the understanding of men . . . with an industrious kinde of confusion,' and he asks, 'Is this the plainnesse and simplicity of a Gospel-preacher . . . to leave the hearers in a mist of words and dark expressions ? . . . when the very Text itself is more easie, plain and familiar.'[4] Samuel Rutherford is more severe on the 'loftiness, high riding and soaring of words . . .

lively Definitions and Variety of Latin, English, Scriptural Examples, Pertinent to each of them apart. Conducing very much to the right understanding of the Sense of the Letter of the Scripture, (the want whereof occasions many dangerous Errors this day) . . . (1657).

[1] Such for instance as *Similies Divine and Morall. Touching the great Work of Redemption . . . Consisting of One Hundred Centuries and approved by sundry learned Authors* (1647).

[2] In his reply to Thomas Hall's defence of learning, Thomas Collier declares that many uneducated people have more 'natural Retorick' than the educated. *The Pulpit-Guard Routed*, p. 38.

[3] Jones *et al.*, *The Seventeenth Century*, pp. 111–42. In his *English Pulpit Oratory from Andrewes to Tillotson*, W. Fraser Mitchell has found a plain style in Baxter and other better educated puritans. But the preachers who frightened men like Waterhouse and Gauden were the less educated and more fanatical kind.

[4] *A Sermon*, p. 10.

capacious swelling bagges or blathers of wind,' and more to the same effect.[1] Obviously the attacks on humanistic rhetoric, when accompanied with this kind of practice, could do little to further a plain style. This was not the case, however, with the stylistic movement associated with science, which, when it moved into the Restoration, grew in strength and influence, not only in the secular but also in the religious world, when Anglican ministers attacked rhetorical preaching as vehemently as the puritans had previously done. It is the nonconformists who are now on the defensive, and who in some cases go so far as to defend eloquence.

The famous preacher Robert South furnishes a clear example of the reversal which took place in the Anglican attitude toward rhetoric. On July 29, 1660, at the time of the King's Commissioners meeting at Oxford, he preached a sermon at St. Mary's Church on the text 'The Scribe Instructed,' which was a humanistic defence of learning of the same general nature as those already discussed, for its purpose was to show that 'largeness of natural and exquisiteness of acquired abilities are not only consistent with, but required to the due performance of the work and business of a preacher of the gospel.'[2] He vigorously defends rhetoric, employing, for the most part, arguments with which we are already familiar. He asserts that in the thirteenth chapter of St. Matthew from which his text was taken, Christ gave the world a discourse 'fraught with all the commanding excellencies of speech . . . furnished with a strain of heavenly oratory far above the heights of all human rhetoric . . . clothing this sense in parables, similitudes, and other advantages of rhetoric, so as to give it an easier entrance and admission into the mind and affections; and what he did himself, he recommended to the practice of his disciples.' In discussing the faculties that qualify a man to preach, he emphasizes invention, which, he says, depends largely upon the power of the imagination, the exercise of which many consider unlawful, yet certainly divinity should not 'be deprived of a most useful and

---

[1] *A Survey of the Spiritual Anti-Christ* (1648), p. 312. 'They have a sort of high and lofty speaking, but far from the Scripture-stile . . . their eloquence is a combing, decking and busking of Christ, and the beauty and glory of the Gospel.'

[2] *Sermons Preached upon Several Occasions* (7 vols., 1823), III, 10.

excellent endowment of the mind . . . which gives a gloss and shine to all the rest . . . piety engages no man to be dull.' The sermon, composed under an acute consciousness of the puritan antipathy to rhetoric, employs the arguments used so frequently before: '. . . in God's word we have not only a body of religion, but also a system of the best rhetorick: and as the highest things require the highest expression, so we shall find nothing in Scripture so sublime in itself, but it is reached and sometimes overtopp'd by the sublimity of the expression.' As examples he cites Job, Moses' song in the thirty-second chapter of Deuteronomy, the Song of Solomon, and the Lamentations of Jeremiah, in which 'One would think that every letter was wrote with a tear, every word was the noise of a breaking heart.' Eloquence, he says, is the natural expression of these passages because the passions of the soul 'being things of the highest transport, and most wonderful and various operations in humane nature, are therefore the proper object and business of rhetorick.' In no writer of the period do we find a more passionate devotion to eloquence and a more vigorous defence of rhetoric than in South.

But let us pass over a period of eight years, during which the Royal Society was founded on an antirhetorical basis, the significance of which was broadcast to the world in Sprat's *History of the Royal Society* (1667). The climate of stylistic opinion must have changed considerably to permit such a sermon as South preached at Christ Church on April 30, 1668, on the fifteenth verse of the twenty-first chapter of Luke: 'For I will give you a mouth and wisdom, which all your adversaries shall not be able to gainsay nor resist.'[1] South interprets

[1] This sermon is found in South's *Sermons* (1843), IV, 134. The change in South's stylistic values could hardly have been due directly to the influence of the Royal Society, for Evelyn tells us (*Diary*, June 9, 1669) that in an oration delivered in the Sheldonian Theatre South made 'some malicious and undecent reflections' on the Royal Society. South had been a student at Oxford during the period when the puritan attacks on the universities, both from the religious and the scientific points of view, were at their height, and it is possible that later he associated the Royal Society with these attacks. A cursory examination of his sermons shows that he kept up very well with the new science, understood what it was about, and admired men like Bacon, Copernicus, Galileo, and Descartes. The Royal Society espoused the ideal of a plain, simple style, but the later was, independently of the Society, part and parcel of the scientific

'mouth and wisdom' as meaning great clearness and perspicuity and an unaffected plainness and simplicity in expression, the same qualities the puritans of the preceding decade had found in the New Testament. From this point of view and with perhaps a glance at Jeremy Taylor, he attacks the difficult nothings, remote allusions, high-flown metaphors, allegories, and starched similitudes of eloquent preachers. He exalts the plain, easy, familiar style of the Apostles, because it presents truth 'just as it is. For there is a certain majesty in plainness; as the proclamation of a prince never frisks it in tropes or fine conceits, in numerous and well turned periods, but commands in sober, natural expressions. A substantial beauty, as it comes out of the hands of nature, needs neither paint nor patch; things never made to adorn, but to cover something that would be hid.' This clearness and simplicity of expression, he says, gave power to the preaching of the Apostles, since only reason and judgment can move the will.

For the next ten years Anglican preachers such as Simon Patrick, Samuel Parker, and Joseph Glanvill, all associated with the new science, engage in the same kind of attacks on the rhetorical preaching of the dissenters which the puritans had previously made upon that of the Anglicans. And it is interesting to see them calling upon the same Biblical witnesses. As we have just noticed, South calls attention to the plain style of the Apostles, and Glanvill also emphasizes their humble origin and plainness of style. The first preachers, he says, were fishermen and mechanics 'without pomp of speech.'[1] One argument previously employed by the Anglicans in behalf of rhetoric, namely the eloquent nature of Job, the Psalms, the Song of Solomon, and other parts of the Bible, is deliberately undermined by the Anglicans of the Restoration, who assert that the writings in question are really poetry, in which rhetoric is

movement. When South says (*Sermons*, I, 258), 'Most of the writing and discourses in the world are but illustration and rhetoric, which signifies as much as nothing to a mind eager in persuit after the causes and philosophical truth of things,' he is expressing a sentiment that could have come from any experimental scientist of the day.

[1] *The Way of Happiness* (1670), p. 6. In *An Essay Concerning Preaching* (1678), p. 20, Glanvill criticizes the style of puritan preaching, and quotes with much satisfaction Paul's 'enticing words of man's Wisdom,' upon which the puritans had formerly based their attack on eloquence.

more justifiable than in prose.[1] Like the defenders of learning in pre-Restoration days, Glanvill answers the attack on philosophy, but in quite a different manner. Glanvill maintains that Paul's 'vain philosophy' referred to the disputing philosophy of the Greeks and not to experimental science, which was not known then.[2] The learning he would justify in the eyes of religion is not humanistic learning. Science has taken its place.

[1] *The Seventeenth Century*, pp. 129–30.
[2] *Philosophia Pia* (1671), pp. 131–34.

R. L. COLIE

Some Paradoxes in the Language of Things

THIS paper attempts to deal with one aspect of the riddling quality, the doubleness, of all creativity, in the arts or in the sciences, though it modestly limits itself to an examination of the natural sciences in their protomethodological state—that is to say, in the early modern period, before natural sciences had established an autonomous rule for themselves, a constitution ostensibly declaring their freedom from the arbitrary rules of the *ancien régime*, the arts. In this period, Milton could still call Galileo the 'Tuscan artist'; and for many scientists, as for many artists, the miraculous and the wonderful had not yet been banished as a test of scientific accuracy, but were still a partial validation for scientific experimentation, sometimes even a total validation of it.

Among the systematic wonders of Salomon's House in Bacon's New Atlantis, were chambers and houses in which the marvellous effects of nature were successfully imitated by the scientists. In some of these 'Great and Spatious Houses' they were able to demonstrate meteors and other weather-phenomena, such as 'Snow, Haile, Raine, some Artificiall Raines of Bodies, and not of Water, Thunder, Lightnings; Also generations of Bodies in Aire; as Froggs, Flies, and divers others.'[1]

[1] Francis Bacon, *The New Atlantis*, in *Sylva Sylvarum: Or, A Naturall Historie* (London, 1627), p. 34.

93

The scientists had models of the heavens (p. 39) which turned and returned to demonstrate God's system in the universe; they had experimental stations where animals and plants were made to grow larger and smaller by art (p. 35), and laboratories devoted to studying the relative sense-impressions of human beings. In the 'Perspective-Houses' the scientists presented

All Delusions and Deceits of the Sight, in Figures, Magnitudes, Motions, Colours: All Demonstrations of Shadowes. Wee finde also diverse Meanes yet unknowne to you, of Producing of Light, originally, from diverse Bodies. We procure meanes of Seeing Objects a-farr off; As in the Heaven, and Remote Places; And represent things Neare as A-farr off; And things A-farr off as Neare; Making Faigned Distances (p. 40).

In the 'Sound-Houses' parallel tricks of imitation and distortion were played:

Wee represent Small Sounds as Great and Deepe; Likewise Great Sounds, Extenuate and Sharpe; Wee make diverse Tremblings and Warblings of Sounds, which in their Originall are Entire. We represent and imitate all Articulate Sounds and Letters, and the Voices and Notes of Beasts and Birds . . . Wee have also diverse Strange and Artificiall Eccho's, Reflecting the Voice many times, and as it were Tossing it: And some that give back the Voice Lower then it came, some Shriller, and some Deeper; Yea some rendring the Voice, Differing in the Letters of Articulate Sound, from that they receyve (p. 41).

In the 'Perfume-Houses' the scientists were able to 'Multiplie Smells' and imitate them synthetically; they could imitate flavours 'so that they will deceyve any Mans Taste' (pp. 41–42). In the 'Houses of Deceits of the Senses' the scientists 'represent all manner of Feats of Jugling, False Apparitions, Impostures, and Illusions; And their Fallaces,' their explications, so that any man could see for himself the way the tricks were done and might, if he wished, learn to perform them himself.

All the tricks listed in the *New Atlantis* were eclectic, however ingenious and new they may have seemed to Bacon's readers: he collected them from the late medieval and renaissance compendia of the natural sciences and selected for his

Salomon's House the examples most striking. Many of his experiments fell into the limbo of 'natural magic,' a study pursued with enthusiasm by some men who had no interest whatever in what we now call 'objective' scientific experimentation; by some who did not distinguish with modern sharpness between 'magic' and 'natural science'; and by others again who were, even by our odd standards, scientists. And all those practitioners might be regarded by the public as magicians, white or black: the lines were not yet drawn between an official and an unofficial science. The ultimate problem raised by magic, natural or otherwise, was that of blasphemy. A man like Faustus attempted to take over the domain of God by means of magic, to imitate God's creation, even to recreate it; like Faustus, the alchemists (when they were not regarded as subjects for comedy, as by Ben Jonson) were considered too nearly to usurp God's proper function. The fact is that science raised problems identical with those raised by magic or alchemy, but expressed them so differently, or in so different a context, that scientific investigation has seemed on the whole an acceptable enterprise for reverent mankind: the terms of its expression have made all the difference.

In Salomon's House, and in scientific activity in general, the problem of imitation involves reproduction and re-creation. In its simplest form, an imitation is not the same thing as the thing imitated; it is demonstrably and recognizably something else. Though we may mistake James Reston's Uniquack for James Reston at times, we do not think that Univac, that non-infallible election computer, is a human being or even a human brain. We recognize that an automaton, or a picture, or a statue, or a poem, or a photograph all belong to the category of imitation and are not 'the thing itself.' But an imitation can also be a 'Chinese copy,' something so close to the original object imitated as to be indistinguishable from it, or in some cases to be 'it,' a sufficient substitute for the original. The representing of 'Small Sounds as Great and Deepe; Likewise Great Sounds, Extenuate and Sharp' is an imitation of one sound by another— and who is to say which is the 'real' sound, the small one, or the one great and deep? When a natural echo is imitated in the laboratory, is it then an echo or an imitation of an echo? When something is made to taste of an apple, does a man fall when he eats of that other thing? The answers to all such questions depend upon our point of view, our perspective; they are relative and, at best, can be answered only with the qualifications of relativity.

The line between imitation and reproduction is not easy to draw, and it is not constant, yet the problems it raises are those of all art and all craft. To 'improve' vegetables or fruit was part of the aim of agronomists in the New Atlantis (as in other sovereignties more recognizable as real), but their efforts at once laid them open to the moral criticism of Andrew Marvell's mower, who complained against the Garden in which man had so meddled with natural arrangement that

> The Pink grew then as double as [man's] mind,

the emblematic result of an impiety practised upon nature.

In the rhetoric of arts and crafts, of *techne*, the problem is a reflection of the general problem of truth, and the answer one gives depends largely on the intention one assigns to the performer. No one who sees a classical marble torso in the apartment of an instructor in English is likely to think either that the statue is an 'original' or that the instructor has been the victim of fraud, least of all that he has dared rob a museum; he will recognize it as a 'Museum Replica' which, though it may be outrageously expensive for what it is (really, for what it is not), is properly within the context and the means of the instructor. But when the same man enters a more elegant drawing room to discover a picture of a man with a bandage over his ear, he thinks twice about it; if he should later read of a lawsuit between the owner of the painting and 'experts' who deny that it is 'a Van Gogh,' he may not be particularly surprised. He has come up against another phase of the problem—intention. Museum Replicas do not pretend that their commodity is the Medici Venus, and the Medici Venus exists to prove that it is not; but the forger of the Van Gogh—if the picture was forged— was not imitating another known picture by Van Gogh; he was making 'a Van Gogh.' Since he was not Van Gogh, he intended a fraud; however much his picture may look like a Van Gogh, it is not one.

All arts, all crafts involve imitation and, if one takes the plain data of nature as one's absolute criterion, they involve deceit. A loaf of bread is, after all, a transmogrification of wheat, yeast, and water not 'intended' in Nature 'most plain and pure,' as Marvell's mower called that power. A typewriter is a great convenience, but at the most, Nature intended us to write with our fists, if we have to write at all. To leave out a great deal, a painting is a picture of a thing and it is a thing—'But it *is* a violin: there it is!' A poem is a form and an experience, both 'like' an actual experience in life and an experience of life. And a play, whatever else it is, is first of all an imitation of action.

The language of imitation in which we discuss the arts is Plato's language, and Plato himself was ambiguous in his attitude toward the arts. His ultimate judgment of the arts is relative: if they imitate good things, they are good; if they do not, they are not. Certainly poetry, closest of all to the language of philosophy, suffered most at Plato's hands in the *Republic*, however honourably he treated it in the *Phaedrus*; but the other arts and crafts also came in for a moral grading in a way dissociated from their intention *as art*; as art, the forged Van Gogh may in fact be 'as good as' a genuine Van Gogh; morally, it never can. Art tips over into deceit naturally enough—when a man paints grapes that birds peck at, and another paints a curtain that the spectator tries to draw aside, his imitation has turned into a deceit, a *trompe l'œil*. Moreover, he is threatening Nature by seeming to replace her, or even, in a pious age, threatening the creating God.

By the time we come to look at pictures, to attend plays, to read poems, we think we know what we are doing—not many of us try to brush the fly off the Metropolitan's Petrus Christus. We have learned to make allowances, to look from a certain point of view. People do not habitually speak in blank verse, we know; we know that perspective is a two-dimensional substitute for three-dimensional existence, that rhyme is a formal device rather than an imitation of ordinary life. We have, by the time we come to take the arts seriously, put behind us, or put aside, all distracting considerations of truth and falsehood exactly so that we can carry on our looking, our reading, our going to plays without being frightened or bewitched or even deceived.

Bacon's scientists were not free to be quite so sophisticated. They stood very self-consciously at the self-elected point of redefinition and reconstruction in their subject; in its reformation they desired above all things clarity and truth. Bacon's great works all are, in one or another way, a call to the truthful, the exact, restatement of *things*. To this end he urged the rejection of the muddling verbal structures used to confine truth and to distort it on what he regarded as rhetorical and logical beds of Procrustes. Bacon stood 'at the beginning,' or very near it, of a technical rhetoric in which things came to replace words in a large area of life; and we may expect in him a certain ambiguity in the question of imitation and deceit, since at the beginning no one can expect firm rules to be laid down.

On the face of it, the scientists made themselves clear enough —they practised the 'deceits of the senses' in their appropriate laboratories, but they were scrupulous always to demonstrate the 'Fallaces' of the deceits, the methods and techniques by which illusions were achieved. As the guide in the *New Atlantis* expressed it to visitors,

. . . surely you will easily beleeve, that wee, that have so many things truely Naturall, which induce Admiration, could in a World of Particulars deceive the Senses, if wee would disguise those things, and labour to make them seeme more Miraculous. But wee doe hate all Impostures, and Lies: Insomuch as wee have severely forbidden it to all our Fellowes, under paine of Ignominy and Fines, that they doe not shew any Naturall worke or thing, Adorned or Swelling; but only Pure as it is, and without all Affectation of Strangenesse (p. 43).

The reason for such strong academic disapproval of cheating is not far to seek: Bacon's whole effort was directed to 'the essential fourme of knowledge; which is nothing but a representation of truth; for the truth of being, and the truth of knowing are one, differing no more than the direct beame, and the beame reflected.' His third vice of learning, 'of all the rest the fowlest,' destroyed that essential form by its two manifestations, 'delight in deceiving, and aptnesse to be deceived, imposture and Credulitie.'[1] Because judicial astrology, natural magic, and alchemy made serious pretensions to learning which

[1] Francis Bacon, *The Twoo Bookes of the Proficiencie and Advancement of Learning* (London, 1605), I, 21.

they could not justify by their actual accomplishments, they fell into Bacon's third category of vice.

Though he deplored deceits and all untruths, whether deliberate or accidental, Bacon did not believe in prejudging them: every statement, every experiment, was to be examined and classified, however unreasonable it might seem, that truth might ultimately be sifted from untruth and imposture. Norms must be established before the deviant can be known; exceptions to rules may prove to be rules in themselves. Thus a complete record was to be kept 'of *Nature* in *Course*; of *Nature Erring*, or *Varying*; and of *Nature Altered* or wroght, that is *History* of *Creatures*, *History* of *Marvailes*, and *History* of *Arts*' (II, 8). From the inherited agglomeration of fables and popular errors the truth, confirmed by observation and experiment, was to be distinguished, and natural miracle established as such. For

from the Wonders of Nature, is the neerest Intelligence and passage towards the Wonders of Arte: For it is no more, but by following, and as it were, hounding Nature in her wandrings, to bee able to leade her afterwardes to the same place againe;

(II, 5)

man's technical effort is just the imitation of natural operations in order to reproduce them in his own context. All man need do was to follow his own potentialities for knowledge and for benevolent action; he need not supplant the God of the Creation but bring to perfection by his ingenuity stages of the creation that God has not seen fit Himself to perform.

The End of our Foundation is the Knowledge of Causes, and Secrett Motions of Things; And the Enlarging of the bounds of Humane Empire, to the Effecting of all Things possible.

(*New Atlantis*, p. 31)

The *Sylva Sylvarum* was Bacon's logbook of 'Causes and Secrett Motions of Things,' but the *Sylva* was not, as the devoted William Rawley wrote in the 'Preface to the Reader,' a mere English replica of such books as Giovanni Battista Porta's *Natural Magick*:

And the Difference betweene this *Naturall History*, and others. For those *Naturall Histories*, which are Extant, being Gathered

99

for Delight and Use, are full of pleasant Descriptions and Pictures; and affect and seek after Admiration, Rarities, and Secrets. But contrariwise, the Scope which his Lordship intendeth, is to write such a *Naturall History*, as may be Fundamentall to the Erecting and Building of a true Philosophy. . . .

Bacon's experiments seem to be the conventional 'Experiments of Fruit' he recommended in the *New Atlantis*, the sweetening of sea water, the improving of the human body, the speeding up of the maturation process in plants and animals, the grafting of fruit trees. He registered in the *Sylva* his disapproval of 'fanciful' interference in natural processes, such as ventriloquism, in which he saw 'no great use . . . but for Imposture, in Counterfeiting Ghosts or Spirits' (p. 65). Similarly, playing games with flowers and fruits was purposeless and a waste of time: 'The *Altering* of the *Sent, Colour,* or *Taste* of *Fruit*, by *Infusing, Mixing,* or *Letting* into the *Barke,* or *Root* of the *Tree, Herb,* or *Flower,* any *Coloured, Aromaticall,* or *Medicinall* Substance; are but *Fancies'* (p. 128).

Even for Bacon, 'fancies' were not always easy to distinguish from 'improvements': though he himself would never 'Aime at the making of *Paracelsus* Pigmey's; Or any such Prodigious Follies' (p. 33), he intended the examination of all acts of creation and transformation available to human experience. Transmutation of one species into another, for instance, 'in the vulgar philosophie, pronounced Impossible,' was a subject which unquestionably required 'deepe Search into Nature' to see if it might be done artificially. Caterpillars become flies, as Bacon had himself observed, and seeds and plants are known to degenerate, to the grief of farmers and gardeners. Man approaches actual transformation when he successfully speeds up natural processes in plants and animals, for 'Acceleration of *Time,* in *Works* of *Nature,* may well be esteemed *inter Magnalia Naturae.* And even in *Divine Miracles, Accelerating* of the *Time,* is next to the *Creating* of the *Matter'* (p. 81). Indeed, Bacon went on,

For this *Writing* of our *Sylva Sylvarum,* is (to speake properly) not a *Naturall History,* but a high kinde of *Naturall Magicke.* For it is not a Description only of Nature, but a Breaking of Nature, into great and strange Workes. (p. 29).

Like Porta's, Bacon's natural magic was one in which 'we overcome those things in Art, wherein Nature doth overcome us.'[1]
Not for nothing was Salomon's House called the College of the
Six Days' Work, where God's creation was studied for the
benefit of mankind, the improvement of the human condition.

II

Seventeenth-century literature is full of preoccupation with
creation—and indeed all literature is in part the record of man's
ideas about the beginning of things. Many a book, poem, or
story begins 'in the beginning,' thus making of itself an image
of what it attempts to represent; in the Western tradition, to
name only the most obvious, two inestimably important books
begin so—Genesis and the Gospel according to S. John. In the
development of Christian doctrine the importance of the creation
was crucial; inspired by doctrinal preoccupation the literature
of the hexaemeral tradition developed, enriched by the accumu-
lation of ideas and details from many non-Christian sources.

The 'beginning' of things inevitably presents a puzzle. How
did 'things,' a whole set of ideas that can only with the greatest
difficulty be thought away, 'begin'? Christian doctrine came to
depend (not without conciliar struggles) upon a paradox
canonized into orthodoxy, that God created the universe *ex
nihilo*; by implication that original act of creation could not be
repeated by any human. When King Lear warned his tongue-
tied daughter that 'Nothing can come of nothing,' he was
expressing what was, in the natural world at least, a truism.
Only God could make something of nothing, and men could
at best 'improve' a little on the original wonder of creation,
before which the human mind properly boggled.

On the whole, minds boggled gladly at the Creation. Reverence demanded it, and man's nature acquiesced, for it is far
simpler to bow to an orthodox paradox than to analyse God's
methods of creation. Even Bacon was careful in this respect to
curtail man's search into essential mystery, since, as he said,
man's mind had occupation enough in the contemplation of the
works of the world without seeking to know God's reasons for

[1] G. B. Porta, *Natural Magick* (London, 1658), p. 2.

making it. As one might expect, though, other forms of creative activity were inevitably likened to God's original act of creation; the alchemist's systems relied upon his analogy to the Creator, and alchemy relentlessly unfolded the implications of the simile in its arcane language and practice. Musicians and artists soon found themselves likened to the divine Creator, and Plato's verb was joyfully expounded to the poet's advantage.[1] The question of imitation and creation invaded literary criticism. George Puttenham, who says so many useful things about the poet and his craft, is even more apt to our purpose than Sidney, whose humanistic presentation of the poet as maker is usually cited in this connection. Puttenham tackles the ambiguities at once:

A Poet is as much to say as a maker. And our English name well conformes with the Greeke word; for of ποιειν to make, they call a maker *Poeta*. Such as (by way of resemblance and reverently) we may say of God: who without any travell to his divine imagination, made all the world of nought, nor also by any paterne or mould as the Platonicks with their Idees do phantastically suppose. Even so the very Poet makes and contrives out of his owne braine both the verse and the matter of his poeme, and not by any foreine copie or example, as doth the translator, who therefore may well be sayd a versifier, but not a Poet. The premises considered, it giveth to the name and profession no small dignitie and preheminence, above all other artificers, Scientificke or Mechanicall. And neverthelesse without any repugnancie at all, a Poet may in some sort be said a follower or imitator, because he can express the true and lively of everything is set before him, and which he taketh in hand to describe: and so in that respect is both a maker and a counterfaitor: and Poesie an art not only of making, but also of imitation.[2]

To call a poet a maker involves the question of category: if there is, in fact, but one Maker, the Creating God, then all other makers are themselves imitations, constructing as best they can imitations of God's creation. But if poets are really

[1] See Ernst Kris and Otto Kurz, *Die Legende vom Künstler* (Vienna, 1934), *passim*.

[2] George Puttenham, *The Arte of English Poesie* (London, 1589), p. 1.

makers, then the category of maker must be enlarged to include them, and though there can be degrees of excellence within the category, the essence of all makers is the same, and thus, presumably, the essence of their creations is the same as well. The sculptor makes a man, the painter makes a *nature morte* or alive, the poet makes a world: and at the same time he has imitated a norm called man, or perhaps even S. George or Balzac; he has imitated an arrangement, natural or artificial, of nature; he has written *Paradise Lost*.

What he does may well be wonderful, and we may properly admire it. Or it may not be—in which case, if we withhold admiration, we usually also try to dismiss the object created (or imitated) from the category of art. If the artist has done something at all admirable, we are likely to accept it as art and to justify it accordingly. Sometimes a 'wonderful' work of art seems to be the product of a nonrational or suprarational operation; sometimes the product of chance, or genius, or happy accident; sometimes recognizably the result of consideration and hard thought, its wonderfulness a contrived or artful wonder.

In literature, such an artful wonder is the rhetorical paradox, or 'Wondrer,' as Puttenham translated the word in his dictionary of domesticated rhetorical terms.[1] The 'Wondrer' may be of several kinds—he may himself wonder, usually ironically, at the condition of which he speaks; or he may make the audience wonder or admire his work, either by cheating their expectation of simply by a display of rhetorical skill so dazzling as to reduce them to astonishment. The traditional rhetorical paradox, for instance, belongs to this category: a 'thing without honour' is convincingly praised, as in Gorgias' praise of Helen or Isocrates' of Thersites, until the auditory is won over to the orator's expressed—if not his real—view. The standard paradox of the late classical period and the renaissance was this sort of rhe-

[1] Puttenham, p. 189. For some of the literature on this subject see Theodore C. Burgess, *Epideictic Literature* (Chicago, 1902); A. S. Pease, 'Things without Honour,' *Classical Philology*, XXI (1926); Warner G. Rice, 'The *Paradossi* of Ortensio Lando,' (Michigan University) *Essays and Studies in English and Comparative Literature*, XII (1931); Henry Knight Miller, 'The Paradoxical Encomium, with Special Reference to its Vogue in England, 1600–1800,' *MP*, LIII (1956); A. E. Malloch, 'The Techniques and Function of the Renaissance Paradox,' *SP*, LIII (1956).

torical display in praise of traditionally worthless things (fleas, lice, baldness, asses, folly) or things on which the audience officially held another opinion (woman's constancy, tyranny, imprisonment, or the benevolent operation of nature). This kind of paradox, the defence of an unpopular opinion, was a light version of a far more serious activity. The paradoxes of Zeno, for instance, either his own or those attributed to him in the *Parmenides*, were expressions of monistic conviction at variance with popular pluralistic belief. Because of their logical structure, these paradoxes were 'paradoxical' in another way— their conclusions often contradicting the premises from which they sprang, or their various conclusions contradicting one another and thus cancelling themselves out—and their purpose was to leave their disillusioned auditors with only the monistic conclusion to fall back on. In all cases, the paradoxes themselves expressed, or expressed from their hearers, wonder, amazement, admiration.

Even Zeno's paradoxes involve tricks of intention. Sometimes he deduces from premises of popular belief his contradictory conclusions—that is to say, he takes the *pseudodoxia epidemica* in bad faith, because his intention is to deny them. Sometimes he takes the negative conclusions flowing from such a premise and deduces his contradictions by that method. Sometimes he begins with his own premise and argues 'purely' to his end; but in the main his argument is at least ironic and usually tricky. The Sophists encouraged the spread of the rhetorical paradox because it gave them a chance to show their skill in *epideixis*; and they brought into great prominence the warfare between form and content, between technique and philosophy, between rhetoric and logic, which Plato so deplored. Intention becomes extremely important in the evaluation of paradox— and intention is just what the paradoxist intends to conceal. He may conceal it by saying two things at once, or by saying one thing outright and meaning another, or by proving logically that opposites are one, or by reducing his opponents or his readers to despair by his impeccable circular reasonings or infinite regressions. And because his themes are often ostensibly serious, he discusses them in a form that is light, or the other way around; the paradox is traditionally an escape from the responsibilities of reasoned conclusion, an amusement, a play with as well as upon words, an illusion, a game, a joke. At its height, a paradox is an escape from moral responsibility that manages all the same to make an important moral point— *The Praise of Folly*, *Utopia*. In the seventeenth century, that great period of professional intellectuals, these recreations of the learned were collected into books of recreation for the learned with fine titles like *Argumenta ludicrorum et Amoenitatum* (Leiden, 1623), *Admiranda Rerum Admirabilium Encomia* (Nijmegen, 1666), or greatest of all, Caspar Dornavius' two folio volumes, *Amphitheatrum Sapientiae Socraticae Joco-Seriae* (Hannover, 1619).

These were recreations, surely, in all the complex meanings of the word; in the rhetorical sense, they were the reorganization of natural proportion, of divine order, into another and arbitrary order of the writer, all the more wonderful if the subject was not officially worthwhile.[1] There were other aspects of Renaissance culture that offered analogies to rhetorical paradox, for example, the *Wunderkammern* and *Kunstschränke*, the cabinets of princes and virtuosi, in which samples of the chain of nature were displayed to the admiration of the beholder. 'Erring Nature' had its place in these cabinets as well as 'Nature in Course'; the virtuosi loved remarkable objects such as fossils of mysterious creatures or stones in the shape of feet, or vegetables shaped like human heads, or wonder-working stones or earths or talismans.[2] The great collections had their

[1] I am at work on a study of paradoxology which ultimately will, or so I hope, lay out fuller documentation and explanation of some of the generalizations made here. Some of the critical theories for Renaissance poetry that are part of the *apologia* for paradox have been discussed, though to another end, by J. A. Mazzeo in his suggestive articles on the aesthetics of the metaphysical style. See particularly his 'A Seventeenth-Century Theory of Poetry,' *Romanic Review*, XLII (1951), 248–49; and 'Metaphysical Poetry and the Poetic of Correspondence,' *JHI*, XIV (1953), 228–29. At this point I should like to refer to the discussions of creation, paradox, and illusion by E. H. Gombrich in his invaluable book, *Art and Illusion* (New York and London, 1960), and to thank him for the Socratic questions which gave to this paper such order as it has.

[2] Julius von Schlosser, *Kunst- und Wunderkammern der Spätrenaissance* (Leipzig, 1908); Gustav Klemm, *Zur Geschichte der Sammlungen für Wissenschaft und Kunst in Deutschland* (Zerbst, 1837). For the tricks of perspective played in the cabinets themselves, see Liselotte Nölter, *Der Wrangelschrank und die Verwandten Süddeutschen Intarsianmöbel des 16. Jahrhunderts* (Berlin, 1956).

quota of ingenious mechanisms as well, the products of an increasingly learned technology, again *joco-seriae* of a particularly admirable kind.[1]

Parallel to these are the scientific exercises and compendia of the Renaissance, also seeking the knowledge of causes, or, as Porta put it, 'the whole witty force of hidden Nature.'[2] Porta's *Magia Naturalis* was a tremendous collection of true 'science,' superstition, experiment, myth, theory and remedy and notion, a major source for his successors, including Bacon. Other great compendia were gathered in the period, partly following the medieval tradition of Vincent of Beauvais, Isidore of Seville, and Albertus Magnus, partly working in the new tradition of the moderns, reforming nature in a new model, recreating her. Cardanus' *De Subtilitate* (Nürnberg, 1550) went into many editions, as did his *De Rerum Varietate* (Basel, 1557); Scaliger's corrective to the *De Subtilitate*, *Exotericarum Exercitationum Liber* (Paris, 1557), was also widely cited by the wonder-collectors following him. Cardanus' book was full of 'witty' similes and analogies from Nature's book, but he himself deplored the uselessness of the mere *joculariae artes*, professional entertainments existing with no more serious purpose or implication:

Nam ludunt, pugnant, venantur, saltant, tuba canunt, coquinarium exercent artem, atque haec omnia ut mirabilia sunt, ita nullius ut dixi utilitatis, et cum resciveris rationem qua oculos fallunt, ea autem duobus constat, instrumentis variis ad hoc paratis, manuumque agilitate, nec si te docere velint precario digneris discere.[3]

Nature was the real artist: the rest is trivial. God played a kind

---

[1] One of the most famous of these collections was that of Athanasius Kircher, often referred to by Schott; in the eighteenth century a catalogue was printed of his collection of antique art, but not of his scientific collections (*Musei Kircheriani in Romano Societatus Jesu Collegio Area* [Rome, 1763]). There are many printed books recording like collections, the names of which Schlosser gives; I have managed to see only two for careful study: *Museum Wormianum, seu Historia Rerum Rariorum* (Leiden, 1655) and M. B. Valentini, *Museum Museorum* (Frankfurt-am-Main, 1714, 2 vols.).

[2] *Natural Magick*, p. 3.

[3] Cardanus, *De Subtilitate*, pp. 342–43.

of game with the world, according to some seventeenth-century commentators. He was a Heraclitan inventor of a world 'compounded of Contraries and Agreement of Discords';[1] his world was a *discordia concors*, a composition to which oxymoron was the appropriate figure of speech. The poet's task was to recreate those marvellous discords with his rhetoric, and the natural scientist's to recreate them in his technological language of things.

Porta's book, with its emphasis on the wonderful, was one such book in imitation of Nature; Johannes Josephus Wecker wrote another, *De Secretis*,[2] and Johannes Jonstonus his *Thaumaturgia Naturalis*,[3] both later translated into English. Daniel Schwenter and G. P. Hartstoerffer compiled the three-volume *Deliciae Physico-Mathematicae* (Nürnberg, 1651–53), full of 'lustiger art' and rather conscientious natural wit; Joseph Furttenbach contributed his *Architectura Recreationis* (Augsburg, 1640) and *Mannhafftern Kunst-Spiegel, oder Continuatio und Fortsetzung Allerhand Mathematisch- und Mechanisch-Hochnutzlich . . . Delectationen* (Augsburg, 1663). The titles alone, so strikingly like those of the collections of paradox, demonstrate the joco-serious nature of these books.

The most important of such compendia were the work of the great Jesuits, Mario Bettini, Gaspar Schott, and Athanasius Kircher. Bettini's beautifully published collection was the first of the major encyclopædias of the light and the grave in science: *Apiaria Universae Philosophiae Mathematicae* (Bologna, 1642, 2 vols.), the subtitle to which produces the desired parallel, *In quibus Paradoxa, Et nova pleraque Machinamenta ad usus eximios traducta*. The 'paradoxes' are of many different kinds—scientific ideas contrary to general opinion, logical and mathematical paradoxes, geometrical problems which had not yielded to solution, curious machines and engines, illusions, games, and tricks. Bettini tackled the 'learned hallucinations' constellated

---

[1] Baltasar Gracian, *The Critick*, trans. by Paul Rycaut (London, 1681), pp. 33–34; cf. p. 35. For a general theory of play in western civilization see J. Huizinga, *Homo Ludens* (London, 1949).

[2] Basel, 1604; translated into English by Dr. R. Read as *Eighteen Books of the Secrets of Art and Nature* (London, 1660).

[3] Amsterdam, 1632; translated into English as *An History of the Wonderful Things of Nature* (London, 1657).

about the quadrature problem, and about the asymptotic lines which go *de infinito in finito*, as well as those that result from deformation of the rules of perspective. Archimedes' screw, wedges, levers (to lift the earth, as usual) all make their appearance, magnificently illustrated. Paradox becomes the normal mode in Bettini's world.

The titles Gaspar Schott chose for his books again spring from the paradoxist's mind—*Magia Universalis Naturae et Artis* (Nürnberg, 1657); *Physica Curiosa, sive Mirabilia Naturae et Artis* (Nürnberg, 1662); *Technica Curiosa* (Nürnberg, 1664); and *Joco-Seriorum Naturae et Artis, sive Magiae Naturalis Centuriae Tres* ([Würzburg], 1674). Schott was Kircher's disciple and colleague, and his books drew heavily on Kircher's idiosyncratic genius, presenting ideas and things that Kircher had published in his own works or had discussed with his colleague. Schott made no secret of his admiration for Kircher and his dependence upon his master's work, stressing in his long introduction the playfulness with which Kircher tackled the problems of natural philosophy, emulating a playful Nature:

> Hic curiositate Theatrum panditur,
> In quo *Ars* et *Natura* ludunt:
> Sed dum ludunt doctis; indoctis illudunt.[1]

From Kircher's tricks, games, and illusions, Schott came to understand, he says, the ultimate mystery of metamorphosis, which can be practised upon Nature by art, so that their collusion, their playing together, may result in protean formations and deformations, in *serio ludere*. The marvellous anamorphic pictures and landscapes Kircher and Schott developed not only exhibited man's technical art but imitated also 'God Himself, the author of Nature, who plays on earth.'[2] Illusion and game are, of course, not the only products of these men's admiration for Nature—and their jealousy of her—and many of their inventions and notions are not 'paradoxical' or ambiguous or joco-serious at all. But the ambiguous, the paradoxical, and the

[1] *Magia Universalis*, Prologus Encomiasticus ad Lectorem.

[2] *Magia Universalis*, p. 170; *Joco-Seriorum*, pp. 1–2. (I do not want to imply that such usual games were peculiar to the seventeenth century—Giuseppe Archimboldo, as well as Erhard Schön, Holbein himself, and many others, practised such *trompes l'œil* and tricks of double vision in the preceding century.)

joco-serious played an essential part in their view of God, of Nature, and of themselves, and gave tone to the wonder and admiration they paid to God's universe.

III

The joco-serious paradox operates across limits, and paradox loves limits—beginnings, as in the Creation, where nothing becomes something (or even everything), and eternity becomes for man's measurement time; ends, where something becomes nothing again, or time loses itself eternity.[1] Paradox operates with especial vigour at the limits of discursive knowledge. Whatever else the riddling *Parmenides* is, it is a demonstration of the problems at the limit of knowledge and of the linguistic and rhetorical problems arising from the attempt to overcome those limitations. Paradox operates in relativity—the many is one, and the one many, two different statements involving two different systems of value; God is Three in One and One in Three, two statements involving but one system of value; 'I lie,' the classic paradox of infinite regression involving more than one concept of truth and more than one philosophy of language, a problem unsolved until the development of the metalanguage.[2] It has been said that wherever the problem of infinity arises, paradox is born[3] (out of nowhere, out of nothing), but one could extend that to say that wherever there are concepts of number there are also paradoxes. Zero is as fertile as infinity in the generation of paradox.

Even the simplest form of paradox, the defence of a belief generally unpopular, is not really very simple, since it involves an unspoken assumption of the wars of truth, an acceptance of pluralism in the truth of sublunary situations and at the same

[1] For some discussion of this, see my article 'Time and Eternity: Paradox and Structure in *Paradise Lost*,' in the *Journal of the Warburg and Courtauld Institutes*, XXIII (1960), 127–38.

[2] Solved in the metalanguage, a conceptual system unhappily unavailable to thinkers of the period under examination. For discussions of this, see Rudolf Carnap, *The Logical Syntax of Language* (London and New York, 1937), esp. pp. 211–22; Frank Plimpton Ramsey, *The Foundations of Mathematics* (London, 1925); Alfred Tarski, *Logic, Semantics, Meta-mathematics*, trans. by J. H. Woodger (Oxford, 1956), pp. 152–95.

[3] Bernard Bolzano, *Paradoxes of the Infinite* (London, 1950), p. 75.

time a conviction that truth is only one and all competing 'truths' are at best but appearances. Of course Zeno knew that the tortoise did not in fact move faster than Achilles, so fleet of foot; but in the monistic universe to which he gave his allegiance such matters were of no importance and did not enter the category reserved for truth. The logical model of pluralism did not coincide with empirical observation: both pluralism and empirical observation were, by Zeno's high standards, trivial mental diversions rather than pursuits of the truth. His paradoxes were a negative weapon, rather 'alarums to truth to arme her then enimies,' as John Donne wrote later of his paradoxes. From Zeno's time on the word 'paradox' carried with it implications of challenge, of warning, or stimulus, or irony.

In its use of the word, scientific writing on the whole conserved the plainest of paradox's complicated meanings. The 'Copernican paradox,' for instance, was the phrase used to refer to the Copernican theory or hypothesis of cosmic heliocentrism, a notion which obviously ran counter to most men's opinions and to the evidence of the senses, paradoxical too insofar as it was a challenge to truth which for a time at least became accepted truth. In the history of scientific thought, the life-history of an hypothesis is often a series of the meanings of paradox: an hypothesis presents itself as a paradox contrary to public opinion; accepted, it becomes 'truth' and incites other investigatory paradoxes; supplanted, it turns out to have been a paradox after all, the defence of a thesis subsequently 'proved' to have been indefensible. All this because scientific paradoxes, like any others, operate at the edge of knowledge, at the limits of man's relations to his physical universe. In his *Philosophia Libera*, Nathanael Carpenter hinted at this relativity in the term:

. . . quorum alii Paradoxi nomen, pro opinione veritate opposita, interpretantes indigne tulerunt ea me inter Paradoxa recensuisse, quae vera esse crederunt. . . .[1]

His book makes fascinating use of mathematical and logical paradoxes to control the physical world and also to delineate theological truth. In 1661, when Robert Boyle published his

[1] *Philosophia Libera*, Oxford, 1622, Praefatio ad Lectorem.

Sceptical Chymist, he gave it a fine subtitle: *Or Chymico-Physical Doubts and Paradoxes, Touching the Spagyrists' Principles Commonly call'd Hypostatical, As they are wont to be Propos'd and Defended by the Generality of Alchymists* (London, 1661). Carneades, the hero of the dialogue, was selected because he was 'so conversant with nature and with Furnaces, and so unconfin'd to vulgar Opinions, that he would probably by some ingenious Paradox or other, give our minds at least a pleasing Exercise, and perhaps enrich them with some solid instruction' (p. 3). That is just what Carneades does: in the traditional debate with his fellow virtuosi, he lays out, gracefully and decorously, his own views and of course wins his friends over to them. At one point in his instruction, Carneades performs a trick of the artful paradoxist most common in the graphic arts and painting—he introduces the composer into the work he is composing:

And, if I could here shew You what Mr. *Boyle* has Observ'd, touching the Various Chymicall Distinction of Salts, you would quickly discern, not only that Chymists do give themselves a Strange Liberty to call Concretes Salts. . . . (p.252)

This is a cute trick for an author so little playful as Boyle, the generality of whose work has an austerity and even a ponderousness that made it easy prey for the wicked young Swift in his paradox and parody, 'A Meditation upon a Broomstick.' Here, though, Boyle reminds his readers at once by this device of the levels of reality involved in any act of creation, either of a new idea or of a book about a new idea; his intention is to jar his readers into some reflection on this point.

Boyle's *Hydrostatical Paradoxes* (Oxford, 1666) gives his reason for using the term in his title, and his reason (stated in the Preface) is involved with concepts of creative wit and with *mirabilia naturae.*

For (first) the Hydrostaticks is a part of Philosophy, which I confess I look upon as one of the ingeniousest Doctrines that belong to it. Theorems and Problems of this Art, being most of them pure and handsome productions of Reason duly exercis'd on attentively consider'd Subjects, and making in them such Discoveries as are not only pleasing, but divers of them surprising, and such as would make men wonder by what kind of Ratiocination men came to attain the knowledg of such unobvious Truths.

In his view, hydrostatics should be rescued from its subservient position to geometry and established as a legitimate subject of its own:

. . . I hop'd I might doe something, both towards the illustrating and towards the rescue of so valuable a Discipline, by Publishing the ensuing Tract; where I endeavour to disprove the receiv'd errors, by establishing Paradoxes contrary to them, and to make the Truths the better understood and receiv'd. . . .

The term 'paradox' was in legitimate chemical employment. Both Jean-Batiste van Helmont and his son, Franciscus Mercurius, used the word in all sorts of connections, theological, physical, and chemical,[1] so that Boyle came to it naturally enough as a term of art. He dealt at considerable length with another problem, in its own nature a paradox of physics, the vacuum. In Schott's *Technica Curiosa*[2] there is a fine illustration of the wonder of the Magdeburg experiment, in which eight horses could not pull apart the two halves of a vacuum-sealed copper ball. Guericke's and Torricelli's experiments on the vacuum were for their contemporaries exercises in the problem of *nothing*, that *nihil* existing before the Creation and on which so many witty paradoxists had composed their lessons.[3] The Torricellian experiment dealt with mercury in a glass tube, and engaged good men in its explanation—Helmont, Gassendi, Kircher, Schott, Charleton, Hobbes, Pascal, Maignan, Fabri, Linus, and Boyle all tackled it, as did Henry More and Sir

---

[1] J. B. van Helmont, *Works* (London, 1664), pp. 284 ff, 690, 693 ff.; F. M. van Helmont, *The Paradoxical Discourses Concerning the Macrocosm and the Microcosm* (London, 1685); J. B. van Helmont, *A Ternary of Paradoxes*, trans. and ed. by Walter Charleton (London, 1650).

[2] See *Technica Curiosa*, plate between pp. 38 and 39.

[3] See Dornavius, I, 730–38, where eight paradoxes on *nihil* are given, of which some of the authors are Goclenius, Passerat, and Beza. Another very interesting *De Nihilo* (Groningen, 1661) is by the mathematician Martinus Schoock.

Matthew Hale.[1] The problem of the vacuum was of the greatest philosophical importance, since if it could be definitely proved to exist, the vacuum tended to confute the theory of plenitude, by which each nook and cranny of the created universe was believed to be occupied by something. The 'corpuscularians,' among them Boyle, Gassendi, and Charleton, all held for a vacuum against the plenists,[2] and were industrious in their defence of its existence. For all sides, however, the problem was a paradox in the plain sense, as well as a problem involving paradox in both words and things, the possible illustration of the impossible nothing.

IV

Illusion of any kind may involve paradox, particularly the paradoxes of relativity, in the sense that one thinks that something is real when in fact another thing is the reality. Though they are not identical, illusion and paradox are close kin and often in alliance. 'My mother: father and mother is man and wife; man and wife is one flesh, and so my mother'—an illicit logic to express an illicit conjunction. In Bacon's chambers of experiment and illusion there are paradoxes aplenty, but paradoxes of a rather different kind from Boyle's. Late renaissance scientific analysis proceeded with incredible speed, and like all analytical processes, it yielded a double result. In the first instance, it resulted in the Baconian proposal to manipulate natural laws to some immediate and practical effect, preferably an effect beneficial to mankind but in any case an effect well within the context of society; in the second, it resulted in recreation, in both senses of that word. Amusement can mean relaxation, often 'marvellous' or tricky, as well as rebuilding, repreparing for action. It can also be the re-creation, making again, imitating, the 'making and counterfaiting' of Puttenham's phrase. When Nature is reassembled after analysis, as in the perspective

[1] See Henry More, *Enchiridion Ethicum* (London, 1671); [Matthew Hale], *Difficiles Nugae* (London, 1674); Henry More, *Remarks upon Two Late Ingenious Discourses* (London, 1676); Matthew Hale, *Observations Touching the Principles of Natural Motions* (London, 1677).

[2] See *An Essay Concerning a Vacuum* (London, 1697), for the antiplenist view; for a standard expression of plenism, Porta, *Natural Magick*, pp. 303–4.

and sound-houses of Salomon's House, she may appear 'as she is' or she may appear deformed and grotesque. In the grotesque recreations paradox lurks, a concealed threat to perception and thus to knowledge. Deceits of the senses that are two things at once, two-or-more-in-one, are the parallel in natural philosophy to the verbal paradox of contradiction, since they raise and illustrate the same puzzles about the nature of perceived reality.

Such deceits were widespread in Europe in the late Renaissance, cultivated in circles of the greatest intellectual concentration upon reason—in the Cartesian group around Mersenne and the Paris Minorites, and among the Jesuits in Rome and Germany gathered about the polymath Athanasius Kircher. Jurgis Baltrušaitis has shown the extraordinary relationship between Cartesian rationalism and the fantastic world of optical illusion created by Cartesian workers in the vineyard, who applied their new understanding of the operations of the eye, not to produce cameras (models of the eye) only, but to produce optical deformations and deceptions as well.[1] Not such an extraordinary relation, when one comes to think of it: technical mastery of a subject often turns against the subject, and when it does, paradox occurs, as when logic turns on itself in circular reasoning or infinite regression, or when rhetoric produces paradoxes that transcend its own rules. The outburst of anamorphosis, the anti-eugenic alliance of technique and art to produce deformed offspring, illustrates the forms such recreations took: pictures which when looked at frontally looked like nothing at all (the dangerous nothing of the paradoxists) or like a chaos (the other, though heterodox, ground of creation), but when looked at from another point of vision resolve into genuine pictures of recognizable things or persons. The most familiar example of this is the skull, so disturbing both technically and intrinsically, painted between Holbein's French ambassadors in the National Gallery in London. Bushy describes the same phenomenon in *Richard II*:

> . . . perspectives, which rightly gaz'd upon
> Show nothing but confusion, ey'd awry,
> Distinguish form. . . .   (II, ii)

[1] Jurgis Baltrušaitis, *Anamorphoses, ou Perspectives Curieuses*, Paris, [1955]. I have borrowed heavily from this fascinating book for the section on optics. See also the important discussion in Gombrich, pp. 242–87.

A picture is always two-in-one, if not more-in-one, containing far more than its form 'should' hold—but this contradiction of elementary physical law is the supernatural of all art, all language. An anamorphic picture contains the usual two-or-more-in-one and another element, deliberate intellectual trickery, like the paradox expressly loaded with ambiguities and designed to amaze, to cause question, doubt and disturbance. 'Real' pictures, paintings with no attempt to 'deceive' the onlooker, such as the Last Judgment of the Sistine Chapel, where the upper registers are for hieratic reasons as well as for reasons of perspective painted larger than the lower, had always adjusted to the spectator's point of vision. Long before the rules of perspective had been properly formulated architects had made the same sort of visual adjustment, of which columnar entasis is the simplest and best-known example. Before modern perspective was invented, optical puzzles were known and played at, like the boxes every schoolchild discovers for himself: ✪

In the late sixteenth century such optical tricks were read out of 'serious' painting and engraving: in the Franciscan Church at the Palais Royal there hung a copy (now lost) of a painting of the Descent from the Cross by Daniele da Volterra, which when seen from two different vantage points presented two different pictures. Jean-François Nicéron, the pupil and friend of Mersenne, mentions it as

... Christum velut primariam tabulae figuram adumbravit tanto artificio ut spectatus e latere sinistro, tabulae plano velut transversè incumbere videatur et ad eandem partem pes illius dexter prosilire; at in dextra parte constitutis totum corpus quasi erectum in tabula, atque idem pes qui prius versus sinistram, iam ad dexteram protensus appareat; quod hic etiam agnoscat qui volet attentè contemplari ectypum illius tabulae quod Ecclesiae Nostrae Parisiensis Hippodromum Regium, altare maius exornat.[1]

In this picture the same lines and brush strokes, looked at from two different angles, produce two different effects, like the liar paradox in logic. There were, by lesser techniques, other ways to produce such a dual picture: Nicéron describes

[1] Jean-François Nicéron, *Thaumaturgus Opticus, seu Admiranda Optices, Catoptrices, Diotrices* (Paris, 1646), p. 189.

pictures layered on to the same surface *par petites bandes*, such as the election buttons some people chose to wear which when viewed from one side read 'I like Ike' and when viewed from the other revealed the candidate's beaming face.

On fait certaines images, lesquelles, suivant la diversité de leur aspect, representent deux ou trois choses toutes différentes, de sorte qu'estant veuës de front, elles representeront une face humaine; de costé droict une teste de mort, et du gauche quelqu' autre chose encore différente; et à la verité des images dans la nouveauté ont eu assez de cours, encore qu'il n'y ait pas grand artifice à les dresser. . . .[1]

But the whole thing was of little consequence, since the cleverness required to construct such an illusion involved 'aucune cognoissance de la perspective, et de ces effets,' no properly analytical knowledge of natural philosophy. Real perspective anamorphoses were pictures drawn on a wall so that as one entered a door into the room where they were, they seemed to double the length of the room, or to continue artificially the actual perspective of the room. Or such a projection might be a view of S. John on Patmos, or S. Francis receiving the Stigmata (both subjects were demonstrated by Nicéron and others), drawn on a wall by one or another projection device that threw properly elongated or foreshortened images on the surface to be covered. Catoptrics, or the science of mirrors—really of lenses, some silvered—was able to produce still more remarkable effects, though it often carried its practitioners into accusations of sorcery. Nicéron loved catoptrics:

La Catoptrique ou science des miroirs nous a fait veoir des productions si admirables, ou plustost des effets si prodigieux, qu'entre ceux, qui l'ont cogneue et practiquée, il s'en est trouvé, qui par une vaine et ridicule ostentation, ou quelquesfoix pour abuser les plus simples, se sont efforcez de passer pour devins, sorciers ou enchanteurs, qui avoient le pouvoir, par l'entremise des mauvais esprits, de faire veoir tout ce qu'ils vouloient, fut-il passé, ou à venir. Et de faict on en a veu des effects si etranges, qu'à ceux, qui n'en sçavoient pas la cause, ny

---

[1] Jean-François Nicéron, *La Perspective Curieuse ou Magie Artificielle des Effets Merveilleux*, Paris, 1638, pp. 50–51.

les raisons, et n'avoient jamais rien veu de semblable, ils devoient passer pour surnaturels, ou bien estre reputez pour de pures illusions ou prestiges de la magie diabolique. Le nombre de ces effects est infiny, et qui voudroit entreprendre de les declarer tous par la maniere de leur construction, en pourroit faire deux beaux volumes.[1]

With concave and convex glasses, and concave and convex cylindrical mirrors, all sorts of deformations were possible, as in modern fun-fairs. By arranging several mirrors in different ways, a figure might be made to seem to fly or walk on the ceiling. A single figure might be multiplied to seem to be an army of men.[2]

Faceted crystals through which light is projected may be cut to produce various images which ultimately fuse into one. That 'one' may be the basis of all the transforming pictures projected, as in Cornelis Drebbel's magic lantern made on these principles,[3] or it may be the unifying picture made from many different and separate pictures:

... l'autre merveille, que nous a produit la dioptrique, est celle, qui par le moyen des verres ou crystaux polygones et à facetes, fait veoir, comme je l'ay exprimé au titre de ce livre, en un tableau, où on aura figuré 15 ou 16 pourtraits tous differents, et bien proportionnez, une nouvelle figure differente des autres, aussi bien proportionnée et semblable à quelque object proposé. Laquelle invention pour sembler en quelque façon moins utile que la premiere, n'est pourtant pas à mespriser, puis qu'elle fournit aux curieux un agreable divertissement, et qu'on se laisse tromper de la sorte avec contentement.[4]

Nicéron's examples were witty in subject as well as in execution —thirteen Ottoman Turks who turn into His Most Christian

---

[1] *Ibid.*, p. 74.

[2] *Ibid.*, pp. 76, 79.

[3] See Drebbel's description of this (Royal Library, The Hague, Kon. Akad. Ms Huygens xlvii, fol. 207) cited in R. L. Colie, '*Some Thankfulnesse to Constantine*,' The Hague, 1956, pp. 97–98; also Porta, *Natural Magick*, p. 356, for a brief description of the operation.

[4] Nicéron, *Perspective Curieuse*, p. 102.

Majesty, or a series of great popes who fuse into Urban VIII.[1]

That these tricks were regarded as paradoxical the title of Giulio Troili's book on optics suggests: *Paradossi per Pratticare la Prospettiva senza saperla* (Bologna, 1683), in which he describes the 'perspective machines' as developed from the time of Dürer through the industrious seventeenth century. Paradoxes of natural science were gradually collected into handbooks of all sorts of puzzles and jokes, of which the optical experiments were an important part.

Other constant experiments of this nature were those with automata, such as the designs of Isaac and Salomon de Caus, who could counterfeit 'The Voices of smal Birds by means of Water and Aire' to deceive the hearer who could not see the machine; and who made fountains in which Galatea was drawn by dolphins or Neptune encircled by moving tritons and horses.[2] Automata, so recognizably not alive and yet so close to life, fascinated renaissance philosophers, so that even so little mechanistic a philosopher as Locke could not help making his reference to the Strassburg clock, and Descartes, Boyle, and Hobbes often referred to it as a sample of what machines and mechanism might accomplish. An automaton of particular fascination was the perpetual motion, attempted by many

[1] Nicéron gives a little poem, extraordinarily bad, on the Turks who 'became' Louis XIII:

> Que va representer cette plate peinture?
> Tu le veois curieux, et ne le cognois pas;
> Tu veois des Ottomans, et sous leur pourtraicture
> Un visage est caché, qui ne se montre pas;
> Si tu veux cognoistre, met l'oeil à l'ouverture
> De ce petit canal, et tu recognoistras
> Du Monarque François la naifue peinture,
> Qui doit des Ottomans l'Empire mettre à bas;
> Qui fera des Croissans de la race infidelle
> De ces Mahometans, surgir les Fleurs de Lis
> De nos Roys Tres-Chrestiens, que la France fidelle
> A tousiours recogneu du ciel les favoris.

Perspective Curieuse, p. 116.

[2] Isaac de Caus, *New and Rare Inventions of Water-Works*, trans. by John Leak (London, 1654), pp. 20, 26, 27, 28; Salomon de Caus, *Les Raisons des Forces Mouvantes* (Frankfurt-am-Main, 1615), *passim*. See A. Chapais and E. Droz, *Les Automates* (Paris, [1949]), for a full discussion of the history and problems of the subject.

scientists in spite of Kepler's discouraging formulation of the behaviour of matter. Cornelis Drebbel made one of the best of these, described in a letter to King James[1] and later in Thomas Tymme's *Dialogue Philosophicall.*[2] To make a perpetual motion was, however, far too close an approximation of the divine creativity for most people, as Caus made clear:

There have been divers Men which have Travelled to find out a motion which they have called (without knowledge) Perpetual, or without end, a thing very ill considered and ill understood, because all that hath a beginning is subject to have an end; and the word Perpetual or without end ought to be applyed to God alone, who as he had no beginning, cannot also have an end, so it is folly and deceit in Men to make themselves beleeve that they can make perpetual Works; seeing that themselves are mortal, and subject to an end: so also are all their works. . . .[3]

But Porta considered the possibility of perpetual flame, and Bettini the possibility of a perpetual motion worked from the earth's gravity all the same.

Another important part of such recreations was mathematics, and there were many mathematical paradoxes, puzzles, and 'impossibilities,' to which great mathematicians from antiquity to the present had contributed. Many such paradoxes are 'fixed,' that is, are either insoluble by present mathematical tools or are verbal or numerical tricks that have but one ingenious answer; so the same questions appear from antiquity to the present. Zeno's query, or the query attributed to him, about which grain makes the noise when a bushel of wheat is poured from its basket (Is it the first?—No. The second, then?—No; etc.) turns up over and over again in the volumes of *Mathematical Recreations* published through the seventeenth century. One of the best of these, Jean Leurechon's *Recréations Mathématiques*, appeared in 1627 and subsequently had other editions, often with additions and improvements of the eminent mathematician Claude Mydorge, another collaborator of Nicéron and Mersenne. It went into English translation, along with Mydorge's *Sections*

---

[1] Drebbel, *Kort Tractaet van de Natuere der Elementen* (Haerlem, 1621).

[2] Thomas Tymme, *Dialogue Philosophicall*, London, 1612. See also Porta, *Natural Magick*, p. 302 for perpetual flame, and Bettini, *Apiaria*, I, Book IV, p. 12, for a perpetual motion based on the earth's magnetism.

[3] I. de Caus, *New And Rare Inventions*, p. 21.

Coniques, (the sort of optical study that made anamorphosis possible), under the auspices of William Oughtred, whose eminence as a serious mathematician did not in the least prevent him from playing games with his subject.[1]

V

Many of the problems in such books involve the 'impossible,' itself a word in the negative philosophy and rhetoric difficult to conceive and difficult to use. Mathematics is a science of relations (called ambiguously 'ratio' by mathematicians), and therefore the problems its language presents and represents are often paradoxes apparently susceptible of no solution but actually soluble from another or a limited 'point of view.' Like anamorphoses, such problems seem to be 'nothing' or chaotic when looked at head on but are quite orderly from the proper point of vision. Elaborate number games in which a man guesses what number another man is thinking of, or guesses which knuckle on a possible ten fingers a man has set a ring on deal in a science with a paradoxical name—the laws of chance.[2] Others less strictly mathematical can be cast into mathematical language. For example, directions are given to weigh the blow of a fist, of a hammer, or of an axe; to weigh the smoke of a combustible body, or its flame; to balance three knives, or even a millstone, upon the point of a pin.[3] Some are trivial in the extreme, such as the injunction to break an apple into equal parts without breaking the skin (with a needle and thread), or to make a cheating scale hang true when empty which can also weigh uneven weights as if it were true, or a bowl falsely weighted so that it amuses by running awry.[4] Some are not amusing at all, though rather marvellous, and certainly recreations in another sense, such as the earphone for the deaf and the spy-mirror that reflects what goes on in another room.[5]

[1] Jean Leurechon [ps., Hendrick van Etten], *Recréations Mathématiques* (Lyon, 1627); trans. William Oughtred, *Mathematical Recreations* (London, 1633), reprinted in 1653 and 1674.

[2] Leurechon, *Les Recréations Mathematiques,* fifth ed. (Paris, 1661), pp. 28, 44, 49, 56, 57.

[3] *Ibid.,* pp. 13, 41, 42, 40, 38.

[4] *Ibid.* pp. 49, 119, 4–8.

[5] *Ibid.,* pp. 138–9, 333–4.

Other problems are, as Mydorge put it, purely metaphysical, such as the receipt for dropping a perfect ball from a great height into a glass of water without breaking the glass, or the arrangement of all the angels and all the men in the world so that they pull upon a spider's thread without breaking it,[1] or the construction of a stone bridge, or ring, around the whole world so that it will hang in the air without support and not fall.[2] Some are logical beauties about the centre of the earth and the poles, riddles asked every teen-ager by one more sophisticated in school. To one of these, 'Comme est-ce qu'un homme peut avoir en mesme temps la teste en haut, et les pieds en haut, encore qu'il ne soit qu'en une place,' Leurechon's answer was, 'at the center of the earth'; but Mydorge remarked with Swiftian matter-of-factness that a man could fulfill the conditions just as easily in his own bed, by lying on it and raising both his feet and his head, and went on to an equally Swiftian but less decent comment of his own.[3]

Numbers bring their own paradoxes, which scientists and logicians love, and so does geometry. Where there are circles there are paradoxes too—and indeed the circle is an emblem for the great paradox of eternity, as well as of the equally paradoxical notion of infinity.[4] The circle is also immeasurable, however small it may be; for efforts to arrive at the correct area of a circle have resulted only in infinite approximation. Therefore the area of a circle cannot be equated to the area of another geometrical figure, though men have made every effort to 'square the circle' or to equate it with any sort of polygon. There is of course an absolute area of a circle to which one can conceive a square of equal area; but until recently that solution was, in Mydorge's words, purely metaphysical; its analytical mathematical proof was absent. Which is cleverer, asks Leurechon, he who draws a circle freehand or he who finds the centre of a circle already drawn? He answered, on the authority of Aristotle and S. Augustine, that the more difficult

[1] *Ibid.*, pp. 109–110.
[2] *Ibid.*, p. 106.
[3] *Ibid.*, pp. 58–60.
[4] See Marjorie H. Nicolson, *The Breaking of the Circle* (Evanston, 1950); and Martin Foss, *The Idea of Perfection in the Western World* (Princeton, 1946), esp. pp. 13–26.

task was to find the single centre of that line of infinite points.[1]

Squaring the circle was an antique recreation that made its way through history with greatest ease. Great mathematicians all had their fling with the circle, and a great many tried to find its equivalent square. Friendly enemies then either gladly demonstrated the futility of their friends' attempts or lent themselves to the same futile task. Medieval scholars left records of their attempts to square the circle, and renaissance mathematicians pursued the problem with fierceness and hate. Porta, Cataldo, Rheticus, Clavius, and Vieta, to name but a handful of the best-known, all quadrated; in the seventeenth century there were first-class quadrature rows, stemming chiefly from the solution of Longomontanus, who stimulated directly and indirectly such men as John Pell, Descartes, Mersenne, Roberval, Golius, Cavendish, Hobbes, and Wallis to tackle the problem. Over and over again, one is struck by the bitterness of this controversy. Though the quadrature of the circle was an official 'game' and was accepted as such by mathematicians, it was a game with the most serious intellectual stakes. For one thing, to render the impossible possible is to conquer the problem of knowledge at one of its bastions, in this case to advance the cause of mathematics both as a language and as an instrument, so that it can both say and do—and thus be—more than it could say or do or be before. In the second place, methods of quadrature sprang from geometrical systems which were in hazard at precisely this point and which, however lightly their inventors undertook to quadrate the circle, were most serious and seriously defended intellectual constructs. So the tone of the quarrel between Hobbes and Wallis, both superb polemicists, became particularly virulent over the Hobbesian quadrature and 'solutions' to other classical problems.[2]

[1] *Les Recréations Mathématiques* (Paris, 1661), pp. 133–4.

[2] A most useful bibliography (though in the nature of the work incomplete) can be collected from Augustus de Morgan's *A Budget of Paradoxes*, particularly from the edition made by David Eugene Smith (London and Chicago, 1915, 2 vols.). See also Ferdinand Rudio, 'Das Problem von der Quadratur des Zirkels,' *Vierteljahrsschrift der Naturforschenden Gesellschaft in Zürich*, 1890, pp. 1–51. For a bibliography of the Hobbis-Wallis battle, see Hugh Macdonald and Mary Hargreaves, *Thomas Hobbes. A Bibliography* (London, 1952), pp. 41–58 and p. 63.

Circle-squaring is a particular teaser not just because it is impossible. To make the circle square is the logical operation, illustrated in this case by geometry, of uniting different categories; and its successful operation is also a denial of geometrical category, an explanation of why one thing is the same as another. Proof and demonstration are not the same thing in such a problem, unless all categories are to be abolished: for although the proof that a circle is 'as good as' a square, or 'equals' a square, certainly supports the Eleatic view of the universe, it implies the annihilation of the very barriers, definitions, and limitations by which geometry exists. In connection with the quadrature problem, Schott remarked that if Zeno is right, then it is both possible and impossible to square the circle, possible because the circle is a finite unity, impossible because the implications of a circle are that it is always in motion.[1] The fact that Snellius, Huygens, Pascal, and a host of other talented mathematicians all had their say about circle-squaring suggests the seriousness of the game: the impossible is better handled *sub specie ludi* in case it doesn't work—or in case it does.

Circle-squaring is 'useless' and became the standard trope for time-wasting intellectual activity. Another fine mathematico-logical paradox, however, had its social and economic uses and was also the object of hard-headed formulation by first-class minds: the study of the laws of chance. The phrase has become so familiar to us that its initial yoking of opposites is almost inaudible, but when Cardanus wrote his *De Ludo Aleae*, he directed it to a moral end, the analysis of deceit, as well as to a scientific end, the study of probability.[2] Arbuthnot's introduction to his adaptation of Christiaan Huygens' *De ratiociniis in ludo aleae*[3] makes quite clear that man has little insight into the distributions of chance or fortune, however much he may say about them:

Every man's Success in any Affair is proportional to his Conduct and Fortune. Fortune (in the sense of most People) signifies an Event which depends on Chance, agreeing with my Wish;

[1] Schott, *Technica Curiosa*, p. 607.

[2] See the English translation by Sidney Henry Gould, in Oystein Ore, *Cardano, the Gambling Scholar* (Princeton, 1953).

[3] Christiaan Huygens, *De Ratiociniis in ludo aleae*, in Franciscus van Schooten, *Exercitationum Mathematicarum Libri Quinque* (Leiden, 1657).

and Misfortune suggests such an Event contrary to my Wish: an Event depending on Chance, signifies such an one, whose immediate Causes I don't know, and consequently can neither foretel nor produce it. . . .[1]

Since gaming has become so common a profession that every man runs some danger from cardsharps, any system that can be descried in the operations of chance may serve, says Arbuthnot, to keep a man's shillings in his pocket. The laws of probability need not be applied only to gaming, either—'It is,' for instance, 'but 1 to 18 if you meet a *Parson* in the Street, that he proves to be a *Non-Juror*, because there is but 1 of 36 that are such [*sic*(!)]. It is hardly 1 to 10, that a *Woman* of Twenty Years old has her Maidenhead, and almost the same Wager, that a *Town-Spark* of that Age has not been clap'd.' Arbuthnot knew the moral applications of the new science of statistics as developed by Petty and Graunt, as well as did the Swift of the *Modest Proposal*; like all the scientists of the period after Huygens and Newton (but quite unlike Swift), for Arbuthnot numerology had turned into mathematics for good:

The Reader may here observe the Force of Numbers, which can be successively applied, even to those things, which one would imagine are subject to no Rules. There are very few things which we know, which are not capable of being reduc'd to a Mathematical Reasoning, and when they cannot, tis a sign our Knowledg of them is very small and confus'd; and where a mathematical reason can be had, it's as great folly to make use of any other, as to grope for a thing in the dark when you have a Candle standing by you.

The mathematical analysis to which Arbuthnot gave his allegiance is the ordinal mathematics of quantitative analysis, the mathematics of one answer, untroubled by the paradoxes of numbers or of logic, and to some extent Arbuthnot's sensible statement marks a temporary end to conscious paradoxology, even in mathematics. For him 'the laws of chance' was not a phrase uniting opposites so much as a limited but direct statement of one aspect of the unknown. Arbuthnot's gamester —unlike Bacon's ever so slightly playful scientists—is not going

[1] [John Arbuthnot], *Of the Laws of Chance, Or, a Method of Calculation of the Hazards of Game* (London, 1692), Preface.

to do tricks; he will at any point tell his method to others. In fact Arbuthnot's aim is egalitarian, to reduce to order one aspect of the unknown so that every man may, if he will, gamble with some safety. The gamester in question is concerned only with practical life. The rest is not his business.

Paradox and deceit in mathematics and science tend to lose their playfulness and their mysteriousness in the course of seventeenth-century thought. Teleology puts a check on wonder, which is or can be a tremendous time-waster. Ends that are aims replace ends that are also beginnings. Though he understood perspective deformation thoroughly, Grégoire Huret did not enjoy anamorphosis as Nicéron, Mersenne, Schott, and Kircher had done. For him its 'dépravations' were monstrous and inartistic; they were

visions de songe lugubres, ou des sabats de sorciers, seulement capable de donner de la tristesse et frayeur, et mesme faire avorter ou dépraver le fruit des femmes enceintes, que pour representer des sujets naturels et agréables à l'ordinaire.[1]

As far as Huret was concerned, such *trompes l'œil* were useful only to disguise the size or shape of an improperly balanced room; figures should be represented as they are and as we see them, not as deformations of actuality. Since we see in perspective, the rules of perspective were to be employed in painting not to deform but to achieve correct representation, as in the work of Rubens and 'Raimbram Holandois.'[2]

Another scientist of the late seventeenth century, Jean Ozanam, began his *Mathematical Recreations* with the same direct analytical intention:

Ignorance keeps the World in perpetual Admiration, and in a Diffidence, which ever produces an invisible Inclination to blame and to persecute those that know any Thing above the Vulgar; who, being unaccustom'd to raise their Thoughts beyond Things sensible, and unable to imagin that Nature implyeth Agents that are invisible and impalpable, ascribe most an end to Sorceries and Demons, all Effects where they know not the Cause. To remedy these Inconveniences is the Design

[1] Grégoire Huret, *Optique de Portraiture et Peinture* (Paris, 1670), pp. 64–65.

[2] Huret, p. 111.

of these Mathematicall Recreations, and to teach all to perform those Sorceries. . . .[1]

Ozanam does not underestimate the power and pleasure of 'Pastimes of the Mind, and Entertainments equally fitted to excite Pleasure, and to give Enlargement of Understanding,' nor does he deny the close proximity of game and speculation; he does, though, always emphasize the 'reasonableness' rather than the wonder of such recreations and believe in their invariable surrender to rational analysis.

This kind of solution, the Baconian demonstration of the 'Fallace' of the scientific paradox or illusion, is one way of disposing of Nature's *discordia concors*. Analysis and explanation ('The End of our Foundation is the Knowledge of Causes') can put a check to the kind of stupefaction that paradox by its nature induces. To the verbal magic of rhetorical and logical paradox another kind of solution offered itself, the discounting of such paradox by the simple demonstration of its self-denial, its absence, in two senses, of end. There was still another kind of attack on this sort of paradox, reserved to the exceptionally talented, the satirical method of proposing one's own made-up paradoxes to undo the paradoxical method.

This was Jonathan Swift's way, who knew all the other ways of paradox as well. He himself had raised the paradoxical encomium to its highest level of irony in the nonpareil *Modest Proposal*; his antirationalism epitomized the rationalist attack upon rationalism. He was past-master of the tricks relativity plays, and could play them himself whenever he chose. Swift's terrifying relativities do not really preach a rigid absolutism, as lesser satirists so often must when dealing the same sort of trick; his relativities plead as eloquently for other relativities, those of common sense, of ordinary social life. In the 'Voyage to Laputa' Swift makes up his own brilliant paradoxes out of the 'real' reports of scientific investigations he found in that staid and serious periodical, the *Philosophical Transactions of the Royal Society*. His method has been demonstrated past doubt— how he combined the real experiments on vegetables, dyes, insects, dogs, and meteorology into the lunatic activities carried

[1] Jean Ozanam, *Recreations Mathematical and Physical; laying down, and solving Many Profitable and Delightful Problems* (London, 1708), The Author's Preface.

on in the Grand Academy of Lagado.[1] His experiments follow
two traditions, the amusing one of the 'marvels of natural
science,' by which readers are supposed to be titillated and
entertained[2] and the satiric tradition, in which he makes a
different kind of fun of what was originally fun in quite another
sense. He rings the destructive changes on the marvels of the
old projectors, for the attempts in Lagado are the same old ones,
really, the stuff of the renaissance scientific compendia. Caus,
Stevin, Kircher, Schott, and the other hydraulic engineers all
found ingenious ways of raising water uphill, to flow out in a fair
fountain, to cleanse a city, to turn mills on hills. The blind man
who could tell colours apart was a stock marvel for those
secretaries of Nature; he existed long before Boyle, Molyneux,
and Locke sent him on his travels through the rationalist
literature of the eighteenth century. Experiments to improve
vegetables and animals, to make better weather indicators and
gnomons, fill the pages of Porta, Wecker, Bacon, Bettini, and
Schott. Their machines to reduce probability to some order
need only Swift's application to the production of imaginative
literature to be satirical; the frame from which all natural knowledge was to be extracted was simply a thing made to seem
ridiculous by its own idea.

Swift's sort of experiment merely exaggerates aspects of
reality. Both the joke and the seriousness of such mechanical
ingenuity are increased, the joke is made more ridiculous so that
the seriousness may enter into a moral context. Swift uses, in
short, one paradoxical rhetoric, the joco-serious expression in
the language of *things* to assert the superiority of an older
rhetoric, that of human experience and understanding. The
great 'Bundle of *things* upon his Back' that the ordinary
Laputan Academician must carry about to have conversation
with his fellows is the Baconian burden carried to the nth
power, or *ad absurdum*, and Swift cuts it off with his two-edged
instrument of rhetorical paradox. In this book of *Gulliver* all

[1] See Marjorie H. Nicolson and Nora Mohler, 'The Scientific Background of Swift's "Voyage to Laputa",' *Annals of Science*, II (1937),
299–334; 'Swift's "Flying Island" in the "Voyage to Laputa",' *Annals of
Science*, II (1937), 405–30.

[2] See Miss Nicolson's suggestion in *Mountain Gloom and Mountain
Glory* (Ithaca, 1959), p. 170, note 28.

the traditions of paradox meet—insistence upon the value of realities as opposed to appearances, recreation of things into a new world, rhetorical persuasions of the limits of rhetoric, joco-serious reconsideration of man's whole activity.

Man's intellectual pride is put into its place. Though men attempt to contrive 'a new Method for building Houses, by beginning at the Roof, and working downwards to the Foundation,'[1] only God can really do that trick:

The proceeding of this Soveraign Architect in the Frame of this great Building of the Universe, not being like to the Architecture of men, who begin at the bottom; but he began at the Roof, and Builded downwards, and in that process, suspended the inferior parts of the World upon the superior.[2]

God's world is the truly paradoxical; the greatest paradoxes are divine, inimitable by mere human ingenuity. Lagado's attempts to imitate the inimitable are doomed to failure, as even Gulliver and the dullest reader can perceive at once; because they are not only foolish in themselves, they are also emblems of man's foolish pride. Lagado is, happily, a utopia, nowhere—we are relieved at that, since they are such fools in that country. But Lagado is, unmistakably also, England and, nowadays, everywhere. Swift has not attempted to build a house down from the roof: he has managed a more daring emulation of divine paradoxology, by creating out of non-being, of nowhere, a major lesson of being.

[1] Jonathan Swift, *Travels into Several Remote Nations of the World* (London, 1747), p. 173.
[2] Matthew Hale, *Difficiles Nugae*, p. 57.

ARTHUR O. LOVEJOY

Milton's Dialogue on Astronomy

THE author of this paper has elsewhere remarked that
when, in the seventh and eighth Books of *Paradise Lost*, Adam
and the 'affable Archangel' Raphael are made to engage in a
long discussion of the theories of seventeenth-century astronomy, the reader of the poem needs some acquaintance with the
doctrines and reasonings of astronomers from Copernicus's
time to Milton's concerning the arrangement and motions of
the celestial bodies if he is to 'form any competent judgment
about Milton's knowledge of *and attitude towards* the new
science of his age.'[1] That subject has recently been studied and
greatly illuminated by several scholars especially well qualified
to deal with it. But perhaps the present attempt at a logical
analysis of the movement and apparent motivations of Milton's
thought in the passage in question may be a not wholly re-
dundant contribution to the same inquiry.

In the case of Milton, as of other writers of the time, it is
essential to keep in mind not only the distinction of the seven
issues which have been discriminated in *The Great Chain of
Being*,[2] but also the different grounds, none of them in the

---

[1] 'The Historiography of Ideas,' in *Essays in the History of Ideas*
(Baltimore, The Johns Hopkins Press, 1948), p. 4; first published in
Proceedings of the American Philosophical Society, Vol. 78, No. 4, 1938;
Italics here added to indicate the principal topic of what follows.

[2] (Cambridge, Harvard Univ. Press, 1936), pp. 103–8.

stricter sense 'scientific,' upon which the then current views upon these issues rested. Milton's position upon four of them can be fairly well gathered from *Paradise Lost*.

I

The argument modestly presented by Adam (VIII.15–38) as a 'doubt' which he hopes his archangelic mentor will resolve, relates explicitly only to the strictly Copernican issue, whether the 'appearances' are to be accounted for by assuming the motion of the earth or that of the sun and spheres. And it is based wholly upon the principles underlying Copernicus's own argument— the principles of the simplicity and economy of nature in the methods by which its effects are produced. It was well known to Milton's contemporaries, and is a commonplace of the history of astronomy and philosophy, that the adoption of the theory of the earth's motion by astronomers rested chiefly upon such supposed axioms as *Natura simplicitatem amat, semper agit per vias brevissimas, non agit per ambages difficiles, nil facit frustra*.[1] These maxims were not, for the most part, for sixteenth- and seventeenth-century writers merely methodological principles, expressions of the desire for economy of thought on the part of men of science. They were aspects of the principle of sufficient reason, and they presupposed a teleological conception of natural processes—the supposition that some phenomena could be readily recognized as ends and others as means to the accomplishment of those ends. If there were processes not valuable in themselves, and instrumental to no rational ends, or if there were processes which, though they realized such ends, did so by extravagant and roundabout methods, the rationality of nature could not be maintained, and therefore the rationality and goodness of its Author would be impugned. It is evident that, as thus applied, the principle of sufficient reason seemed to run counter to the principle of plenitude, in spite of the fact that the latter was itself also often presented (as by Leibniz) as a corollary of the assumption of the rationality of the universe and the goodness of God. The principle of plenitude, in fact, implied the falsity of the assumption that some

[1] Cf. Edwin Arthur Burtt, *The Metaphysical Foundations of Modern Physical Science* (rev. ed. New York, Harcourt Brace, 1932), pp. 26, 42.

parts of the creation are merely means to other parts; it declared that the best and most rational world is that in which everything which possibly *can* exist does exist, down to the very lowest level of being, the creature of which the existence is so meagre that it is barely removed from sheer nonentity. From this point of view, everything that exists, though it may, indeed, be incidentally instrumental to other ends, has a reason of its own for existing—namely, the reason that the world as whole would without it be incomplete, would contain an arbitrary and therefore irrational gap in the great chain of being. The principle of plenitude thus contradicted the principle of the 'frugality' (the word used by Milton) of nature, and did so through a deduction from the same principle of cosmic reasonableness upon which the maxims accepted by Copernicus and Kepler, as by many others, explicitly or implicitly rested.

Now Adam, in lines 15 to 38, applies these maxims in two ways. Assuming that the object in view is simply the production of the terrestrial phenomena of day and night, he argues that the hypothesis that these are due to motions of the sun, planets, and stars implies an immense *waste* of motion. In comparison with the Copernican theory, it requires that far more numerous bodies and far larger ones shall move, and that they shall move at vastly greater speeds; and that the only end accomplished by all this is the diurnal alternation of light and darkness upon a globe not only incomparably smaller, but also—as Adam observes, in accord with the medieval conception—one far less 'noble' than they.

> When I behold this goodly Frame, this World
> Of Heav'n and Earth consisting, and compute
> Thir magnitudes, this Earth a spot, a graine,
> An Atom, with the Firmament compar'd,
>
> . . . . .
> . . . meerly to officiate light,
> Round this opacous Earth, this punctual spot,
> One day and night; in all thir vast survey
> Useless besides, reasoning I oft admire,
> How Nature wise and frugal could commit
> Such disproportions, with superfluous hand
> So many nobler Bodies to create,
> Greater so manifold to this one use,
> For aught appeers, and on thir Orbs impose

Such restless revolution day and day
Repeated, while the sedentarie Earth,
That better might with farr less compass move,
Serv'd by more noble then her self, attaines
Her end without least motion, and receaves,
As Tribute such a sumless journey brought
Of incorporeal speed, her warmth and light;
Speed, to describe whose swiftness Number failes.

Now from the assumptions expressed in this reasoning of the first of astronomical theorists, either of two inferences *might* conceivably have been drawn. It might, first, have been argued that since the assumption of the motions of the sun, planets, and fixed stars cannot be reconciled with the principle that Nature does nothing uselessly or extravagantly, they serve some other end than that of 'officiating light' and warmth to the earth. And this was, as we know, one of the current arguments for the plurality of inhabited worlds. Thus the principle of nature's frugality could be used to justify the same conclusion as was drawn from the principle of plenitude. Because nature does nothing in vain, it must be assumed that there are utilities—and utilities for finite beings—to which the number, size, and motion of the other globes are instrumental. But this is *not* the consequence explicitly drawn by Adam. It is solely to the alternative consequence that his argument inclines him. He assumes that the other celestial bodies and their movements are means only to the production upon the earth of day and night, light and darkness, heat and cold; and since these effects could be so much more simply and economically produced by supposing the earth to move and the others to remain stationary, it is implied that the truth of the Copernican theory, so far as this point is concerned, would follow.[1]

[1] The argument being a commonplace of the Copernican polemic, Milton might have learned it from any of a number of previous writers. Perhaps the most likely source is the following from John Wilkins's *Concerning A New Planet* (1640): 'Another argument to this purpose may be taken from the chief end of the diurnal and annual motions, which is to distinguish between night and day, winter and summer; and so consequently, to serve for the commodities and seasons of the habitable world. Wherefore it may seem more agreeable to the wisdom of providence, for to make the earth as well the efficient as the final cause of this motion; especially since nature in her other operations does never use any

Raphael's reply to this argument (VIII.65 ff.) is to the effect not that its conclusion is necessarily false, but that its premises lack cogency. Though the reasoning of the archangel is not quite so clear as one could wish, it seems to resolve itself into five objections to the assumptions made by Adam.

1. The assumption that the celestial bodies are 'nobler' than earth is groundless. Raphael is made by Milton to say:

> . . . Great
> Or Bright inferrs not Excellence: the Earth
> Though, in comparison of Heav'n so small,
> Nor glistering, may of solid good containe
> More plenty then the Sun that barren shines,
> Whose vertue on it self workes no effect,
> But in the fruitful Earth; . . .

2. In any case, if the motions of the sun, planets, and stars are simply instrumental to terrestrial effects, it is to man's use that they must be supposed serviceable; it is not a question of a larger and 'nobler' mass of matter being subservient to a smaller and less noble one.

> Yet not to Earth are those bright Luminaries
> Officious, but to thee Earths habitant.

tedious difficult means to perform that which may as well be accomplished by shorter and easier ways. But now, the appearance would be the same in respect to us, if only this little point of earth were made the subject of these motions, as if the vast frame of the world, with all those stars of such number and bigness were moved about it. It is a common maxim (Galen). Nature does nothing in vain, but in all her courses does take the most compendious way. It is not therefore (I say) likely, that the whole fabric of the heavens, which do so much exceed our earth in magnitude and perfection, should be put to undergo so great and constant a work in the service of our earth, which might easily save all that labour by the circumvolution of its own body; especially, since the heavens do not by this motion attain any further perfection for themselves, but are thus made serviceable to this little ball of earth. So that in this case it may seem to argue as much improvidence in nature to employ them in this motion, as it would in a mother, who in warning her child, would rather turn the fire about that, than that about the fire. . . . Can we imagine that (nature) should appoint those numerous and vast bodies, the stars, to compass us with such a swift and restless motion, when as all this might as well be done by the revolution of this little ball of earth.' *Mathematical and Philosophical Works*, (2 vols., London, 1802), I, 238.

3. To man the realization of the disproportion between his own abode and the magnitude of the heavens is useful for edification; it helps him to realize his littleness and weakness in the presence of these evidences of the power and splendour of his Creator.

> And for the Heav'ns wide Circuit, let it speak
> The Makers high magnificence, who built
> So spacious, and his Line stretcht out so farr;
> That Man may know he dwells not in his own;
> An Edifice too large for him to fill,
> Lodg'd in a small partition. . . .

4. But even though it be assumed that the heavenly bodies and their motions are means to useful ends, it is unwarranted to assume that they are meant to serve terrestrial ends only; 'the rest' may be 'Ordain'd for uses to his Lord best known.' This is the argument from man's ignorance.

5. Finally, there is perhaps a hint of the principle of plenitude, in its theological form.

> The swiftness of those Circles attribute,
> Though numberless, to his Omnipotence,
> That to corporeal substances could adde
> Speed almost Spiritual; . . .

In other words, one would expect that an omnipotent cause would produce, among other things, velocities reaching the maximum (whatever that may be) of which corporeal substance is capable. It is not legitimate to apply the principle of parsimony to the action of such a cause.

> What if the Sun
> Be Center to the World, and other Starrs,
> By his attractive vertue and thir own
> Incited, dance about him various rounds.

This supposition, he points out, undeniably *is* simpler than the Ptolemaic; upon the latter theory the changes of day and night must be ascribed 'to several sphears'

> Mov'd contrarie with thwart obliquities,
> Or save the Sun his labour, and that swift
> Nocturnal and Diurnal Rhomb suppos'd,
> Invisible else above all Starrs, the Wheell

Of Day and Night; which needs not thy beleefe,
If Earth industrious of her self fetch Day
Travelling East, and with her part averse
From the Suns beam meet Night, her other part
Still luminous by his ray. . . .

Thus, though Milton avoids pronouncing definitely in favour of either the geocentric or heliocentric theories, he gives the latter the last word, and puts this in the mouth of an archangelic authority. He may, on the whole, then, be said, up to this point, to have been unable to make up his mind, but probably to have felt that of the two rival systems Copernicanism had the better arguments.

II

More noteworthy is the fact that Milton shows a manifest inclination towards the belief in other inhabited planets and even in the plurality of inhabited worlds. For the archangel does not limit his reply to the purely Copernican question raised by Adam. He proceeds to suggest the possibility not only that there may be inhabitants on the moon (VIII.145–148), but that 'other suns perhaps, / With their attendant moons' may similarly contain 'some that live.' And the reason why he suggests this, Raphael explains in substance, is that it is difficult to suppose that there is in nature so prodigious a waste of materials, so strange a failure to utilize actual possibilities of being. He argues, in other words, on this question from the same premise which Adam assumed in expressing his doubts about the theory of the 'sedentary Earth':

For such vast room in Nature unpossest
By living Soule, desert and desolate
Onely to shine, yet scarce to contribute
Each Orb a glimps of light, conveyd so farr
Down to this habitable, which returnes
Light back to them, is obvious to dispute.

Which is to say that pertinent reasons for the plurality of inhabited worlds can be offered. And against this hypothesis, no positive argument is propounded. This omission is, in Milton, very curious. For there was a possible and familiar argument against it which one might have expected to be peculiarly potent with him. If there were admitted to be rational

beings on other globes, it seemed necessary to assume either
that no Fall took place on any of them, or else that the Incarnation and Crucifixion were repeated in other, perhaps in many
other, planets. The latter alternative not only would have ruined
the machinery of Milton's epic, but would surely have been, at
the least, exceedingly difficult to reconcile with his religious
beliefs. In truth, any admission of the plurality of inhabited
worlds was inconsistent with the logical presuppositions of
Paradise Lost. No modern man ever more naïvely represented
the general success or failure of the creation as wrapped up
with the course of terrestrial history. And yet Milton never
raises this objection; can it be that it did not occur to him? If he
recognized it and felt its force, one would have expected him at
least to refrain from putting into the mouth of Raphael an
effective statement of one of the usual arguments *for* this part
of the Brunonian doctrine. Yet he not only introduces this
argument in the dialogue between Adam and the archangel, but
also at the end of Book VII has all the heavenly host, as they
chant to the Creator of the wonders of his 'new-made World,'
express—though with a dubiety a little odd under the circumstances—their belief that all the celestial orbs may be inhabited.
The creation, they sing, is

> Of amplitude almost immense, with Starr's
> Numerous, and every Starr perhaps a World
> Of destind habitation; . . .

In an earlier passage (III.460–463) Milton comes close to a
positive affirmation that there are inhabitants on at least one
other globe. The moon, he declares, is not, 'as some have
dreamed,' the abode of nature's abortions, and of those who have
during life, been given over to vanity and folly,

> Embryos, and Idiots, Eremits and Friers,
> White, Black and Grey, with all thir trumperie.

For these the 'Limbo large and broad' called 'the Paradise of
Fools' is reserved:

> Those argent Fields more likely habitants,
> Translated Saints, or middle Spirits hold
> Betwixt th' Angelical and Human kinde:[1]

[1] It is clear from the context that 'likely' here does not mean 'probable'
but 'fitting,' 'suitable.'

The 'translated saints' could not, obviously, have been an indigenous population. Milton is here naïvely mixing astronomy and eschatology. But the alternative supposition places in the moon what may be called natural inhabitants; and it was a part of a familiar hypothesis, recommended by the generally accepted assumption that the chain of being is continuous and 'full.' Thus Wilkins had remarked in 1638: 'There is a great chasm between the nature of men and angels; it may be the inhabitants of the planets are of a middle nature between both these.'[1] But on the whole, Milton here too seems in the end to remain somewhat dubious, like his archangel—who might have been expected to be informed on the point; but that the argument for other inhabited worlds, which might well have been most of all repellent to him, in fact appealed strongly to him seems clear.

III

His position with respect to the doctrine of the infinity of the universe and the 'worlds' contained in it is not quite so easy to determine; but on the whole there can, I think, be little doubt that he consciously rejected it. It is true that he sometimes speaks of the stars as 'numberless,' but the adjective is a common hyperbole and need not be taken literally. The evidence of his adverse position is to be found, in the first place, in the passage last quoted; he is careful to have the angelic choirs sing—with a restraint not altogether usual in hymnody—of the world's amplitude as '*almost* immense' and of stars 'numerous' rather than innumerable. And in the second place, throughout *Paradise Lost* he assumes the conception of a bounded and spherical universe. The uncreated 'Abyss' before the world was fashioned,

> The womb of Nature and perhaps her grave,

was, indeed, a 'void and formless infinite' containing in inexhaustible abundance 'th' originals of Nature in their crude conception'—these, however, being, not Platonic Ideas but the material elements confusedly mixed together.[2] And this infinity

---

[1] *Discovery of a New World*: in *Philosophical and Mathematical Works*, I, 102.
[2] *PL*, II, 890.

was somehow, for Milton, an implicate of the infinity of the Absolute Being.

> Boundless the Deep, because I am who fill
> Infinitude, nor vacuous the space.[1]

Here, then, is a vestige of the principle of plenitude. But this 'wilde Abyss,' where 'Chance governs all,' was apparently not created by God, but was always coexistent with him, while, in its nature, utterly antithetic to him. It was not an overflow of his perfection. The essence of 'creation' was limitation. When the Son, attended by a great retinue of angels, went forth

> Far into Chaos and the world unborn,

to exercise the creative function, his first act was to set bounds:

> He took the golden compasses, prepar'd
> In God's Eternal store, to circumscribe
> This universe, and all created things:
> One foot he center'd and the other turn'd
> Round through the vast profunditie obscure,
> And said, thus farr extend, thus farr thy bounds,
> This be thy just circumference, O world![2]

Thus 'the formless Mass . . . came to a heap,' and 'vast infinitude stood confined.' And this meant an actual physical enclosure of the world; there remains a sphere of fixed stars (whether it were motionless or moving) which for Milton still 'in circuit walls this universe.'[3] It is, I think, impossible to regard all this as merely a part of the machinery of the poem, not intended to be taken seriously. The details of the pageant were doubtless figurative; the emphasis upon the circumscription of the created world cannot be so construed.

If this were all that Milton had said about the new cosmography, one might with plausibility describe him as keenly interested in these controversies, as markedly inclining to Copernicanism, and also to the doctrine of the plurality of

---

[1] *PL* VIII, 168–69; also cf. VI, 405, 956 ff.; VI, 477 ff., 509 ff.

[2] *PL*, VII, 218–232. Milton was here, no doubt, elaborating upon Proverbs, VIII, 25–30, with perhaps a reminiscence of Dante, *Paradiso*, 19, 40.

[3] Cf. *PL*, III, 708–723. For other references to the finitude of the created world, cf. *PL*, II, 102d, 1037 f.; VII, 168 f.

inhabited worlds within the solar system, but as not quite able
to make up his mind on these questions—an unusual attitude of
the mind of John Milton towards the controversies of his age.
We should also be compelled to describe him as still a believer
in a finite and walled-in world. But, unfortunately, he said
certain other things—again through the mouth of Raphael and
of Adam in Book VIII—which forbid us to regard him as on the
whole sympathetically sharing in *any* of the new tendencies.
The celestial choirs, when hymning the creation on the Sabbath
following its completion, appear to be left in ignorance: 'every
star *perhaps* a world of destined habitation,' they sing dubiously.
And the final attitude which Milton makes his spokesman take
upon the cosmographic questions of the poet's day is not merely
a suspension of judgment; it is the conclusion that these are
matters which it is not permissible for man even to speculate
about:

> Think onely what concernes thee and thy being;
> Dream not of other Worlds, what Creatures there
> Live, in what state, condition or degree,
> Contented that thus farr hath been reveal'd
> Not of Earth onely but of highest Heav'n.
> . . . not to know at large of things remote
> From use, obscure and suttle, but to know
> That which before us lies in daily life,
> Is the prime Wisdom, what is more, is fume,
> Or emptiness, or fond impertinence,
> And renders us in things that most concerne
> Unpractis'd, unprepar'd, and still to seek.[1]

These lines have sometimes been interpreted as the expression of a judicious scientific scepticism and an evidence of
Milton's sympathy with the temper of Baconian experimental
science. But Milton does not say that the new hypotheses are
generalizations based on insufficient evidence; he says that they
deal with questions which ought not to be asked and cannot be
answered. And he takes this position not only with respect to
the then, and perhaps for ever, scientifically insoluble question
of the plurality of populated globes; investigation into the
truth of the Copernican theory is equally discountenanced:

[1] *PL*, VIII, 176–197. The concluding lines are put into the mouth of
Adam. The temper of this is, of course, very different from that of the
Areopagitica.

> This to attain, whether Heav'n move or earth,
> Imports not, if thou reck'n right, the rest
> From Man or Angel the great Architect
> Did wisely to conceal, and not divulge
> His secrets to be scann'd by them who ought
> Rather admire; . . .[1]

There survives, too, in Milton's theology not a little of that primitive, equally un-Christian and un-Platonic idea, fundamental in the Jewish Babel-myth and in Greek popular religion, of the 'jealous' or invidious God, swift to thwart man's intellectual and other ambitions, lest his own position be impaired.

> God to remove his ways from human sense,
> Plac'd Heaven from Earth so far, that earthly sight,
> If it presume, might err in things divine,
> And no advantage gain.

It is even suggested that the stellar system may have been so constructed as to be an insoluble enigma to astronomers in order that the Creator may chuckle over their blunders;

> . . . He the Fabric of his Heav'ns
> Hath left to thir disputes, perhaps to move
> His laughter at thir quaint Opinions wide. . . .[2]

A singularly detestable being was the God—that is, this one of the several mutually incongruous Gods—in which even such a Christian humanist of the seventeenth century as Milton could sometimes believe. That it was only one of several should, of course, be emphasized; it should not be inferred that Milton habitually thought of his Creator in this fashion, as a humorous celestial sadist devising intellectual pitfalls for the human mind, to provide amusement for himself when some men fall into them. Milton's usual conceptions of deity, though they *are* mutually incongruous, are, at any rate, elevated and edifying. What is astonishing is that he could ever have entertained such an idea, and have suggested it to his readers—even with a 'perhaps.' For to a consistent and devout adherent of the historic Christian theology there could have been no 'perhaps' about it; such a conception would have been simply unthinkable.

[1] *PL*, VIII, 70–76.
[2] *PL*, VIII, 75–77.

However, though this observation is, I think, of some psychological and biographical interest as showing how widely Milton could, in the heat of controversy, deviate from his more usual and more serious religious beliefs, it is not the point that it is important for the historian to bear in mind. That point is that, in the half-century in which the science of astronomy was making its most memorable advances, three decades after Galileo's masterpiece and two decades before Newton's *Principia*, Milton went out of his way to attack, not any specific astronomical hypothesis but the study of astronomy as such. For the dialogue between Raphael and Adam, in so far as it relates to seventeenth-century astronomy, obviously had no natural place in an epic of the Fall of Man; it was not a part of the 'plot' of the poem nor of the dramatic characterization of the human protagonist. The subject was violently introduced— 'dragged in'—because Milton had in mind his contemporary readers and wished to bring them to accept a theorem of his own. The motivation of the theorem was mainly theological; it was a derivative of the same primitive conception of a 'jealous' deity, fearful lest his human creatures should, through *hybris*, become forgetful of their inferiority and seek to exercise powers reserved for himself. In Adam's speech on the prohibition against eating the fruit of the Tree of Knowledge (IV.421–434), this conception is attenuated and all but negated; there is no explicit suggestion that the prohibition is prompted by fear or envy of man on the part of the Creator. It was only Satan who asked what was, after all, a very pertinent question (IV.515–526):

> . . . Knowledge forbidden?
> Suspicious, reasonless. Why should thir Lord
> Envie them that? Can it be sin to know,
> Can it be death? And do they onely stand
> By Ignorance, is that thir happie state,
> The proof of thir obedience and thir faith? . . .
> Envious commands, invented with designe
> To keep them low whom knowledge might exalt
> Equal with gods, . . .

But in Book VIII the old strain returns, and is used to justify the condemnation not only of the investigations of astronomers but of every quest of knowledge 'of things remote from use, obscure and subtle.'

Thus the final conclusion which Milton expresses through his spokesmen in the dialogue—the thing, apparently, that he most wanted to say on the subject—is that these are matters about which it is useless and 'impertinent,' and even sinful, for men to employ their minds. Milton's position, in short, is pragmatic, in the most vulgar sense of that ambiguous term, the sense in which it designated an obscurantist utilitarianism hostile to all disinterested intellectual curiosity and to all inquiry into unsolved problems about the physical world. Of this sort of pragmatism no more extreme expression is (so far as my reading goes) to be found in English literature. And in no other book and at no other time could the expression of it have been more incongruous or, unwittingly, more ironic.

GRETCHEN LUDKE FINNEY

Music, Mirth, and Galenic Tradition in England

Notions of the medical value of music in the Renaissance were based, broadly speaking, on two different attitudes toward music. In Pythagorean and Platonic tradition, music, because it imaged the harmony of the universe, could move the soul to its own motions, and, through soul, body. On the other hand, many medical writers regarded it, not as something divine, but as amusement, and while they granted its beneficial effect on state of mind, denied its power to alter the soul. They found authority in Aristotle, but primarily in the apocryphal book of Ecclesiasticus. These ideas (occasionally tempered by Platonism) they then attempted to fit into Galen's formula for preservation of health, an attempt that resulted in a unique pattern of thought.

This episode is an essential segment of musical-medical history, for it raised questions that were revived and clarified long after Galen had lost his position as 'Prince of Physicians,' and after music, too, had been reevaluated.[1] The chief interest of this background for literary scholars, however, lies in the extent to which it throws into relief the place of music in one of the most charming poems of all time—Milton's *L'Allegro.*

[1] A study of this subject is in progress.

I

Galen, in his *De sanitate tuenda*, had treated causes and cures of disease under two general headings—congenital conditions that 'take beginning at our Nativity' and are thus beyond physicians' power to change, and things nonnatural, which can be controlled by man. Of these nonnatural things there were six: air, food and drink, sleep and watch, evacuation and repletion, exercise (or motion and rest), and affections of the mind. These things 'beinge orderly, conveniently, and competently used,' it was said, 'have great power and efficacie to keepe man in health.'

Where should music (it was difficult completely to ignore music in the Renaissance) be placed in these Galenic categories? Most often it was a part of exercise, partly no doubt because of the long tradition of the value of singing to exercise lungs, diaphragm, or 'entrayles,' or to draw in pure air to revive the spirits, a usage that had little to do with music as such. But listening to music found a place, also, under 'exercise.'

Most physicians agreed that nothing is more wholesome or more available for health than exercise, but they realized too that any excessive activity, physical or mental, can cause harmful weariness—that rest, too, is essential. As was often said, 'the string ever stretched will end by breaking.' Yet there was danger in complete idleness, 'the bane of body and mind . . . the chief author of all mischief, one of the seven deadly sins.' Through idleness, wrote William Bullein in the *Governement of Healthe*, 'be engendered all disease both of soule and bodie.'[1]

The solution, which avoided excessive activity on the one hand and idleness on the other, was recreational exercise. As Aristotle had written in his *Ethics* (x.vi.6), 'amusement is a form of rest,' not as an end in itself but as 'a means to further activity.' Many were the sports and pastimes suggested, but almost always, largely on the authority of Aristotle's *Politics* (viii.v.1), music had prominent place. Music was 'rest' from arduous toil, but the physician maintained also that it shared with other activities the virtues of 'motion.' Listening to music, as well as singing, was a kind of exercise (whether of body, senses, or mind) that moved the spirits and hence the blood,

[1] London, 1558, fol. 85.

whereby noxious (especially melancholic) humours were dissipated.

Any moderate activity, wrote Levinus Lemnius in *The Touchstone of Complexions*, may strengthen and refresh the body and mind of man 'wearyed wyth troublesome busynesse and cares . . . for by it the quicknes and vigour of the mynde is revyved, the faynt drowsye Spirits styred up and awaked.' And to the least troublesome exercises (all drawn from ancient writing) of being carried in wagons or rowed in boats, frictions, or walking, he added 'singinge and musicall melodie, chaunted eyther with lively voyce, or played upon swete Instrumentes.' In his *Exhortation* (in lines recalled by Burton), he extolled music in similar terms and still as exercise. Husbandry, hunting, hawking, travelling to far places—not in reality but in imagination—all refresh spirits and mind, as does music:

For this by a consent of voices and instruments sounding tunably, doth not onely delight our ears with variety of sounds but doth raise our spirits vital and animal with a noise that is spread every where through the arteries, discussing all clouds and sadnesse from our minds, and making them to be lively and ready for employment.[1]

Thomas Cogan agreed, and Timothy Bright also. 'Bodily exercise,' Bright advised, may serve to recall the soul to 'fellowship' with the body, from which, through 'Speculation,' it 'after a sort disjoyneth it selfe.' But 'actions' of sense may serve the same purpose—use of things 'sweet in taste, pleasant in smell, soft to be felt,' and especially cheerful music, for it moves the spirits, 'allowing them to stirre the bloud, and to attenuate the humours.'[2]

Aside from the 'fact' that pleasant distraction released them from strenuous duties, why and how did music move the spirits? Did mind work on body or body on mind, as classification of 'exercise' implies? Lemnius suggests, at least, that benefits of music derive from direct action on the spirits. Music

---

[1] *The Touchstone of Complexions*, tr. Thomas Newton (London, 1576), fols. 51ᵛ–53ᵛ; *The Paraenesis, or Exhortation. How to lead a life that shall be most excellent. . . .* published with *The Secret Miracles of Nature* (London, 1658), pp. 365–66.

[2] Cogan, *Haven of Health* (London, 1584; 1612 ed.), pp. 20–21; Bright, *Treatise of Melancholie* (London, 1586), pp. 243–50.

pleases the ear, but by a kind of vibrating motion, by 'noise' that is spread everywhere through the arteries, vital and animal spirits are 'raised,' and melancholy *subsequently* dissipated. Bright (although he makes a similar suggestion) was tempted to accept the Platonic notion that because the soul is harmony, there is an 'agreement betwixt concent of musicke, and affections of the minde.' The majority of physicians, however, had a still different explanation—one that confused opinion about music's place in the Galenic framework.

By delight alone, it was said, music has far-reaching effects, a belief derived not from Aristotle but from *Ecclesiasticus* and the book of *Proverbs*. 'Give not over thy minde unto heavinesse [*tristitiam*],' wrote 'Jesus the sonne of Sirach' in the book of *Ecclesiasticus* (30.21–24). 'Heavinesse hath slayne many a man . . . Zeale and anger shorten the dayes of the life, carefulnesse and sorrow [both nouns in translation of *cogitatus*, deep thought] bring age before the time.' To this rule Proverbs (17.22) added authority, for Solomon said, 'A merie heart maketh a lusty age: but a sorrowful minde drieth up the bones.'

These ideas medical men explained in physiological terms. Sorrow and care, wrote Bullein in a *Bulwarke of Defence*, wound the heart and 'draweth it togeather as a purse.' 'The vitall partes by little and little do wither & wast away.'[1] Care cooled the blood and hastened ageing. Pleasant emotions on the other hand, had opposite effect: they warmed the blood and sent spirits throughout the body to give good colour, wipe away wrinkles and confirm health.

How then was man to be merry? The answer was again in Ecclesiasticus (40.20): 'Wine and musicke rejoice the heart.' 'For, that musicke causeth mirth,' wrote Thomas Wright, 'besides the dayly experience which prooveth it, we have Gods word to confirme it, *Vinum & musica laetificant cor*.[2] Whatever

---

[1] *Bulwarke of Defence againste all Sicknes* (London, 1579), 'The Booke of the use of picke men and medicines,' fol. 25ʳ.

[2] *Passions of the Minde* (London, 1601; 1604 ed.), p. 162. To the authority of Scripture could be added that of Aristotle's *Politics* (VIII. iv. 3) where Aristotle, elaborating on possible uses of music, associates it with wine in its force to drive away care. Why or what kind of music caused mirth were questions that few physicians attempted to answer. They usually blindly followed Scriptural authority. They did not, either, face the widely-expressed theory that melancholics do not like music at all.

the virtues or danger of wine, music, and mirth (whether cause or effect) became well-nigh inseparable. Between them they postponed old age and cured melancholy, which, in popular opinion, 'for the most part nourisheth all diseases.'

Use of the word 'mirth' was not accidental. Granting exceptions, 'mirth' was distinct from 'joy.' Mirth (or merriment) was less permanent and was aroused by lighter amusements. Mirth (*laetitia*), it had been explained, is a motion toward some present good, joy (*gaudium*) toward eventual good.[1] Mirth was associated with laughter, as it is today, with hilarity and jocundity. It revealed itself in lively motion.

Surely, thinks the modern reader, music, as a provocation to mirth, should be discussed under the Galenic heading 'affections of the mind.' Elizabethan physicians, however, were in a quandary. If music is merely entertainment, if mirth is jollity, we can imagine them argue, surely they can have no deep effect on passions of the soul, whose control should be left to reason and religious counsel. William Bullein was outspoken in denial of the usefulness of medicines or sensory pleasures to cure spiritual perturbations. When his patient cries out in despair that delights of the Muses no longer please him, seeming as 'playne vanity,' the physician exclaims:

What sickenes is this, that neyther Physicke, nor all these delights, can gyve cure unto? it is a merveilous disease, bee lyke it shoulde appeare, that it is no sycknes of the body, but rather the passions or perturbations of the mynde.

For 'griefes of Mynde,' he counsels, 'imbrace the heavenly Phisicke, contayned in Goddes woorde, whych is the pryncipall Regiment.'[2]

---

[1] Ludovico Vives, *De anima & vita* (Basel, 1538), Lib. III, p. 215. He was often quoted. Even 'delight' and 'pleasure' had different implications than 'mirth,' but shades of meaning differed in different context and were often confused. Loose mirth might lead to neglect of duty or to lust as in *The Faerie Queene* (ii. vi) when 'Guyon is of Immodest Merth / Led into loose desyre.' The 'Riot, and ill manag'd Merriment' of *Comus* (172–74), 'Such as the jocond Flute, or gamesom Pipe / Stirs up among the loose unleter'd Hinds,' stand for vulgar sensuality. At the other end of the spectrum was the 'Musicke and Ethereal Mirth' referred to by Milton in 'The Passion.'

[2] *Bulwarke of Defence*, fol. 23 and 29ᵛ ff.

The mirth roused by music was closely related to recreation. Music made merry the heart; it lightened heaviness of mind, 'carefulness' and sorrow. But 'superfluous care and sollicitude' was equated with 'thought.' If mirth drives off care, or counteracts the undesirable effects of mental concentration, its benefits resemble those of recreational exercise. Lemnius, for one, retained his comments on wine, music, and mirth under the heading of 'exercise,' in company with husbandry or hawking.[1] Other physicians solved the problem by adding another category. Bullein, in advice for avoiding pestilence, in the *Governement of Health*, associated music and mirth with exercise but under a separate heading. William Vaughan recommended them in two different sections, proximate to 'The Soules qualities and affections,' although he still classed music with leeching and diet.[2]

Medical writers won over to Platonism discussed music under the heading of 'affections of the mind' without question, but they granted to music a power far above that of provoking mirth. Singing is indeed exercise, wrote Richard Mulcaster, and music may be so defined in the sense that it gives 'delite & pleasures,' but 'As Musicke is compounde of number, melodie, and harmonie, it hath nothing to do with gymnastick, and exercise.' Music remedies 'desperate diseases,' because it 'hath naturally a verie forcible strength to trie and to tuche the inclination of the minde.'[3]

These divergent points of view Robert Burton tried, with small success, to reconcile in *The Anatomy of Melancholy*, by including music under both exercise and 'perturbations of the mind,' and by attributing to it a variety of benefits. Its value, as

[1] *Exhortation*, p. 367.

[2] Bullein, *Governement of Health*, fol. 85ᵛ; Vaughan *Directions for Health, both Naturall and Artificiall* (5th ed., London, 1617), pp. 184–85, 278–81.

[3] Mulcaster, *Positions wherein these primitive circumstances be examined, which are necessarie for the training up of children, either for skill in their booke, or health in their bodie* (London, 1581), pp. 59 and 37–38; cf. Andreas Laurentius, *A Discourse of the Preservation of the sight...*, trans. by Richard Surphlet (London, 1599), pp. 191–92, 107. John Jones, in *The Arte and Science of ... Healthe* (London, 1579), pp. 12–14, considered music of benefit to health, not because it amused but because it moderated the passions.

exercise, is for recreation—to give a 'moderate' employment, avoiding 'unseasonable exercise' on the one hand, 'too much solitariness and idleness on the other,' a balance most conducive 'to the general preservation of our health.' He followed in general the programme of Lemnius (no less a mélange for being given guise of order): hawking, hunting, fishing, gardening, travel to see cities, palaces, triumphs, weddings, and combats. See or take part in masques or theatre, he writes. In the country, join in merrymaking, listen to tabors and bagpipes, or tales of fairies and goblins. 'Walk amongst orchards, gardens . . . rivulets . . . pools.' And with these diversions (in addition to more fleshly pleasures) are those of rowing upon the waters with music, and listening to the 'heavenly music' of birds or the exquisite singing of beautiful women.

Music has more significant place, however, under the general heading of 'Perturbations of the Mind rectified,' where it is included both because it is an amusement inseparable from mirth (which Burton recognized as an affection of the mind), and—in a separate section—because it is 'divine.' Reason, Scripture, prayer, are man's chief ways to serenity of mind, Burton affirms, but he had no compunctions, even as a clergyman, in admitting the value of sensory pleasure. Nothing is 'so apposite,' he writes, 'as a cup of strong drink, mirth, music, and merry company' to 'mollify the mind.' 'Mirth and merry company may not be separated from music.'

But having been influenced, too, by metaphysical ideas, Burton was not content to leave music in common company. So powerful is music, he continues, quoting Cassiodorus, 'that it ravisheth the soul'; it carries the soul 'beyond itself, helps, elevates, extends it.' At this point, he reveals further confusion, however, for he tried, inconsistently, to explain the elevating power of music both by the theory, drawn from Scaliger, that music moves the spirits corporeally and by the Platonic idea that soul is harmony.[1]

---

[1] Part 2. sec. 2. mem. 4, and mem. 6, subs. 3 and 4. He refers to Cassiodorus' *Variarum*. Lib. II. Epist. XL, in Migne, *PL*, LXIX, 570 ff., and to J. C. Scaliger, *Exotericarum Exercitationum Liber XV de Subtilitate, ad Hieronymum Cardanum Exercitat.* CCCII.

II

This episode in the history of medicine was closed, however, neither by physician nor Divine but by a poet, who, through the synthesizing power of poetic genius, translated this confused body of ideas into language of the imagination free of controversy and absurdity. Belief that recreation, especially music, could join with mirth to banish care and melancholy has been immortalized in Milton's *L'Allegro*.

L'Allegro is in no sense a 'medical' work: there is no mention of humours or spirits, no advice directed toward maintaining 'universal health of the body.' The melancholy exorcised by mirth is the dread affliction treated by Galenic physicians, but it is psychological only, not physical. The poem does not survey the Galenic categories; but it does refer to one aspect of them—the power of mirth.

Here again we meet 'heart-easing Mirth,' accompanied by Jest and Laughter, all of the 'unreproved pleasures free' that deride 'wrincled Care.' To describe the activities of Mirth, Milton follows Burton closely (as Burton had followed Lemnius, and Lemnius more ancient writing)—listing recreations that Burton had included both under exercise and, with mirth, under 'perturbations of the mind.' From country pleasures, to those of city (visited in imagination only, as Lemnius advised), from pleasures of sight and hearing to those of mind and fancy, the mirthful man follows Burton's 'regimen.'[1]

Of these amusements, music—not rustic minstrelsy, but art song—is the climax, and Milton refers certainly to the same passage in Cassiodorus used by Burton, for in this passage Cassiodorus (alone of ancient writers, as has been pointed out)[2] attributed to the Lydian mode, condemned by Plato as lascivious, power to dissipate cares and worries of the soul:

[1] Similarity between Burton's recommended recreations and Milton's has been pointed out by George Wesley Whiting, *Milton's Literary Milieu* (Chapel Hill, Univ. of North Carolina Press, 1939), pp. 136–38. See also William J. Grace, 'Notes on Robert Burton and John Milton,' *SP*, CII (1955). Neither author relates the passages to medical history and neither investigates musical references.

[2] By James Hutton, 'Some English Poems in Praise of Music,' *English Miscellany*, Vol. I (1950), whose translation I use later.

> And ever against eating Cares,
> Lap me in soft Lydian Aires.

Here, as in Burton, are Platonic echoes, but music is still, in *L'Allegro*, one of the pleasures of mirth and not a means of spiritual elevation.

From these activities, so often seemingly incongruous, Milton eliminated confusion both in classification and effect. There is nothing incompatible between mundane recreations and the music of Elysium: all are placed on middle ground between exercise and ways to alter the soul.

Even though the poem is filled with movement, activities of labourers, merry-making youths and maids, the busyness of men in cities, dancing motion of music—

> with many a winding bout
> Of lincked sweetness long drawn out,
> With wanton heed, and giddy cunning,
> The melting voice through mazes running[1]

—this activity is dissociated from physical exertion. Milton is spectator, not participant; he does not forgo, even in *L'Allegro*, the pleasures of solitude. These experiences are refined of physical sensation: they are delights of the higher senses, of eye and ear, closer to mind than body.

But as Milton avoided all physical, so he avoided also metaphysical or religious connotation. He did not in any way link mirth with Scriptural solace, as Burton did. Mirth is a motion of the soul toward present, not permanent, good. Her delights are not those of common conviviality, or tactile gratification, but neither are they delights of contemplation of realities above sense—pleasure reserved for the thoughtful man of *Il Penseroso*.

In the musical imagery we find, also, adroit maneuvring between commonplace and divine, between the Galenic view of music as recreational exercise and the Platonic view that

---

[1] This motion is earthly counterpart of the 'Mystical dance' of the planets described in *Paradise Lost* (v.620–627), moving in

> mazes intricate,
> Eccentric, intervolv'd, yet regular
> Then most, when most irregular they seem,

motion that is both dance and music.

granted it unique power over the soul. Milton did not, like
Burton, fall into conflicting ideas about music (as he himself
did in the tractate *Of Education*)[1] in an attempt to combine
physical with occult effects.

A comparison of *L'Allegro* with the Cassiodorus passage that
Milton and Burton both used reveals not only Milton's debt to
his source, but his skilful avoidance of its distracting suggestions. 'Music enters our ears,' Cassiodorus wrote, 'and alters
our spirits . . . as queen of the senses . . . [it] drives out other
thoughts.' It arouses from indolence and lethargy. 'We are
told that celestial Beatitude enjoys it for ever, and it never fades.'
The Ionian mode 'sharpens the intellect and turns the desires
heavenward,' he wrote. Lydian restores us with relaxation and
invigorates with delight, 'being invented against excessive cares
and worries.'[2] He then commented on the occult power of
numbers in music by which Orpheus drew animals to listen,
and turned finally to Virgil to prove that even those in the
underworld enjoy, in the Elysian fields, the pulsation of the
seven-stringed lyre.

Reference to Orpheus' lyre leads us to the sixth book of
the *Aeneid*, and a passage that was a favourite with occult

[1] Milton discussed music under the heading of 'Exercise' (following a
recommendation of military games), as a pleasant way to rest the mind
and recreate 'travail'd spirits,' but he said both that it aids digestion and
that it tempers the soul.

[2] Ludovicus Caelius Rhodigenus, in his *Lectionum Antiquarum, Libri
trigenta* (pub. 1513, 1566, 1620, etc.), Book IX, chap. II, quoted Cassiodorus, but exchanged the effects of Ionian and Lydian modes. Lydian, he
wrote, sharpens the wit and leads to desire of celestial joys; Ionian
produces jocundity. Charles Butler in *The Principles of Musik* (London,
1636), pp. 1–3, quoted Cassiodorus via Caelius and repeated the error.
Lydian mode, he wrote (with credit both to Cassiodorus and Caelius),
'Throogh his heavenly harmoni, ravisheth the minde with a kinde of
ecstasi, lifting it up from the regarde of earthly things, unto the desire of
celestiall joyz . . . which it dooeth lively resemble.' Ionian is 'for honest
mirth and delight, chiefly in feasting and other merriments.' I cannot
agree with Harris Francis Fletcher (*The Intellectual Development of John
Milton*, [Urbana, 1956], I, 35–151) in his opinion that Milton and Butler
'use . . . Lydian in the same sense' and that Milton's lines are intended
to be 'reminiscent of . . ., "mournful things".' Lydian mode, as Butler
described it, is more suggestive of the musical imagery of *Il Penseroso*,
where music dissolves into ecstasies and brings 'all Heav'n' before the
eyes. Milton and Burton, too, surely knew Cassiodorus at first hand.

philosophers of the Renaissance who saw deep significance in reference to the seven strings of Orpheus' lyre, which were thought to symbolize and account for his magical power.[1] The happy ones in Elysium, wrote Virgil, enjoyed exercises and pastimes of life on earth, and there, too, was Orpheus, who 'with only the tuneful strings of a Thracian lyre / To aid him could conjure forth the ghost of his wife.'

> Some exercise upon the grassy playing fields
> Or wrestle on the yellow sands in revelry of sport;
> Some foot in rhythmic dances and chant poems aloud.
> Orpheus, the Thracian bard, is there in his long robe,
> To accompany their measures upon the seven-stringed lyre.

Others on the greensward, or 'amidst a fragrant grove,' in a realm of light, feast and sing jovial paeans. 'All was the same beyond the tomb.'[2]

From Cassiodorus comes the emphasis in *L'Allegro* on the power of the Lydian mode to expel care and invigorate with delight, to rouse from lethargy, and like Cassiodorus, Milton proceeded to the Orpheus image and the delights of music in Elysium suggested by Virgil. As in Virgil, the Orpheus setting is in a land of fragrant landscape and golden light, of 'golden slumber on a bed / Of heapt *Elysian* flowres'; and like Virgil, Milton recalls Orpheus' power, not to charm beasts, but to draw Eurydice from the underworld.

But digression from source is equally significant. Milton did not associate music, as did Virgil, with active exercise. Only the most languid motion stirs the somnolent Elysium of *L'Allegro*, where Orpheus merely lifts his head from slumber to listen. Conversely, Milton ignored the occult significance of Orphic

---

[1] Lines 119–120, 540–658. 'In 1589 Fabio Paolini, a professor of Greek at Venice, published a large volume, entitled *Hebdomades*, which is a commentary, divided into seven books, each containing seven chapters, on one line of Virgil' (*Aeneid* vi.646) to discourse on the virtues of the number 'seven.' D. P. Walker, *Spiritual and Demonic Magic from Ficino to Campanella* (London, 1958), p. 126. The translation of the *Aeneid* used here is that of C. Day Lewis (London, 1954).

[2] The fallen Angels of *Paradise Lost* (II.526–548) also entertained 'the irksome hours' with these same sports—with mock battle or 'swift race' as in 'Olympian Games' on earth. 'Others more milde, . . . sing / With notes Angelical to many a Harp.' This parallel has been pointed out by numerous scholars.

music suggested to other Renaissance writers by Virgil's lines, a notion that dominated *At a Solemn Musick* where music breathed sense into the dead and made the soul celestial. The music of *L'Allegro*, in spite of reference to penetration of the soul, does not, like that of *Il Penseroso*, lead the mind beyond sense. It does not, as Burton wrote, 'ravish the soul . . . help, elevate, extend it.' It does not expell passions of the mind, as in Platonic tradition. Music is neither an 'exercise' nor an image of universal harmony. Even for Orpheus it is a pleasure of the sense.

By nature Milton preferred intellectual pleasures. Yet he saw, as did medical men of the Renaissance, value in mirth. He wrote later in his life to his friend, Cyriack Skinner:

> To day deep thoughts resolve with me to drench
> In mirth, that after no repenting drawes;

'Attic tast, with Wine,' and

> To hear the Lute well toucht, or artfull voice
> Warble immortal Notes and *Tuskan* Ayre

were commended in the sonnet to Lawrence as delights for which an hour may wisely be spared. Wine, mirth, music, 'make merie the heart,' and of all companions of Mirth— 'putter away of all diseases,' foe of Care and Thoughtfulness— music was chief.

MARY ANN NEVINS RADZINOWICZ

Eve and Dalila: Renovation and the Hardening of the Heart

J OHN MILTON writes about moral regeneration as a poet of medicinal comfort. He is not cold, proud and incapable of charity.[1] Rather, he writes 'to inbreed and cherish in a great people the seeds of virtue and public civility, to allay the perturbations of the mind and set the affections in right tune.' Milton is sure that men are capable of remaining uncorrupted in the presence of strong desire or fear, and equally are capable of rehabilitation if they fail.[2] The theme of moral regeneration is not incidental to other themes in his poetry: it is one of his primary subjects. Whether 'Israel still serves and all her sons' after his efforts, Milton never doubts but that individual men among the faithful need not.[3] Milton intends to free his

[1] See 'Milton and Magnanimity' in *Ikon: John Milton and the Modern Critics*, ed. by Robert Martin Adams (Ithaca, Cornell Univ. Press), 1955.

[2] John S. Diekhoff, *Milton's Paradise Lost*: A Commentary on the *Argument* (New York, Columbia Univ. Press, 1946), chap. VII, 'The Way of Virtue,' contains a notable exposition of this point.

[3] B. Rajan, *Paradise Lost and the Seventeenth Century Reader* (London, Chatto and Windus, 1947), p. 78. ' . . . Milton's faith in man's goodness is splendidly affirmed. It is a faith which if anything has grown deeper and more tolerant with the years. . . . Before [Adam in *Adam Unparadis'd*] can see the error of his ways he has to be reasoned with by Justice, admonished by the Chorus, and intimidated by the masque of evils which Milton postponed to the eleventh book of the epic. The draft shows us a

countrymen to let them work. Among the impediments to that poise of spirit which leads to action, the severest is the inner struggle of pride, despair, contempt, and anger which he calls 'the hateful siege of contraries.' Milton theorizes about regeneration in *De doctrina Christiana* and about the liberation of the self-enslaved within a faulty marriage in the divorce tracts. He dramatically presents his findings in Eve and Dalila: he has depicted in Eve the process of renovation and in Dalila the process of the hardening of the heart.

Milton views human existence as a perpetual series of minute-to-minute choices and acts undertaken by a total person free from minute to minute to decide. The liberty to act is not sacrificed totally by a false choice; rather it is kept alive by the very exercise of liberty, each deed opening up new alternatives among which man must continue to choose.[1] Since a fall does not absolutely predetermine subsequent action, but rather prepares the circumstances of the next choice, fallen men have copious matter for rethinking.[2]

What in the fall Milton insists upon is that the failure can be mended. The story of the fall with creation destroyed, restored, returned to instant readiness for new choice is the life history of the human race. The truth which Milton emphasizes is not that God's power and goodness suffice to prevent the triumph of evil and turn it to good, present as that truth undoubtedly is.[3] What Milton stresses is that the fall having happened once, criminal driven by fear to confession. *Paradise Lost* shows us two people ennobled by adversity, acknowledging their unworthiness of their own free will. The twenty-five years which separate the two versions, those years which brought Milton defeat and disillusion, have taught him nothing except to believe in Man. It is an unusual lesson and one which ought to qualify the charge of pessimism which is levelled against the last books.'

[1] Twice Milton shows us true liberty which does not fall, once in Abdiel in *Paradise Lost*, once in Christ; in these portraits he displays exemplars of growth in responsibility. More often he examines temptation yielded to.

[2] Initial liberty does not consist in initial perfection: 'Assuredly we bring not innocence into the world, we bring impurity much rather: that which purifies us is trial.'

[3] To correct the emphasis of A. O. Lovejoy and others upon the theme of the paradox of the fortunate fall in Milton, see Irene Samuels, 'The Dialogue in Heaven: A Reconsideration of *Paradise Lost*, III, 1–417.' *PMLA*, LXXII (1957), 611.

may again, but need not; what was once lost is precious, inward, and of supreme concern. With the educative example of its loss before him, each man must tend the preservation of his liberty with utmost diligence. When Adam says,

> . . . full of doubt I stand
> Whether I should repent me now of sin
> . . . or rejoyce
> Much more, that much more good thereof shall spring,

he is on the point of thinking Eden well lost in a universe suffused with protective love. His next words are apprehensive, however:

> But say, if our deliverer up to heav'n
> Must reascend, what will betide the few
> His faithful left among th'unfaithful herd. . . .

And Michael answers that the destiny of God's chosen people is refinement by trial not prosperity in the days of their lives.[1] The angel translates the war between good and evil into man's concern. What is fortunate about the fall is not that God will make all losses good in a triumphant war against the forces of darkness, it is that human beings may fight in their own hearts, knowing victory possible if their wills be resolute. The war of Christ and anti-Christ is no such war in Milton as in John. When Adam anticipates a heroic combat such as John describes, Milton gives him instead the Epistle to the Romans, a struggle of the old and new Adam in the human breast.

> Dream not of thir fight
> As of a Duel, or the local wounds
> Of head or heel: not therefore joynes the son
> Manhood to God-head, with more strength to foil
> Thy enemie, nor so is overcome
> Satan, whose fall from Heav'n, a deadlier bruise,
> Disabl'd not to give thee thy deaths wound:
> Which hee, who comes thy Saviour, shall recure
> Not by destroying Satan, but his works
> In thee and in thy seed . . .

[1] Even the promised Comforter is not one who wipes the tears for ever from men's eyes but one 'who the law of Faith working through love upon their hearts shall write.' He is more like a pedagogue than a paraclete.

The true second coming is when God calls upon the believer to become the new Adam. Milton moves the images of Heaven and Hell on to the inner stage of the human heart, a final step in the elimination of Satan as a dramatic character. Little is said about the Passion, for the crucifixion of Christ is in the sinner's heart; little of the method of Atonement, for the work of atonement is rehabilitation.[1] The whole of human history comes simply to mean the struggle for the individual regeneration of the individual soul. Reform is possible to each, to 'as many as offered life neglect not, and the benefit imbrace by faith not void of workes.'

Paradise Lost is written from Milton's conviction that error can be redressed, in the desire to 'send [his readers] forth, though sorrowing yet in peace.' There is no other way for man to redeem his mistakes than through remaking the decisions which caused them. Each must break the pattern of mischoice in fresh choice. Change is predicted upon freedom: the mercy of providence can be no other than permitting parallel choices.[2] Man is released from siege of contraries when he becomes simultaneously conscious of loss and restoration of freedom and knows he may choose again.

In the phrasing of the demand for freedom in the *Treatise of Civil Power* is a useful recapitulation:[3]

If then both our beleef and practice . . . flow from faculties of the inward man, free and unconstrainable of themselves by

---

[1] C. A. Patrides, 'Milton and the Protestant Theory of the Atonement.' *PMLA*, LXXIV (1958), 13, shows that what little is said by Milton is in no way peculiar to Milton. There is no 'personal emphasis' in Milton's theory of the Atonement.

[2] The *De doctrina Christiana* discussion of renovation rejects even a benevolent despotism by God. 'But if the will of the regenerate be not made free, then we are compelled to embrace salvation in an unregenerate state.' Though he is speaking of the inheriting of the kingdom after death, Milton denies the possibility of one being surprised by grace beyond his willing.

[3] Arthur Sewall, in *A Study in Milton's Christian Doctrine* (London, Oxford Univ. Press, 1939), p. 187, argues that this passage shows Milton holding that liberty is not a psychological condition involving control of the passions but rather is an enriched spiritual condition. It is my impression, however, that the passage shows freedom as natural to man, once lost, then supernaturally restored, and now the only element in which he can grow.

nature, and . . . from love and charitie besides, incapable of force *and all these things by transgression lost, but renew'd and regenerated in us by the power and gift of God alone,* how can such religion as this admit of force. . . .

Here Milton grounds his morality not simply upon the nature of God and the sense of revelation, but upon the nature of man and the reality of human experience, upon the actual faculties of the inward man as he knows them to work. He says that man's experience is of transgression and loss, of renewal and regeneration; this experience demands freedom. Choice, rechoice, and change is a process of mental and spiritual health. Conscious of both the loss and restoration of freedom, Milton calls man to heroic action.

II

Among Milton's diverse dramatizations of renovation are the stories of Eve and Dalila. That both are women makes the treatment especially interesting, not because Milton views women with an especially fascinated loathing,[1] but because he in common with all seventeenth-century expositors locates women a little below men in the great chain of being. He places them in a natural social sphere, able to grow only as they cope with other human beings. He limits their capacities just enough to make them seem especially preconditionable, likely to be determined from without, unlikely to experience much renovation. Yet 'natural' renovation is shown in Eve, and 'hardening of the heart,' a confirmation in self-enslavement, is seen in Dalila. They are studies in the process of moral regeneration, particularly effective because particularly natural and human. Light is thrown on the role of each as a woman by the discussion of regeneration in the *De doctrina Christiana,* on the role of each as wife by the divorce tracts.

Although their primary aim is to argue the freedom of earnest Christians to divorce upon deliberation, Milton's divorce tracts

[1] Among Denis Saurat and others, see James Holly Hanford, *John Milton, Englishman* (New York, Crown, 1949), p. 221; W. B. C. Watkins, *An Anatomy of Milton's Verse* (Baton Rouge, Louisiana State Univ. Press, 1955), p. 141.

consider the nature and purpose of marriage, its place in human life, and love's place in it.[1] The main objects which prompt man to marry are the propagation of children, the relief of concupiscence, and, primarily, the consolation of loneliness. Milton defines marriage as an inner loving relationship between husband and wife and says that anything may be forgiven a partner in marriage—sterility which prevents the propagation of children; adultery which misdirects the relief of concupiscence—save failure to solace loneliness by cheerful mutualness. He asserts not just that husbands and wives ought to love one another, but that they must.[2] A marriage is no marriage without 'love fitly disposed to mutual help and comfort of life.'[3] Milton's divorce reform follows from this premise: if no marriage of true minds obtains in a union, it is no union in the eyes of God, and the partners are free to dissolve it to seek true wedlock. Deny them that right and it is the right to marry itself, not just to divorce, which is lost.

Milton first establishes marriage upon the nature of man rather than the external command of God. Before the fall, Adam had the law of nature innate in him to teach him 'whatever is agreeable to right reason, that is to say, whatever is intrinsically good.'[4] What led him to marry was either his own good head and heart, concurring with God's advice, or it was an arbitrary command outside the law of nature. Milton says that it was the former, Adam's rational awareness of his own

[1] For evidence that Milton's view of women and marriage accords with seventeenth-century humanist and Puritan thought in its idealizing and hierarchical aspects see: Arthur Barker, 'Christian Liberty in Milton's Divorce Pamphlets,' *MLR*, XXXV (1940), 160 ff.; A. H. Gilbert, 'Milton on the Position of Women,' *MLR*, XV (1920), 7 ff; William Haller and Malleville Haller, 'The Puritan Art of Love,' *Huntingdon Library Quarterly*, V (1942), 235 ff.; Evian Owen, 'Milton and Selden on Divorce,' *SP*, XLIII (1946), 237 ff.; W. R. Parker, *Milton's Debt to Greek Tragedy* (Baltimore, Johns Hopkins Press, 1937); C. L. Powell, *English Domestic Relations*, 1487–1653 (New York, Columbia Univ. Press, 1917); F. L. Utley, *The Crooked Rib* (Columbus, Ohio State Univ. Press, 1944).

[2] Haller and Haller, p. 250.

[3] *Tetrachordon*, p. 664. All of the quotations from Milton's works in this paper are taken from *The Student's Milton*, ed. by F. A. Patterson (New York, Crofts 1946).

[4] *De doctrina Christiana*, p. 986.

needs.[1] For Milton, God's advice in the matter is binding because it is good, not because it is God's.[2]

But as Milton not only argues that divorce corresponds to right reason, but also holds that God sanctioned it as an instance of the liberty suitable to the faithful,[3] he is compelled to explain why of the four Biblical texts discussing divorce the two from the Old Testament are more permissive than those from the New Testament. Moses had written, 'If a man find his wife undesirable, he shall write her a bill of divorcement so she can remarry'; but Jesus said, 'Whoso shall put away his wife, except it be for fornication, and shall marry another committeth adultery.' To resolve the dilemma of agreeing with Moses to permit what Christ reproves, Milton substitutes for the usual sense of fornication a new sense. By fornication Jesus means spiritual disunion, not physical, for since Jesus holds the spirit to be purer and more important than the flesh, he would not displace reason to draft a rule based simply upon the flesh. Milton then reminds us that God's intention is always freeing, merciful, and charitable. Since Christ fulfils the law and removes slavery, what he commends in the gospel is a priori more compassionate than anything Moses commends in the law.[4]

The moral part of Mosaic law Christ cannot have abrogated; that is based upon eternal principles. Hence divorce is legal. Christ freed men simply from the menace of the law. With Him comes Christian liberty, which means that that Mosaic morality still in force is expressed only within the conscience of each Christian.[5] What Christ does is 'to restore us in some compe-

---

[1] In *Tetrachordon* (p. 656), Milton quotes God saying 'It is not good for man to be alone' and points out that God 'presents himself like to a man deliberating' to show 'that he intended to found marriage according to natural reason, not impulsive command, but that the duty should arise from the reason of it, not the reason be swallowed up in a reasonless duty.'

[2] Owen, p. 239.

[3] Barker, p. 155.

[4] *Tetrachordon*, p. 677. 'If our Savior took away aught of law, it was the burdensome of it, not the ease of burden; it was the bondage, not the liberty of any divine law that he removed; this he often professed was to be the end of his coming.'

[5] *Ibid.*, p. 675. 'If the law of Christ shall be written in our hearts . . . how can this . . . be a law of Christ, so far from being written in our hearts that it injures and disallows not only the free dictates of . . . moral law, but of charity also and religion in our hearts.'

tent measure to a right in every good thing both of this life and the other.'[1] Milton moves well beyond the normal Puritan definition of Christian liberty: that Christians are freed from the imposed righteousness of the law; their obedience to it is a product of grace, not compulsion. He has added that Christian liberty frees the believer from the compulsion of all external precept whatsoever. The only law that binds is the law written in the heart of the believer, his conscience. Milton thereby extends Christian liberty from the management of spiritual affairs to all of earthly life as well.[2] Upon such absolute freedom from constraint Milton depends in his theory of regeneration. It places the responsibility for his purification squarely upon man, who repeatedly must use right reason to choose and re-choose.

Marriage consists 'in the mutual love, society, help and comfort of the husband and wife,' with, however, 'a reservation of superior rights to the husband.'[3] His superiority is not arbitrary but natural, stemming from his 'indelible character of priority.'[4] The mundane sphere was made for man. The first need he felt, even before sin, was a need for woman; the first intervention of God on his especial behalf was to create her. As she was made for him, she was his inferior; as, however, she was made to complement him, she was made very little inferior. And in one respect she was created his equal: that is, in the inheriting of grace. Woman is not less valuable as a soul than man. Wives are commanded to obey their husbands, but like all subjects of higher powers, they are commanded first to obey their Lord. In a conflict of duty, a wife must deny her husband to obey God. Moreover, the very freedom of divorce which Milton proposes carries with it a final equalizing con-

---

[1] *Ibid.*, p. 658.

[2] *Ibid.*, p. 653. 'God hath called us to peace, and so doubtless left it in our hands how to obtain it seasonably, if it be not our choice to sit ever like novices wretchedly servile.'

[3] *De doctrina Christiana*, p. 987.

[4] The subjection is neither inevitable nor invariable. 'Not but that particular exceptions may have place, if she exceed her husband in prudence and dexterity, and he contentedly yield; for then a superior and more natural law comes in, that the wiser should govern the less wise, whether male or female.' *Tetrachordon*, p. 653. Milton instances Abagail as worthier to rule than Nabal, for example.

sequence. His proposal is that either partner finding marriage intolerable should escape through divorce. The belief that a husband enjoys a prior prerogative is essentially ineffectual when they stand on the same level of privilege in all contentions.

From such limited distinctions in their natures, distinctions in role follow. Man is made to know and love God, love and assist his fellow man, learn and labour truly, and do his duty in whatever state of life he may be called to. Woman is created to be a help meet for him in these tasks. Her qualities fit her to be one. Milton solemnly rebukes Augustine for rusticity in affairs of the heart because he thinks a friend would have been more helpful.[1]

Upon the distinctions in nature and function also rests the symbolic significance of marriage. The husband is to love his wife as Christ loves the Church; the wife is to be to her husband as the Church to Christ, loving like Rachel, wise like Rebecca, faithful and obedient like Sarah.[2] God recommends marriage because He designs it as the source and pattern of all human relationships, a little church, a little state.[3] It is easy to find the myth of Adam and Eve in Eden a repository for political and social speculation, for ethical and philosophical, even indeed, for psychological—for the union of male and female in marriage was endlessly likened to unions of might and passivity, mind and imagination, spirit and flesh in the individual personality. This true, little wonder that marriage should have been Satan's chosen battlefield in Paradise.

A bad marriage does personal damage equal to that done by all forms of enslavement. It psychologically cripples the individual with despair and anger, hopelessness and rebellion. Unless some issue out of the calamity is offered to man 'he will

[1] *Colasterion*, p. 718. 'Nor was it half so wisely spoken as some deem, though Austin spake it . . . for which opinion he might justly be taxed with rusticity in these affairs. For . . . there is one society of grave friendship and another amiable and attractive society of conjugal love.'

[2] Haller and Haller, p. 250.

[3] And inasmuch, also, as Paul said not only 'wives, submit yourselves unto your husbands' but also 'husbands, love your wives'; and not only 'children, obey your parents in all things' but also 'fathers, provoke not your children to anger' and 'servants, obey in all things your masters according to the flesh,' he was taken to be discussing the reciprocal responsibilities of the whole structure of society.

be ready to . . . mutiny against Divine Providence.'[1] Thus Milton says, 'Whoso prefers either matrimony or other ordinance before the good of man and the plain exigence of charity, let him profess papist or protestant, or what he will, he is no better than a pharisee and understands not the gospel.'[2]

Within the divorce tracts Milton, upon such arguments, urges a thesis whose implications are larger than the specific reform he advocates. The useful lives of sensitive people are not to be thrown away to gain nothing more than a solemn consistency to a sterile rule made in less rational days and persisted in though God himself allow liberty. The virtuous life consists in free choices made by reason, each choice influencing but not irrevocably determining the future, so that at any point in the process an error not only exposes the individual to new choices but also exposes to the individual the predilections of his own nature in a way fruitful of change. Hence, to disregard the freedom God has given in order presumably to live more virtuously than God suggested is to fail in genuine virtue.[3]

III

Milton's theory of regeneration is set forth abstractly in *De doctrina Christiana*. It begins in God's decree predestining man though as yet uncreated. Predestination (by which Milton means only election and never reprobation) designs all believers for eternal salvation. Its purpose is the saving of all. God predestines no specific individuals but gives grace to all sufficient for attaining knowledge of the truth. Since He left free the will, only those who repeatedly reject offered grace are punished. They become by their own acts self-enslaved; the

[1] *Doctrine and Discipline of Divorce*, p. 585.

[2] *Ibid.*, p. 577.

[3] *Tetrachordon*, p. 688. 'Him I hold more in the way to perfection who undergoes an unfit, ungodly, and discordant wedlock, to live according to peace and love, and God's institution in a fitter choice, than he who debarrs himself the happy experience of all godly, which is peaceful conversation in his family, to live a contentious and unchristian life . . . the remedy whereof God in his law vouchsafes us. Which not to dare use, he warranting, is not our perfection, is our infirmity, our little faith, our timorous and low conceit of charity. . . .'

sinner at any time may be saved by repentance, which is an internal change in his view of himself.

'The calamity or punishment consequent upon sin'—Milton's wording suggests a natural inevitability, not a supernatural interference—is death, which Milton distinguishes into four degrees, regeneration being man's deliverance from them. The degrees are:[1] first, the evils leading to death—guilt and shame; second, spiritual death—the obscuring of right reason and the enslavement of the will; third, death of the body—the extinction of the whole man, not the separation of body and soul; and last, death eternal. The first three are states of awareness, reflected in the physiognomy or physiology though they be. When Milton speaks of renovation, he consistently means an experience of a conscious rational man. Man's restoration begins, however, in an action done for him without his willing it, in his redemption, whereby God through Christ delivers him into a state of grace, Christ voluntarily paying the price of His own blood for all mankind. He performed and continues to perform everything needful for obtaining reconciliation with God, automatically and without man's willed concurrence. What the individual makes of his understanding that the old Adam fell and the New Adam atoned for that fall so that he himself freely stands or falls is what composes his particular renovation or the hardening of his heart.

Redemption initiates renovation, which Milton distinguishes into natural and supernatural renovation. The natural mode of renovation influences the natural affections alone and includes the calling of the natural man. The call renews his mind and will so that he seeks knowledge of God and alters for the better. Its effects are repentance and faith—but the penitence leads to abstaining from sin through self-interest, dread of damnation; and the faith is only a half-trust, acknowledging the truth of scriptures or believing in miracles. These are not enough to save man. Supernatural renovation creates afresh the inward man and infuses new faculties in his mind. Milton's distinction is not doctrinaire; it is a distinction in felt motives. The natural man is a utilitarian. His faith has the aroma of bribe-taking. The supernatural man spontaneously chooses good, though even he is not bound to persist in his new enlightenment. Supernatural

[1] *De doctrina Christiana*, p. 999.

165

renovation follows progressive steps through conviction of sin, contrition, confession, departure from evil, and conversion to good.

In *De doctrina Christiana* Milton also looks at regeneration from a historical as well as an individual, psychological perspective. After treating 'renovation as it is developed in this life,' he turns to 'its manifestations in the covenant of grace.' These two perspectives combine to enable Milton to imagine Adam and Eve both as every man and woman and as summaries as well as exempla of the life history of mankind. Milton coalesces the story of every man and the scriptural story of the chosen people. Every man is born the fallen Adam, undergoes natural regeneration in fear as Israel rested under the law, passes from the law to the gospel at his calling as Israel and the Gentiles together were called and redeemed at the resurrection, and then lives under the covenant of grace, as does every nation after the apostolic ministry. The distinction between Israel and the Gentiles was broken when revelation abolished the old Mosaic law. The result of the abrogation was Christian liberty, whose proper use leads to good works and a free life, whose misuse to self-enslavement, and whose perpetual misuse to the hardening of the heart.

Hardening of the heart is first discussed in the divorce tracts. The drawback to the phrase from Milton's point of view is that it is taken by the orthodox Protestant to describe an action on the part of God which incapacitates man from acting freely. Milton gives in *Tetrachordon*[1] against this sense two other definitions of the term. First, 'when it is in a good man taken for infirmity and imperfection, which was in all the apostles, whose weakness only, not utter want of belief, is called hardness of heart.' This infirmity is not a static condition; it is a process which God meets with suggested remedy, causing Him to suffer man to establish the 'secondary law of nature and of nations.' The law of nations secures a world where the results of man's actions educate but do not annihilate. The second sense of hardness of heart, Milton says, signifies in the sinner a stubborn resolution to do evil. Even that is met by the extension of the freedom to persist. In fine, where hardness is merely the weakness of a good man, nothing softens it save trial; where it is the

[1] *Tetrachordon*, p. 686.

end of a psychological process, it has come about through choices. There is but one way to achieve virtue; that hazards all on free choice repeatedly made. The repetition of decent acts leads to 'good habits, or as they are called, virtues'; repetition of self-willed acts progressively blunts the sensibility, coarsens the understanding and depraves the will.[1]

The divorce tracts set forth one area of remediable error; *De doctrina Christiana* draws the general route towards rehabilitation. Eve and Dalila are dramatizations of the struggle to achieve true freedom and virtue after a fall. Despite many studies of the divorce tracts, the portraits of Eve and Dalila have not been interpreted in their light. Despite many reconstructions of *De doctrina Christiana*, the personal development in Eve and Dalila has not been seen as part of the eternal warfare of good and evil. As a result, the readings of the characters of Eve and Dalila suffer two particular distortions. Studies of Eve concentrate upon reading her fall out of her created nature: they tend to stop there.[2] Dalila is misread when her past treason is

---

[1] Milton summarizes his concept of the true Christian warfare which produces either renovation or hardening of the heart in *Areopagitica*. Human beings do not bring innocence into the world at their birth; they bring impurity. That which purifies them is trial, perpetual rechoice, and the condition for trial is that alternatives be present. 'Wherefore did [God] create passions within us, pleasures round about us, but that these rightly tempered are the very ingredients of virtue.' The presence of evil itself is necessary to the gradual triumph of good. 'Look how much we thus . . . expel of sin, so much we expell of virtue: for the matter of them both is the same: remove that, and ye remove both alike. This justifies the high providence of God, who, though he command us temperance, justice, continence, yet pours out before us even to a profuseness all desirable things, and gives us minds that can wander beyond all limit and satiety. Why should we then affect a rigor contrary to the manner of God and of nature, by abridging and scanting those means which are both to the trial of virtue and the exercise of truth.' *Areopagitica*, p. 741.

[2] Arnold Stein, *Answerable Style* (Minneapolis, Univ. of Minnesota Press, 1953), chap. V, 'The Fall'; E. M. W. Tillyard, *Studies in Milton*, (London, Chatto and Windus, 1951), 'The Crisis of Paradise Lost'; A. J. A. Waldock, *'Paradise Lost' and Its Critics* (Cambridge, Cambridge Univ. Press, 1947), chap. II, 'The Fall (I)'; John S. Diekhoff, *Milton's Paradise Lost*, chap. IV, 'Man's Guilt'; E. L. Marilla, *The Central Problem of 'Paradise Lost': The Fall of Man* (Upsala, Upsala University Essays and Studies on English Language and Literature XV, 1953)—all helpfully describe the stages in the fall: Eve's preliminary gestures of weakness

thought to have determined her character absolutely.[1] But Eve and Dalila have much in common beyond their ruining their husbands. Where critics stop in their examination of Eve, her path begins a systematic deviation from Dalila's; where critics tend to ignore the stages in Dalila's growth into a hard-hearted taunter, those stages are step-by-step rejections which match Eve's affirmations.

IV

At her creation Eve is already an individual, endowed with fully grown traits. Introduced in reminiscences of First Corinthians, she and Adam yet seem Greek in quality. Every attribute has symbolic significance as it squares Scriptural dicta with human-istic doctrine. Paul advises her submissiveness; yet since man's duty is not primarily to command but to love, both the authority of Adam manifest in 'his fair large front and eye sublime' and the obedience of Eve apparent in 'her golden tresses wav'd as the vine curles her tendrils' are transmuted into a love which, the humanist teaches, elevates the individual. Eve

(Stein); her defiance of divine providence (Marilla); her conduct through-out the great pivotal single scene of temptation, fall, and reconciliation (Tillyard); her sequential fall in contradistinction to Adam's single failure (Waldock); her failure in the necessary consistent intellectual surveillance (Diekhoff). What is missing from these portraits is the examination of the initiation of regeneration after the fall in a being for whom choices continue to be present.

[1] A new controversy over the grounds for Dalila's appearance to Samson is developing, and over the possible seeds of sincerity and virtue in her, which contains several interesting new studies. See, e.g., Arnold Stein, *Heroic Knowledge* (Minneapolis, Univ. of Minnesota Press, 1957), 'A Little Further On' (in which Dalila appears as the symbol of feminine injustice); Don Cameron Allen, *The Harmonious Vision* (Baltimore, Johns Hopkins Press, 1954), chap. IV, 'The Idea as Pattern: Despair and *Samson Agonistes*' (in which a sincere and contrite Dalila prompted by her lecherous feelings for Samson reposes to him a supreme temptation); David Daiches, *Milton* (London, Hutchinson Univ. Library, 1957), pp. 241 ff. (in which a Dalila equipped with arguments drawn from the courtly love tradition comes not insincerely to Samson). The traditional view of the doubtfully motivated malicious temptress expounded by James Holly Hanford in *A Milton Handbook* (New York, Crofts, 1933), is continued by W. B. C. Watkins in *An Anatomy in Milton's Verse*. Neither side has presented the evidence of the consistency in her portrait deriving from Milton's processive view of the hardening of the heart.

acts out of and bodies forth a noble synthesis of Biblical and classical theory.

When Adam and Eve begin to speak, Adam's first theme is the freedom God bestows in conjunction with responsibility. Eve's is her love and obedience. Their marriage at once represents the balance and harmony of reason and imagination, love and submission, freedom and responsibility. The characterizations exemplify hierarchy. Adam the superior uses the higher faculties of man: he reasons and explains to Eve. Eve is not irrational—if Adam demonstrated reason in naming the animals, she also in naming the plants—but she is less rational than Adam, more imaginative, more sensuous; therefore she describes, she recreates, she narrates her experiences with variety and charm. She salutes Adam in graceful and intelligently Pauline words, 'O thou for whom and from whom I was formed, flesh of thy flesh, and without whom am to no end, my guide and head,' and continues a richly individual as well as ideally womanly speech about her creation. Her story may reflect the vanity and credulity of woman as well as her power over man, but in manner its charm is Eve's alone. When Adam attempts to explain to Raphael how deeply Eve moves him, he hits upon an exact formula: 'yet when I approach her loveliness, so absolute she seems, and in herself compleat, so well to know her own, that what she wills to do or say seems . . . best.' It is Eve's completeness in herself, her awareness, the vividness and precision of her experiences of herself to herself which make her infinitely believable.

As she has independent womanhood, Eve has independent experiences, of which the dream of temptation is an important example. Because she has memories, dreams, ambitions, sensory delights, correctible inexperienced wonder, Eve must suffer the dangers of rich variableness. The abundance of her nature, strength of her pleasures, acuteness of her responses—these are the very ingredients of virtue which she must rightly temper. Eve's relief at the end of her dream leaves in the reader a foreboding of trouble. She has not objected when Satan praised night, although at night 'nothing abroad do you see except thieves and light-shunning rogues.' She has allowed to go unanswered his regret that the moon shines in vain since unobserved, although Adam has just explained to her how millions

169

of unseen spiritual creatures enjoy it. And finally she has listened to the plausible unreason in which Satan mourns the untasted fruit of the interdicted tree, not permitted to object that the tree is not forbidden as a tree but as a sign of obedience, and to refuse to dispute the symbol as a concrete issue. Instead in the dream she has eaten and awakens to a 'sweet remorse and pious awe, that feard to have offended.' In the way in which Adam consoles Eve, her first 'choice' is ruled no choice at all. But nonetheless Eve in her susceptibility has experienced alone the pattern choice which she repeats in the Fall.

The temptation of the Fall itself displays both Eve's nature and the importance of marriage to her fulfilment. Upon her first suggesting to Adam that they divide their labours in the garden, Adam approves the application of her thoughts, 'for nothing lovelier can be found in woman, than to studie household good.' He argues counter to her because man's role is not 'irksome toil,' but 'delight to reason joyn'd'; therefore their companionship itself is an integral part of his work. He wonders whether Satan's design be 'to withdraw our fealty from God or to disturb conjugal love.' Adam has seen that their harmony is their Paradise, to be guarded. Eve just short of his wisdom offers a truth but not the most profound one, an argument for facing temptation unsupported which she adapts from *Areopagitica*: 'And what is Love, Vertue unassailed alone, without exterior help sustain?' Adam returns the real point, 'wouldst thou approve thy constancie, approve first thy obedience,' but he has felt the force of Eve's words. As a perfect husband he duplicates in his matrimonial bearing towards Eve God's attitude towards him and says, 'Go; for thy stay not free absents thee more.' As little will Adam compel Eve's love and obedience as God compels his.

Confronted by the speaking serpent, Eve blunders. She speaks of miracles, and the serpent says he has been improved by his diet. Accepting the explanation which anticipates the future Popish heresy of transubstantiation, Eve asks not how can eating change essences but what has Satan eaten. When in the presence of the tree, however, she is faithful, the tempter repeats the entrapment of Eve's dream and asks why the tree should be forbidden. Drawn into discussing the tree as a tree, she neglects to say as Adam had that it is the 'only *sign* of our obedience among so many signes of power and rule.' She will discuss it and not obedience as the concrete issue and that error made, she succumbs to argument. She has been talked into holding false reasoning true and has persisted in her initial mischoice.

Eve's total reactions illustrate systematically the first three of the four degrees of death. Sewing fig leaves together 'to hide their guilt and dreaded shame,' she exhibits the first, terrors of conscience. She shows the second, the triumph of passion over reason, in her genuflecting to the tree, greedy gorging on its fruit, her 'swimming in mirth,' and her lasciviousness. She feels the third, the death of the body which extends from man to all created nature, in the changed chill of Eden, when 'through the still night with black air accompanied' she goes to find Adam outstretched on the ground, having reluctantly justified God's ways and plunged in despair. He has understood God's justice but been unable to feel his mercy. Eve's encounter with Adam begins her rehabilitation and enables his. She comes with soft words and is violently reproved. Feeling her evil, she is sorry and begs Adam's forgiveness and God's. Rehabilitation commences in contrition and confession. Eve needs Adam's aid, counsel, support, compassion, and reacceptance; she submits her fate perfectly to his.

> . . . both have sinned, but thou
> Against God onely, I against God and thee,
> And to the place of judgment will return,
> There with my cries importune Heaven, that all
> The sentence from thy head remov'd may light
> On me, sole cause to thee of all this woe.

Made for God in Adam, her renovation cannot proceed without reconciliation to him. Adam must restore to her that scope for action in which alternatives exist. She offers the only possible restitution, submission and assumption of all guilt.[1] Her recognition that she is entitled to no consideration creates the atmosphere in which Adam can feel again. What he feels is their identity in each other. He is enabled to restore her because her

---

[1] Joseph H. Summers, 'The Voice of the Redeemer in *Paradise Lost*,' *PMLA*, LXX (1955), 1082–89, treats Eve's confession as the pivotal passage in the theme of redemptive love in the poem.

pain echoes his and in it he sees their common situation. He gives her his renewed love and tenderness, which returns to her the possibility of action.

> But rise; let us no more contend, nor blame
> Each other, blam'd enough elsewhere, but strive
> In offices of love, how we may light'n
> Each others burden in our share of woe.

Eve's regeneration begins as natural rather than supernatural. Her confession ought to be followed by conversion to good. In fact it has stemmed from misery and issues into despairing shifts rather than patience. To limit punishment for the Fall to themselves, she suggests preventing conception or committing suicide. Although her ideas are escapist, her method of proposing them is not, for it reveals realistic submissiveness unclouded with morbid self-chastisement. Her words inspire Adam to a dual mood—sincere repentance and patient resolution. He and Eve repair to the judgment place where 'in lowliest plight repentent,' they pray:

> Prevenient Grace descending had remov'd
> The stone from thir hearts, and made new flesh
> Regenerat grow instead.

Dalila likewise is given individuality as a woman, transgresses as a wife, and yet fulfils a role in relation to the major action of the poem, Samson's growth in rehabilitation. Since she bulks less large in *Samson Agonistes* than Eve in *Paradise Lost*, her personality is sketched less fully and yet the brevity is telling. Her nature is suggested in the Chorus's wondering description of her arrival before Samson, another Cleopatra gliding like a stately ship 'bedeckt, ornate and gay.' Her outward ornament exceeds her inner strength, but it is of power to awe the Chorus, which an instant before had prayed 'so deal not [unevenly] with this once thy glorious Champion.' In answer to that prayer, God has sent Dalila, a trial and a temptation; by trial comes purity. The combination of sensuousness and sorrow in Dalila represents a mixture of sincerity and adroitness. She speaks a curiously seductive cadence, hesitation embodied in feminine lines, the unaccented last syllables and plentiful caesuras of which emphasize lightly breathed dubiety:

> With doubtful feet and wavering resolution
> I came, still dreading thy displeasure, Samson,
> Which to have merited, without excuse,
> I cannot but acknowledge.

So far she seems to stand like Eve penitent before her Lord, confessing and contrite. Actually, she is in a more neutral position, suspended between regeneration and hardening of the heart. Shortly in defending her earlier choice, she will repeat it and reenact her betrayal. Then she will have hardened her heart. But each blandishment along the way will permit Samson also to remake the decision which led to his fall. Milton lists the stages of hardening of the heart in *De doctrina Christiana* when he discusses the evils corrupting the 'Virtues connected with the Duty of Man towards himself.'[1] Opposed to confession as a stage of regeneration is arrogance and desire for vain glory; opposed to contrition is extenuation of one's own merits to extort praise, and a passion for esteem from whatsoever quarter; opposed to departure from evil is glorying in iniquity; and opposed to conversion to good is exultation over others and self-glorification. When, after acknowledging her sin, Dalila attempts to make restitution, her suspension between regeneration and hardening of the heart is delicately exposed. She says

> . . . yet if tears
> May expiate (though the fact more evil drew
> In the perverse event then I foresaw)
> My penance hath not slack'n'd . . .

Amid penitence she slips in a self-justification, so that rather than grieving that she unnaturally asserted her will against Samson, she grieves that she miscalculated the effect; she repents the lucklessness as much as the evil of her deeds.

Samson is made to answer the probing of her falling cadences with a violent shift in style, with chains of harsh verbs. When Dalila resumes, she is less contrite, more plainly using self-criticism as a cover to incriminate Samson: 'E're I to thee, thou to thy self wast cruel.' Having dispersed her fault among all womankind, removed the onus to Samson, and refused

---

[1] *De doctrina Christiana*, p. 1064. These are all violations of the virtues of magnanimity and lowliness of mind, virtues peculiarly appropriate to those in high station.

responsibility for unexpected effects, Dalila hardens her heart a little more and proceeds to 'crafty extenuation of her own merits to extort praise.' She claims she was prompted by love to betray Samson, she sought to keep him love's prisoner. Asking Samson to forgive her on these grounds, Dalila asks him to conspire in his own ruin. When he rejects her reasoning: 'Love seeks to have Love,' not mere possession, Dalila moves toward even stronger self-gratulation. She claims she was pressed into acting against an enemy of her people by public motives, 'vertue, as I thought, truth, duty so enjoyning.' This new line of argument contains a deeper depravity which consists in a 'passion for esteem and praise from whatsoever quarter.' Her plausible reasoning 'that to the public good private respects must yield' is specious. Samson justly replies that the country planning evil is no state but an 'impious crew'; that a religion cannot be served by irreligious acts. Dalila sought neither public weal in supporting the murderous intent of a rabble nor religious service in projecting ungodly deeds. She sought esteem from a wretched quarter and concealed her aims under 'feign'd Religion, smooth hypocrisy.'

Dalila does not yet openly embrace her old treachery, but she repeats it. She changes the subject, brushes aside the past, and offers Samson present consolation. She poses as a benefactress: 'what by me thou hast lost thou least shall miss.' Her words are at an extreme from Eve's submission: she offers a sick 'domestic ease,' peace on her terms or misery alone. She succeeds in raising Samson to a height of competent reason, and he states the theme of inner freedom in final certitude. The only slavery is voluntarily to serve the unworthy. 'This Gaol I count the house of liberty to thine whose doors my feet shall never enter.'

Dalila resorts to one more stratagem, before she glories in her past treason and exults over Samson. She tries the bribery of passion. That refused violently, Dalila speaks her final lines transparent with self-satisfaction. She sees herself as she is and admires her own reflection. The process of hardening of the heart is complete when Dalila has left herself no other alternative but to go forward happily seeking her own vain glory, proud of her victory, scornful of Samson. She charges him with implacability, ignoring her own ruthless will to power. She alludes to 'double-mouthed fame' which ensures that if condemned in Israel her name will be sung in solemn festival in Philistia. Anticipating public honour she concludes:

> At this who ever envies or repines
> I leave him to his lot, and like my own.

Her self-gratulation and exultation over others goes so far that she lays claim to sublime indifference. Persuaded that good is just what she chooses, she rests in the false magnanimity of the absolute relativist, 'think whatever you like,' hard-hearted and thoroughly corrupt.

Symptomatic of the moral states of Eve and Dalila are their deeds as wives, for to women renovation is intimately connected with marriage.[1] While Eve stands, her faith issues not only into perfect conversation but also into appropriate good works.[2] In almost the same order in which in *De doctrina Christiana* Milton discusses them, she performs good works. Her first act is worship; she and Adam pray as Puritans, standing and extemporaneously praising, no set postures, phrases, or rites having been enjoined even under the law. Her second act is comprehended under man's duty to others, love and righteousness. When she and Adam retire, she reveals her love for him with spontaneity and innocence. In the morning in Milton's

---

[1] In Book VIII of *Paradise Lost* Milton expatiates upon the analysis of marriage undertaken in the divorce tracts. Once again God saying 'It is not good for man to be alone' presents himself like a man reasoning to show that marriage is not arbitrarily established. This time, God teases his new creature. Adam saw all creation while naming the animals, nothing in it looked suitable company, so he asked about his solitude. 'What call'st thou solitude,' God replies. Adam's answer desires marriage —an inner relationship of rational harmony with a fit conversing mate. 'Of fellowship I speak such as I seek, fit to participate all rational delight.' At his request for society, God tests Adam further; is society necessary to felicity: 'Seem I to thee sufficiently possesst of happiness who am alone from all Eternity?' Adam answers that man although perfect in kind, is imperfect in degree, having been made to be improved by passage of time. His imperfection is an insufficient unity, which to repair demands communion, collateral love, social communication. Adam needs a wife to complete himself, to solace his defect and to compose his experience.

[2] Adam has expounded to Eve the markedly Puritan morality: though man is not saved by good works, the saved man does work. *De doctrina Christiana*, p. 1018. 'We are justified . . . by faith, but by a living, not a dead faith; and that faith alone which acts is counted living.'

benedicite omnia opera, they again praise God, and turn to the regulation of the garden. At noon Eve prepares luncheon. Despite Milton's detailed insistence upon the vegetarian domesticities of Eden, there is no need to dwell lengthily upon the individual virtues comprehended under Eve's chores. But while she is doing them, Raphael descends toward earth. Eve began her cookery governed by temperance, including sobriety, modesty, decency, frugality, and industry. When Raphael appears, since temperance admits of liberality, she 'turns on hospitable thoughts intent' to entertain him. When after luncheon Adam enquires about cosmic order, Eve leaves. She withdraws, Milton tells us, not because not delighted with astronomy and not intelligent enough to understand, but because she would rather Adam instructed her privately. Various of man's neighbourly duties she fulfils even in going: meekness, 'that sense of delicacy which precludes us from saying or doing everything indiscriminately,' humanity, simplicity, courtesy, and urbanity.

The day of her Fall Eve begins peacefully performing her share of the reciprocal obligations of husband and wife, as she and Adam commune 'how that day they best may ply their growing work.' She is submissive, cheerful, constant, and dutiful. What follows betrays virtue, and yet to that moment Eve has perfectly justified her creation. Every deed has met a divorce tract desideratum: she has been in her 'apt and cheerful conversation' a refreshment against solitude; a sociable delight; a satisfaction of the mind as well as a sensitive pleasing of the body; she has shown mutualness of interest, peaceful joy in talk, a proportionate, affectionate, and lively mind, and a congeniality of soul. Adam praises her to Raphael in phrases from the divorce tracts:

> Neither her outside formd so fair . . .
> So much delights me, as those graceful acts,
> Those thousand decencies that daily flow
> From all her words and actions, mixt with Love
> And sweet compliance, which declare unfeign'd
> Union of Mind, or in us both one Soule.

As *Paradise Lost* draws to an end, Milton commences a modulation from individual back to stylized figure which enables him to end his poem in gradual silence on a quiet note in a not altogether minor key. Eve's role shifts then, and she is best describable at the close in relation to the central themes of the epic.

As consistently as the wife Eve is successful, Dalila is wanting. Milton altered the Biblical source to change her from Samson's harlot into his wife not solely so that Samson's chastity could not be impugned but also so that her betrayal would be fully spiritual and psychological, not merely commercial. Samson's motives, however, in marrying Dalila are the reverse of Adam's: Samson seeks occasion through Dalila not to perfect himself but to smite the Philistine.[1] In the divorce tracts, Milton had considered the marriage of persons of mixed religion. He explained that to the believer all God's creatures were pure, so he might marry an infidel in the hope of converting her. But he added that no believer was compelled to abide in his choice, dwelling against hope and strength in a marriage which might corrupt his own faith. Divorce was open to him, who ought to forbear putting the pagan away while hope of conversion remained. When he married, Samson was primarily motivated by his vocation to war against Philistia; yet he seems to offer a secondary motive, when he reminds Dalila of the shift of allegiance she owed him. He says that he chose her out of, 'from among,' his enemies. Almost he seems to submit that he loved her to save her, but loved her too uxoriously to love helpfully. Dalila fails in wanting a sense of gratitude and love to her Creator as to Samson. She is a pagan whom it was lawful to marry but whom it is equally lawful to 'hate and forsake.'

In brief, within the marriage the virtues which Milton ascribed to understanding are subverted when for wisdom Dalila displays folly, a false conceit of her own wisdom, and a prying into hidden things. Those ascribed to will are lost when for sincerity she displays hypocrisy. She violates the virtues of neighbourly duty when she governs her affections so ill that she cannot govern her tongue; when for charity, she shows a meddling disposition; for good will, possessiveness and pretended sincerity; for integrity, dishonesty; for obedience, fraud and treason. The virtues associated with her duty to herself she

---

[1] *Samson Agonistes*, 11. 231–33

> I thought it lawful from my former act,
> And the same end; still watching to oppress
> Israel's oppressours.

contravenes when, rather than contentment, she seeks glory in riches. And she abuses the duty of wife towards husband most piercingly when she is clamorous, contentious, brawling, and nagging. Her 'heart is snares and nets, and her hands are bonds.' She is more than an obstacle in Samson's good works; she candidly subverts them. Her fatal flaw is the opposition of her own strongly urged will to his.

Dalila has always known her own interest too well, but she has only gradually been made to see the implications of her deeds. When she leaves and the Chorus words its shock, 'a manifest Serpent by her sting, discover'd in the end,' what has been discovered is not only her malice to the Chorus, her persistence in treachery discovered to Samson, but also her fullest will discovered to herself. She knows now what she could not know when she came to Samson: that she is sublimely indifferent to his fate, satisfied with her estimate of herself, ambitious and firm in the course she has taken and now vigorously headed toward a new future.

Eve and Dalila serve the theme of rehabilitation not only in themselves but also for others. While Eve copes with the chaos she has caused, it is when she is dejected that she most fulfils the subtle function Milton sees her created for. When Adam restores the fallen Eve, he restores a balance more precious because once shattered. Each is again free to stand in the precariousness of new understanding. At first Eve does not grasp the judgment against man. She thinks man will die *in Eden*. Michael's words of expulsion stun Adam into an appalled silence and Eve into a pitiful lament. She does not see how she can leave the walks and shades of Paradise, until the Angel advises her:

> Thy going is not lonely, with thee goes
> Thy husband, him to follow art thou bond;
> Where he abides, think there thy native soile.

The effect of Michael's speech to Eve is described upon Adam. He recovers heart and his scattered spirits return because he sees he is responsible for Eve still. Once again the impact of Adam's experiences comes to him through Eve. She is the occasion of his choice and change; she softens and humanizes her husband in order to elevate him. When he pities her, he recovers responsibility.

In Adam's reacceptance, Eve too recovers balance. She says:

> . . . but now lead on;
> In me is no delay; with thee to goe
> Is to stay here; without thee here to stay,
> Is to go hence unwilling; thou to mee
> Art all things under Heaven, all places thou. . . .

Adam hears her well-pleased as she sounds the accepting note of Ruth. Her words communicate the muted hope, her bearing the grace and responsibility, the intermingled sorrow and assurance with which *Paradise Lost* ends. The hope of the future lies in regeneration after fall, growing from self-knowledge, which produces that responsibility towards others implicit in her words. The quality of her lines is grave; she does not despair, though dejected; she trusts the future, she trusts Adam, and she trusts herself, if warily. She wills the good.

Dalila wills her own not Samson's good, but her behaviour has worked his regeneration even while she hardened her heart. She revives him to mental clarity. Though she stands in his way to virtue, yet

> . . . vertue which breaks through all opposition
> And all temptation can remove
> Most shines and most is acceptable above.

Dalila supplies Samson scope to change in rechoice; she purifies him through trial no matter what hostility and scorn she wills.

The conclusion to be drawn from these portraits rests upon the theoretical point that the married relationship epitomizes God's ways toward man, that the heavenly plan is evolutionary, permissive, and historical. It not only takes account of change, it is predicated upon it. An upward and refining process was meant to be normal for man. When Raphael outlines the heavenly plan, the great myth of Adam and Eve is for a space suspended; the epic cosmos melts away and without encumbrance the motion of grace emerges distinctly:

> O Adam, one Almightie is, from whom
> All things proceed, and up to him return,
> If not deprav'd from good, created all
> Such to perfection, one first matter all,
> Indu'd with various forms, various degrees
> Of substance, and in things that live, of life;

But more refin'd, more spiritous, and pure,
As neerer to him plac't or neerer tending
Each in thir several active Sphears assignd,
Till body up to spirit work, in bounds
Proportiond to each kind. So from the root
Springs lighter the green stalk, from thence the leaves
More aerie, last the bright consummate floure
Spirits odorous breathes. . . .
. . . Time may come when men
With Angels may participate. . . .
Your bodies may at last turn all to Spirit
Improv'd by tract of time, and wingd ascend
Ethereal.

All creation was meant to ascend in even upward stages. The fall has not stopped that movement; it has affected the manner and ease of the process, the circumstances of it; it has done nothing to change the end or means. The means are free: freedom with love, God offers man; love with freedom, man returns to woman; obedience chosen of love and understanding, man yields to God; uncompelled obedience, woman presents to man. And should man fall, as he surely will, regeneration is not occasional or remarkable; it is as likely an effect of trial as is self-enslavement. That heavenly grace is requisite to renovation needs no special emphasis; readers of Milton have never been slow to see his God as omnipotent. What needs emphasis is the point that human patience, tolerance, and forgiveness are necessary to rehabilitation. Release for the self-enslaved comes only by association with other men, in growing self-knowledge, arising from community. But release need not come. Dalila convinced that she is her own woman, entirely self-disposable, does bind, commit, and dispose of herself. She limits scope to her chosen reality; her error stands unrectified and she embraces it as her good.

Change in the tragedy has a different quality from change in Raphael's picture in the epic, of course, but it is a compatible quality. The question hanging over *Samson Agonistes* is why does God do things this way—why is the good so easily lost, why restored with such pain. Samson comes to show what kind of god God is. The Chorus's final words summarize what the drama revealed. God resembles the Aristotelian tragic poet, and human existence an Aristotelian tragedy. God purges us of passion and evil by the educative experience of suffering and trial. We are dismissed from human life as from the play 'with new acquist of true experience . . . with peace and consolation and calm of mind, all passion spent.' We are, that is, if our response to choice and trial has been rational. Otherwise life is not a reforming tragedy to us as to Eve, it is the meaningless comic little mirror of self-will that Dalila finds it when she flounces from Samson, liking her lot.

The rehabilitation of Eve and the hardening of Dalila's heart have a realistic psychological complexity not usually admitted to be one of Milton's strong points. They convince us as characters and powerfully reflect the possibility of moral regeneration. It is only an additional pleasure to note how the apparent misogynist Milton displays his fullest compassion and most secure faith in man's ability to change when his theme is the rehabilitation of one woman; and how acutely he displays the inner quality of evil, with what psychological skill, when his theme is the damnation of another.

ANNE DAVIDSON FERRY

The Bird, the Blind Bard, and the
Fortunate Fall

THE closing lines of *Paradise Lost* evoke the mysterious
sense of finality that Milton achieved first in the ending of
Lycidas and once more in the closing chorus of *Samson Agonistes*.
However the banishment of Adam and Eve may be interpreted,
these lines seem to express some 'calm of mind all passion
spent' which is the fulfilment of the poem's meaning. However
we may define the mood of the conclusion, we feel it to be somehow in harmony with the total poem.

Our sense of the rightness of these lines can be measured by
the strength of our feelings of outrage when we read Bentley's
notorious revision of the original ending:

> Then hand in hand with social steps their way
> Through Eden took, with heavn'ly comfort chear'd.[1]

It is not only our belief in the sanctity of the text which is
violated by these lines. Like Tate's version of the ending of
King Lear, Bentley's revisions coarsen, flatten and sentimental-
ize the marvellous complexity of attitude, the fine adjustment of

[1] Quoted by C. A. Moore, 'The Conclusion of *Paradise Lost*,' *PMLA*,
XXXVI (1921), 2. Mr. Moore points out that Bentley's was only one of
numerous eighteenth-century attempts to cheer up the end of the poem.
Addison in *Spectator* 369 suggested omitting the last two lines while
Peck in his *Memoirs of Milton* of 1740 wished to rearrange the last five
lines.

tone, the beautiful appropriateness of feeling of the original. They destroy all the richness of mood and meaning which the poem demands of its conclusion.

Yet if twentieth-century readers have agreed that a text should be preserved as the author intended it, and if we have also agreed on the rightness of Milton's final lines, we have certainly reached no agreement on their meaning. The debate about the ending of *Paradise Lost* which enlivened our journals approximately forty years ago was not settled even by A. O. Lovejoy's now classic article on the paradox of the fortunate fall.[1] This article provided a name for our dilemma by demonstrating that Milton knew and used the orthodox theological doctrine of *felix culpa*, but it apparently did not define for all readers the mood of the end of *Paradise Lost*. For throughout the last decade scholars and critics of Milton have argued opposite opinions of the importance of the doctrine of *felix culpa* in Milton's attitude toward the fall of man, and therefore opposite readings of the final lines of the poem.[2]

Yet even the arguments of opposed critics have so far tended to follow a single pattern in interpreting the final lines. Unlike Bentley and his contemporaries, modern critics have not judged the end of the poem by traditional principles of epic theory, have not measured its conformity to the critical dictum that epics should end 'prosperously.'[3] Instead they have interpreted the ending in the light of the *dramatic* character of the poem, reading it in relation to the actions and speeches of characters elsewhere in the poem.

This method of arguing the mood of the conclusion grows from the eagerness of many modern critics to emphasize the dramatic character of Milton's poem, an approach which has

[1] 'Milton and the Paradox of the Fortunate Fall,' *ELH*, IV (1937), 161–79.

[2] Among numerous examples see: R. M. Adams, 'Empson and Bentley,' *Partisan Review*, XXI (1954), 178–89; M. Bell, 'The Fallacy of the Fall in *Paradise Lost*,' *PMLA*, LXVIII (1953), 863–83; H. S. V. Ogden, 'The Crisis of *Paradise Lost* Reconsidered,' *PQ*, XXXVI (1957), 1–19; W. Shumaker, 'The Fallacy of the Fall in *Paradise Lost*,' *PMLA*, LXX (1955), 1185–87, 1197–1202.

[3] See 'Original and Progress of Satire,' in *Essays of John Dryden*, ed. by W. P. Ker (Oxford, 1900), II, 29; Addison, *The Spectator*, ed. by G. G. Smith (London, 1925), No. 369, III, 196; No. 297, II, 174.

produced helpful revaluations of his methods and intentions.[1]
Yet it is possible that there has been too much emphasis on the
dramatic character of *Paradise Lost*. Readers have lately seemed
almost to forget that this is an epic, not a play, and that the
simplest and most obvious distinction between the two genres
is that epic is a narrative form. Its story must be *told*, not acted
out, and our interpretation of the actions and speeches of its
characters must be controlled by the narrative voice. When we
ask, therefore, the meaning of the closing lines, our first question should not be how episodes and speeches earlier in the
poem have prepared us to understand these lines. Our first
question should be simply, 'Who is speaking these lines?' We
should define the narrative voice we hear interpreting the
banishment of Adam and Eve from Eden. We should question
the nature of the speaker here and throughout the narrative,
descriptive, and discursive parts of the poem, should explore
his relation to us, his readers, and to the characters and events
of his narrative. Only when we have determined who is
speaking, and to whom, can we evaluate the tone of these
final lines, and therefore the mood of the end of *Paradise
Lost*.

The necessity for these questions about the narrative voice
has been obscured by the habit in criticism of referring to the
speaker in the poem as 'Milton.' In *Paradise Lost*, Milton's
narrator speaks in the role of author (as the narrative voice in
an epic was traditionally expected to speak), but the role of
author is also conventionally assumed, for example, in *Lycidas*
and in Sonnet xii on *Tetrachordon*. All these speakers might
with equal justice and equal vagueness be called 'Milton'; yet
our experiences of the sonnet, the pastoral elegy, and the epic
are experiences of totally different voices, each speaking in the
role of author. To define the tone of the closing lines of *Paradise
Lost*, we must first be more precise about the identity of the
speaker. We must analyse the particular and distinctive
character of the narrative voice which Milton has carefully
created and elaborately defined in his epic.

[1] Among the first to argue this approach was J. H. Hanford in 'The
Dramatic Element in *Paradise Lost*,' *SP*, XIV (1917), 178–95. For a
recent illustration of this tendency see Arnold Stein, *Answerable Style*
(Minneapolis, 1953), pp. 122 ff.

In numerous prose statements Milton left a record of his steady concern with conventional distinctions among literary types, and everything he wrote demonstrates that he always thought of his own poems in living relation to literary traditions. In *Paradise Lost* in particular he reminds us repeatedly of the deliberateness of his choice of epic form and biblical argument; he also reminds us of the consciousness of his artistry, the care with which he has sought a style 'answerable' to the traditional epic form and to his special 'higher Argument' (IX.1–47). This choice of 'answerable style' involved him immediately in the choice of speaker, in the problems of creating a distinctive voice capable of narrating and interpreting his argument. The narrative voice is as deliberate an invention as the other characters in the poem.

The passages in *Paradise Lost* especially devoted to creating and defining the narrative voice are those at the beginnings of Books I, III, VII and IX, in which Milton adapts the conventional device of the epic introduction. It is precisely these passages which Addison and Johnson called 'digressions' or beautiful 'superfluities';[1] yet they are as essential to the structure and meaning of the epic as the so-called 'digressions' in *Lycidas* are now generally recognized to be integral to its total design. To understand the complex nature of the narrative voice and its complex relation both to argument and to reader, it is necessary to analyse a number of these passages in detail. They will be seen to create and define a speaker whose identity and characteristic tone are sustained throughout the epic and control the meaning of its final lines.

Milton's epic opens with a traditional statement of story and theme, given in the conventional form of an invocation:

> Of Mans First Disobedience, and the Fruit
> Of that Forbidden Tree, whose mortal tast
> Brought Death into the World, and all our woe,

[1] Addison, *Spectator*, No. 297, II, 177; Johnson, 'Life of Milton,' in *Lives of the English Poets* (London, 1950), I, 103. The relation of these epic introductions to the total poem is argued from very different points of view by J. Diekhoff in 'The Function of the Prologues in *Paradise Lost*,' *PMLA*, LVII (1942), 697–704, and by F. J. Pequigney in chap. 4 of '*Paradise Lost*, Epic of Inwardness,' Unpublished Dissertation, Harvard University, 1959.

> With loss of *Eden*, till one greater Man
> Restore us, and regain the blissful Seat,
> Sing Heav'nly Muse . . .
>
> (1.1–6)

The speaker assumes our familiarity with the story, assumes
that we can identify '*that* Forbidden Tree' and '*one* greater
Man.' His purpose in these lines is therefore not so much to
familiarize us with the events to come as it is to identify for us
which story we are to hear, what it means to us, and who is to
tell it. We the readers are immediately included in the events
of the narrative with the first line of the poem, because its
subject is '*Mans* First Disobedience' (not 'Adam's' or the
'first man's'), and we are included in Man. We are more
explicitly included in the poem's story when we are told that the
Fall brought 'all *our* woe' until Christ 'Restore *us*.' We are the
heirs of Adam; it is to us and to the poet that Adam speaks
directly when after his fall he laments his legacy of corruption:

> . . . Fair Patrimonie
> That I must leave ye, Sons; O were I able
> To waste it all my self, and leave ye none!
> So disinherited how would ye bless
> Me now your Curse!
>
> (x.818–822)

This first epic introduction therefore tells us that not only
are we to hear a story familiar to us, but one which in a sense
happens to us and to the poet narrating it. We will at least
partially share his angle of vision because we share his humanity,
and more specifically his fallen nature. Like us, the speaker-poet
is limited because he is human, corrupted because he is fallen.

Yet even in the introduction to Book I we feel the identity of
the poet and his relation to us to be more complex than the
fact of our common nature and condition would imply. Although
we may in part share the narrator's point of view, we hear no
easy intimacy in these lines. The diction is formal and general,
the sound sonorous, the syntax remote from speech. The
speaker-poet pictures himself as a bird 'That with no middle
flight intends to soar' in pursuit of a vision of 'Things un-
attempted yet in Prose or Rhime.' He assumes the more than
human authority to '*assert* Eternal Providence' and even to

'*justifie* the wayes of God to men.' Here the word 'men' includes us, the readers, as did the earlier word 'Man,' and it is to us that the poet is to explain God's ways. He is therefore not only one of 'us' because he shares 'our woe'; he is also apart from us, instructing us in his role as poet. The source of his vision is the same divine spirit which inspired Moses to sing of the Creation or which flowed in Siloa's brook, whose waters purged the vision of the blind man.[1] The fallen poet prays to this spirit in his invocation, and, the prayer being granted, he can see 'Above th' *Aonian* Mount,' the imaginations of mortal poets. As inspired poet-prophet, the narrative voice claims the instruction granted to Moses and the illumination granted the blind man. He can interpret to us Adam's story and our own share in it because, like a bird, he can soar beyond the limits of our mortal experience and our fallen vision.

It is this speaker who penetrates for us the 'darkness visible' of Hell and the 'Illimitable Ocean' of Chaos, guiding us to the verge of the lighted world and in Book III transporting us to Heaven. The invocation to light which opens Book III not only provides a transition from one world to another. Its most important function is to reinforce and elaborate the character of the narrative voice created in the introduction to Book I.

After the opening lines of invocation to light the poet develops the metaphors used first in Book I to express his nature and his relation to reader and argument:

> Thee I re-visit now with bolder wing,
> Escap't the *Stygian* Pool, though long detain'd
> In that obscure sojourn, while in my flight
> Through utter and through middle darkness borne
> With other notes then to th' *Orphean* Lyre
> I sung of *Chaos* and *Eternal Night*,
> Taught by the heav'nly Muse to venture down
> The dark descent, and up to reascend,
> Though hard and rare . . .
>
> (III.13–21)

The bird is a metaphor for the poet's double nature. Because a bird is a creature—mortal and limited—and because its song can have moral meaning only if that meaning is endowed from

---

[1] This allusion is discussed by J. Cope in 'Milton's Muse in *Paradise Lost*,' *Modern Philology*, LV (1957), 6–10.

a source outside itself, the bird can be a metaphor for the poet as fallen man, whose song must be inspired by the 'heav'nly Muse.' But because a bird is the one creature who can soar above the limits of man's experience and beyond the clouds obscuring his vision, the bird can serve also as a metaphor for the poet as inspired seer, whose song has the divine authority of prophecy. The pattern of these lines, the terrible descent and reascent of the bird's flight, recalls the pattern of loss and restoration in the first lines of the poem, which included in their circular syntax the history of Adam and of mankind, of the reader and of the poet.

In the next passage of the introduction to Book III, Milton develops his second and parallel metaphor for expressing the nature of the narrative voice. Here the image shifts from the poet as bird to the more elaborate and more moving metaphor of the poet as blind bard:

> . . . thee I revisit safe,
> And feel thy sovran vital Lamp; but thou
> Revisit'st not these eyes, that rowle in vain
> To find thy piercing ray, and find no dawn;
> So thick a drop serene hath quencht thir Orbs,
> Or dim suffusion veild. Yet not the more
> Cease I to wander where the Muses haunt
> Cleer Spring, or shadie Grove, or Sunnie Hill,
> Smit with the love of sacred song; but chief
> Thee *Sion* and the flowrie Brooks beneath
> That wash thy hallowd feet, and warbling flow,
> Nightly I visit: nor somtimes forget
> Those other two equal'd with me in Fate,
> So were I equal'd with them in renown,
> Blind *Thamyris* and blind *Maeonides*,
> And *Tiresias* and *Phineus* Prophets old.
>
> (III.21–36)

In these lines the pattern of descent and reascent, of loss and restoration, of departure and return is interrupted. The light 'Revisit'st *not*' the poet's eyes. 'Dawn,' the assurance of reascent, restoration, return is lost to him. His own light is 'quencht,' his vision 'dim' and 'veild'; and like the blind poets and prophets of old, he can 'find no dawn.' Yet despite his loss he retains his 'love of sacred song,' his dedication to poetry.

Like the man born blind in the Gospel according to John, he is
marked by blindness which is not a special curse on his wickedness but a sign 'that the works of God should be made manifest
in him' (John 9.3). Because he is afflicted with the more than
human suffering we associate with blindness, we feel him to be
capable of more than human profundities of experience. Because he can no longer see the colours and surfaces of things, we
feel him to have special powers of inner illumination which
penetrate the veils dimming out mortal vision.

Once Milton has elaborated these two metaphors for the
speaker-poet's role—the images of the bird and blind bard—he
fuses them in a single simile:

> Then feed on thoughts, that voluntarie move
> Harmonious numbers; as the wakeful Bird
> Sings darkling, and in shadiest Covert hid
> Tunes her nocturnal Note.
>
> (III.37–40)

When the speaker as blind poet compares himself here to a bird
whose song rises in the darkness from an unseen source, Milton
explicitly unifies the two metaphors as part of the total expression of the speaker-poet's nature. The fact that Milton himself
was blind must of course have partly determined his choice of
metaphors, and our knowledge of that fact gives added poignancy to these lines. But the habit in criticism of referring to
this and other passages about blindness as 'autobiographical'
(like the habit of referring to the speaker as 'Milton'), blurs
our awareness of the metaphorical function of the lines. The
language about blindness, vision, darkness, light is metaphorical
here (as it is in *Samson Agonistes* and indeed in *Areopagitica*,
written almost a decade before Milton's own loss of sight)[1]
in the same way that the language about birds, song, wings,
flight is metaphorical. Both images express the complex nature
of the narrative voice in the epic—the speaker-poet as limited
human creature whose vision was dimmed by the fall (just as
Satan's brightness was eclipsed by his sin and Adam's eyes were
darkened by disobedience) and the poet as inspired seer whose
divine illumination transcends the limits of mortal vision.

[1] See for example 'Areopagitica' in *The Student's Milton*, ed. by F. A.
Patterson (New York, 1947), pp. 733, 748, 750, 751, 752.

To see the way Milton exploits the metaphorical language about blindness, it is necessary to analyse the remaining passage of this epic introduction. In these lines Milton extends the metaphors developed in the passage until they include the total pattern of the poem—the cycle of loss and restoration announced in the opening sentence and expressed in the mood of its final lines:

> Thus with the Year
> Seasons return, but not to me returns
> Day, or the sweet approach of Ev'n or Morn,
> Or sight of vernal bloom, or Summers Rose,
> Or flocks, or herds, or human face divine;
> But cloud in stead, and ever-during dark
> Surrounds me, from the chearful waies of men
> Cut off, and for the Book of knowledg fair
> Presented with a Universal blanc
> Of Natures works to mee expung'd and ras'd,
> And wisdome at one entrance quite shut out.
> So much the rather thou Celestial light
> Shine inward, and the mind through all her powers
> Irradiate, there plant eyes, all mist from thence
> Purge and disperse, that I may see and tell
> Of things invisible to mortal sight.
>
> (III.40–55)

In this passage syntax and imagery work together in two contrasting sentences to express the double nature of the narrative voice. The first sentence is extended for ten lines through a long list of nouns, then a series of clauses and qualifying phrases, punctuated with many pauses. The second sentence is only five lines long, consisting of four imperatives marked by full stops and contained by the end-rhymes of 'light' and 'sight.' The contrasting syntax of these two sentences reinforces the contrasting images of light, and these images control the tone in which the narrative voice interprets to us his 'great Argument,' what man has lost and what he has gained.

The images of light in the first sentence describe the light which is now dark to the blind poet. They are images of the passing year, of the cycles of sunrise and nightfall, the seasonal changes of foliage and scenery. This simple, general, idealized language is deliberately conventional. The images of light falling on 'flocks' or 'herds,' on the 'Summers Rose' or the 'vernal bloom' are obviously intended to remind us of pastoral poetry, which traditionally celebrated the pagan myth of the simpler and purer world at the origins of our history, but they also refer us to passages elsewhere in *Paradise Lost* in which the narrative voice describes existence in the Garden of Eden.[1] Perhaps the most familiar of these passages is one in which the Garden is explicitly compared to the world of pastoral poetry:

> Thus was this place,
> A happy rural seat of various view;
> Groves whose rich Trees wept odorous Gumms and Balme,
> Others whose fruit burnisht with Golden Rinde
> Hung amiable, *Hesperian* Fables true,
> If true, here onely, and of delicious taste:
> Betwixt them Lawns, or level Downs, and Flocks
> Grasing the tender herb, were interpos'd,
> Or palmie hilloc, or the flourie lap
> Of som irriguous Valley spread her store,
> Flours of all hue, and without Thorn the Rose. . . .
>
> (IV.246–256)

Earthly Paradise is the pagan Golden Age once true, and the images in which the narrative voice describes it remind us specifically of those in the introduction to Book III. The day's cycle, from which the blind bard is cut off, here frames this first description of Eden:

> . . . the Sun
> Declin'd was hasting now with prone carreer
> To th' Ocean Iles, and in th' ascending Scale
> Of Heav'n the Starrs that usher Evening rose. . . .
>
> (IV.352–355)

The sentence in the introduction to Book III in which the speaker as blind bard describes the changing light of the seasons and the day refers us then to the world of the pagan Golden Age, the world of pastoral poetry, and also to his own descriptions of the Garden of Eden. Again and again in the poem Eden is described in images of the rotating light of sun, moon and stars, and Adam and Eve both repeatedly sing the praises of

[1] My indebtedness will be clear here and throughout the essay to ideas suggested by William Empson in *Some Versions of Pastoral* (Norfolk, Conn., n.d.), pp. 149–91.

sunrise and nightfall. To them before the fall, this cyclical pattern was an emblem of order, a cycle whose constant renewal was an assurance of permanence. The endless rotation of day and night told them that nothing in nature was lost or wasted, just as we are told that before the fall the bower of Adam and Eve 'Showrd Roses, which the Morn repair'd' (IV.773). But to the fallen reader and the fallen poet, the changing light of nature means what it means to Adam and Eve *after* the fall— that nothing in nature is permanent, that everything vulnerable is threatened and everything beautiful will fade, like the garland that Adam weaves for Eve which after her sin 'Down drop'd, and all the faded Roses shed' (IX.893).

The sense of loss shared by poet and reader from the beginning of the epic is experienced by Adam and Eve after the fall, when their minds become darkened like the poet's eyes, and they too are cut off from the Garden of Eden. The blind bard's lament for his personal loss of the world of pastoral nature is echoed by Eve when she first learns that she must be banished from her native home in Paradise:

> O unexpected stroke, worse then of Death!
> Must I thus leave thee Paradise? thus leave
> Thee Native Soile, these happie Walks and Shades,
> Fit haunt of Gods? where I had hope to spend,
> Quiet though sad, the respit of that day
> That must be mortal to us both. O flours,
> That never will in other Climate grow,
> My early visitation, and my last
> At Eev'n, which I bred up with tender hand
> From the first op'ning bud, and gave ye Names,
> Who now shall reare ye to the Sun, or ranke
> Your Tribes, and water from th' ambrosial Fount?
> Thee lastly nuptial Bowre, by mee adornd
> With what to sight or smell was sweet; from thee
> How shall I part, and whither wander down
> Into a lower World, to this obscure
> And wilde, how shall we breath in other Aire
> Less pure, accustomed to immortal Fruits?
>
> (XI.268–285)

The loss of innocence is the loss of Eden and the loss of Eden is the loss of the pastoral world. What was true of man's

experience before the fall has become merely a fable.[1] Adam and
Eve, like the fallen reader and the blind poet, are irrevocably
cut off from the light of Eden, the true pattern of pastoral nature,
and are forced to 'wander down' into the world of chance and
change, the world in which the reader and the blind poet now
live.

Yet if we are to understand how Milton would have us interpret their banishment and our own, we must remember that
in the epic introduction to Book III the speaker-poet contrasts
the lost light of Eden with a different kind of light. This is the
light of divine inspiration shining within the purified heart of the
blind bard, the light which is granted to him as fallen man when
he prays for divine illumination to purge the mists obscuring
his vision. It is a steadier light than the changing light of nature
and it enables the blind bard to see beyond the colours and surfaces of things. It is a celestial, not a mortal light. It can 'plant
eyes,' and that verb suggests a new creation of a new nature.
This is the light which gives authority to the voice of the blind
bard, granting him the power to 'see and tell / Of things invisible
to mortal sight.' It is the same illumination which is granted to
Adam and Eve at the end of the poem when they come to
realize that they must seek a 'Paradise within' them, happier
far. It is the light which enables Eve to see that the lost pastoral
world of Eden is less precious than the Eden within the soul. In
Book XII she is finally reconciled to her banishment from the
pastoral world, as the speaker-poet is reconciled to his blindness.
She expresses her acceptance when she says to Adam:

> . . . but now lead on;
> In mee is no delay; with thee to goe,
> Is to stay here; without thee here to stay,
> Is to go hence unwilling; thou to mee
> Art all things under Heav'n, all places thou. . . .
>
> (XII.614–618)

In the final passage of the epic introduction to Book III, the
contrasts of syntax and imagery help to create the complex tone
which characterizes the narrative voice. The tone of the last

[1] For a discussion of Milton's treatment of the legend of Eden as true
myth see I. G. MacCaffery, *Paradise Lost as 'Myth'* (Cambridge, Mass.,
1959), *passim*.

sentence assures us that the light which the blind bard has gained is better than the light he has lost because it is stronger, steadier, truer, because it illumines the mind with immortal vision. Yet the tone of the preceding sentence reminds us that this inner light is not gained without painful sacrifice, and that sacrifice is the loss of the sweetness and simplicity of nature's rotating light, the loveliness of the rose which bloomed perpetually and without thorns in the true pastoral world of Eden. The poet approves the sacrifice, as Eve is reconciled to her banishment, because the light which is gained illumines his prophetic song with the beauty of unwavering truth, but like Eve he mourns the loss, because the light which is lost had its own beauty and value, and he grieves that what is gained must be at the cost of so much pain and waste.

The voice which we hear in the epic introductions to Books I and III explicitly defines itself through the metaphors of the bird and the blind bard, metaphors sustained and elaborated in the introductions to Books VII and IX.[1] It is the voice which we hear throughout the narrative and descriptive passages of *Paradise Lost* and in the closing lines of the poem, and the complex tone created in these epic introductions is consistently characteristic of that voice.

This complexity of tone depends upon the fact that both poet and reader are involved in the epic argument, that we are made to interpret our own lost innocence by the light of our own experience in the fallen world. In the introduction to Book III, for example, or in Eve's lament for her banishment or in the descriptions of the Garden of Eden, our nostalgic feelings about the lost light of innocence are evoked not only by the lovely simplicity of the lines, but also by their references to the tradition of pastoral poetry. That tradition, although it celebrates the world of innocence which we and the poet have lost, belongs itself to the fallen world. The tradition of pastoral is the tradition of Hesperian fables, feigned by mortal imaginations, but because of the fall, the poet and the reader can only interpret Eden through these fables, unless their minds are illumined by the inner light.

Throughout the poem not only our longing for Eden and our sense of poignant loss, but still other attitudes and quite different

[1] See VII.3–4, 12–20, 27–30; IX.44–47.

emotions are evoked in us by the poet's references to the poetry
of the fallen world. In another passage from the introduction to
Book III, for example, the speaker associates himself with poets
and prophets of ancient renown:

> Blind *Thamyris* and blind *Maeonides*,
> And *Tiresias* and *Phineus* Prophets old.
>
> (III.35–36)

It is significant that he lists Greek rather than biblical names,
and it is significant that he describes his dedication to poetry
not only by the Old Testament reference to the waters of Sion,
but also in pagan imagery:

> Yet not the more
> Cease I to wander where the Muses haunt
> Cleer Spring, or shadie Grove, or Sunnie Hill,
> Smit with the love of sacred song. . . .
>
> (III.26–29)

Here the verb 'wander' does not suggest what it means in
Eve's lament for her banishment, the sense of being bereft and
aimless, lost without direction or guide. Here the verb 'wander'
suggests freedom and a rich variety of choices, the sense of
leisure to experience abundance. The same notion of a variety
of possible choices is suggested by the contrasts of 'shadie
Grove' or 'Sunnie Hill,' contrasts which a blind man could feel
as welcome coolness or warmth. This appeal to the senses, this
feeling of freedom and variety of choice is evoked in these lines
by the references to pagan poetry. Yet pagan poetry belongs
to the world in which the fallen reader and the blind poet *now*
move, not the world of innocence, the pastoral world once true,
which we lost when Adam and Eve were banished from Eden.
Here, and throughout *Paradise Lost*, the allusions to the fables
feigned by pagan poets evoke a sense of all the wealth of knowledge and feeling which has entered the world since Adam's
fall. By his disobedience we lost our original simplicity and
innocence, but we gained a multiplicity of choices; we gained
the beauty, the poignancy, and the variety of mortal experience.

This world in which we and the blind poet now live is presented to Milton's Adam in a vision only after the fall, but to
the reader it is always the ground from which he looks back at
the lost pastoral world of Eden. We know that we are con-

tinually meant to view the events of the poem from this lower world of chance and change because from the first lines the narrative voice repeatedly reminds us of our experience in this world. It is the fallen world which is the source of all the heroic similes, the negative comparisons, the literary allusions, the 'corporal forms' (v.573) by which the inspired poet helps us to envision things which since the fall are 'invisible to mortal sight.'

The tone which is controlled in part by these literary figures and allusions, the tone which characterizes the narrative voice throughout *Paradise Lost*, derives its complexity from paradox, the paradox expressed in the double nature of the bird and the blind bard. Just as the poet has been granted a truer vision in his blindness, and *because* he is blind, so Adam and Eve are granted what the Angel calls 'A Paradise within thee, happier farr' (xii.587) only *after* they have lost their first Paradise. So the reader can experience the abundance and variety of the fallen world— the source of image and allusion which gives the poem its richness and its scope—only after he has lost the true pastoral world, the innocence and simplicity of Eden. The tone implies that for the blind bard, for Adam and Eve, and for the reader, the world that is gained is more precious than what is lost, yet this implication is preserved from complacency by the awareness in the narrative voice of the terrible reality of the pain and loss, and also of the splendid precariousness of the freedom and variety of the fallen world.

This paradox, which is presented in the opening lines of the epic (what we lost by Adam's fall is restored by 'one *greater* Man'), is sustained by the narrative voice throughout the poem. Yet despite our continuous sense of the poet's complex tone, it is only at the end of the poem, only after we have *experienced* the events of the narrative which is a reenactment of our own spiritual history, that we can fully understand the paradox which the poet expresses from the beginning.

In Books xi and xii Adam is granted a vision of the future, which is the history of our fallen world. At first the vision seems only to increase his sense of horror and guilt, for he sees that his sin lets loose in the world an endless variety of diseases, vices, idolatries, and crimes which are paraded before his eyes. Yet when he sees as the fulfilment of history the redemption offered by Christ for man's sins (the redemption predicted to

the reader in the first epic introduction and explained in the
Council in Heaven of Book III), and sees the final restoration
of Paradise, his lament turns to joy and wonder:

> O goodness infinite, goodness immense!
> That all this good of evil shall produce,
> And evil turn to good; more wonderful
> Then that which by creation first brought forth
> Light out of darkness! full of doubt I stand,
> Whether I should repent me now of sin
> By mee done and occasiond, or rejoyce
> Much more, that much more good thereof shall spring,
> To God more glory, more good will to Men
> From God, and over wrauth grace shall abound.
>
> (XII.469–478)

Adam has here apprehended as a theological truth the paradox
that Eve has come to understand intuitively when she accepts
her banishment from Paradise because she recognizes the true
Eden within the soul. Just as without the fall there would have
been no occasion to demonstrate divine love in the redemption,
so without the knowledge of evil that sin brought to Adam and
Eve, they would never have learned the nature of good. The
theological paradox of *felix culpa* which Adam has apprehended
leads him to understand its ethical counterpart. His experience
of sin and his vision of its consequences enables him to recognize
the true nature of heroism:

> Greatly instructed I shall hence depart,
> Greatly in peace of thought, and have my fill
> Of knowledge, what this vessel can containe;
> Beyond which was my folly to aspire.
> Henceforth I learne, that to obey is best,
> And love with feare the onely God, to walk
> As in his presence, ever to observe
> His providence, and on him sole depend,
> Merciful over all his works, with good
> Still overcoming evil, and by small
> Accomplishing great things, by things deemd weak
> Subverting worldly strong, and worldly wise
> By simply meek; that suffering for Truths sake
> Is fortitude to highest victorie,
> And to the faithful Death the Gate of Life. . . .
>
> (XII.557–571)

The ethical paradox which this speech expresses, and its theological counterpart in Adam's earlier speech, provide the logic for Milton's justification of the 'wayes of God to men.'

But *Paradise Lost* is neither an ethical nor a theological treatise; nor is it a drama in which any verbal meanings must necessarily be presented in speeches by characters. It is an epic poem and its chief means of making us *feel* the paradox is through the tone of the narrative voice. The speaker-poet, whose double nature is revealed by the metaphors of the bird and the blind bard, has from the beginning shared 'our woe' at the same time that he has prophesied to us, and his prophetic song declares the great paradox that man's tragic fall brings his glorious redemption. This is the voice which speaks the closing lines of the poem and this the paradox which controls the tone of these lines:

> Som natural tears they drop'd, but wip'd them soon;
> The World was all before them, where to choose
> Thir place of rest, and Providence thir guide:
> They hand in hand with wandring steps and slow,
> Through *Eden* took thir solitarie way.
>
> (XII.645–649)

The speaker here is the blind bard—himself banished from Eden to a dark and painful world yet guided by celestial light through its abundance and variety. Here the word 'wandring' suggests again the sense of aimlessness and bewilderment that her banishment meant to Eve, when she feared to 'wander down' into the world of chance and change. Yet it also suggests the freedom and variety that the verb 'wander' earlier meant to the poet, cut off from the light of pastoral nature yet able to 'wander' in the abundant world of poetry. This second meaning is reinforced in these lines by the accented word 'all,' suggesting again variety and abundance, and the word 'choose,' endowing fallen man with the power to act and to discriminate.

This mingling of attitudes pervades the closing passage. Adam and Eve weep, and yet 'soon' find comfort and resolution. They are 'solitarie'—smaller, frail, and forlorn since the fall— and indeed they are the only people in the whole unknown world; yet they are 'hand in hand' again as before the fall, with a one-ness which in their affliction gains new dimensions of solace and responsibility.[1] They must leave the simplicity and loveliness of their home in Eden for a strange world which seems to them wild and dark, and yet they have a goal, which will bring them 'rest,' and a 'guide' which is the celestial light within them. We feel the world opening out before them, vaster, more complex, more dangerous than the Garden of Eden, and therefore richer in possibilities. We feel their loss of simplicity and innocence, and we never forget the greatness of that loss, yet we also feel their growth in self-knowledge and experience. We feel that they have lost the true pastoral world of Eden and entered the true heroic world of perilous yet glorious choice.

Our feelings are controlled here by the tone of the narrative voice, the mingling of attitudes which has characterized that tone from the opening of the epic. Yet these lines have a special quality. Almost as explicitly as the closing lines of *Lycidas*, they seem to reflect a change in the angle of vision. The speaker seems now at a greater distance from his subject. The figures seem to recede and grow smaller until we see them through his eyes as if framed in perspective. Like the speaker-poet in *Lycidas*, the blind bard has assimilated the events of his own 'great Argument,' made them part of his personal experience and the reader's. The story of the fall of Adam and Eve, by being reenacted in his epic, has become one with his own private loss, and their hopeful restoration includes the pattern of his own recovery. All the cycles in the poem of descent and reascent, loss and restoration, departure and return are fully and finally harmonized for the reader and for the poet in the tone of the closing lines, which conclude the song of the bird and the vision of the blind bard.

[1] The description of Adam and Eve walking 'hand in hand' has special weight at the end of the poem because before the fall they are almost always pictured either hand in hand or embracing (see for example IV.339, 488–89, 501, 689, 739, 771; V.27) while their disunity in sin is foretold by Eve's symbolic gesture of softly withdrawing her hand 'from her Husbands hand' (IX.385–86).

WILLIAM HALLER

The Tragedy of God's Englishman

I n the poem of graceful compliment and deft allusion which
he addressed to Manso at Naples in 1638, Milton expressed a
resolution to serve the muse in his cold northern clime by
composing a heroic poem about Arthur's war against the Saxons.
Again upon his return to England he said in his elegy for
Diodati that he intended to write such a poem on a British
theme. He would do for his own people what Tasso and Virgil
had done for theirs. Later, as if not yet decided on a subject, he
asked himself what king or knight before the conquest would
best serve. The result, if he had been a different kind of
character writing when times had changed, might have been
another neoclassic epic for future generations to leave unread.
Its subject might have been the legendary Brut fleeing like
another Aeneas to found another Rome in Britain or a legendary
Arthur triumphing over the Saxons like another Aeneas over
another Turnus. But Milton was what neoclassical poets
usually were not, a heroic poet of heroic temper with an
imagination seized upon by epic events in his own time. He
wrote no Arthuriad, but it was long before he gave up the idea
of a heroic poem expressing an exalted idea of England's
vocation and destiny, and his great poem when it finally came
still sprang from his early devotion to that theme, even though
in its final embodiment it turned out to be a tragedy.

What happened to the poet in Milton when he took up the

201

cause of revolution was that the literary Virgilian notion which had been occupying his thoughts of a Britain rising phoenix-like out of the ashes of Troy was not so much discarded as transfigured in his mind by that dream of a new Jerusalem rising on English ground which had haunted the English imagination ever since the accession of Elizabeth. That is to say, he embraced the idea that in scripture and history taken together there was revealed a purpose and a design which England was especially and instantly called upon to serve. What he wrote therefore in the crisis of 1640–41 was a statement of what he believed God's purpose and design for England to be, a history of what had been done and left undone to bring divine intention to fulfilment, a prescription of what now demanded to be done, and an announcement of the heroic poem which he intended to write when the process of history had reached the consummation now indicated to be imminent. But when Milton wrote his account of the English reformation, what did he actually know about the subject? Where did his information and point of view come from? What did he think the history of mankind was all about?

His early poems show of course an intimate acquaintance with the body of delightful legends which had come down through various channels with various accretions from Geoffrey of Monmouth, but he knew that these things were the stuff of poetry not of history. His academic exercises suggest that he had read some of the Roman and Greek historians before leaving Cambridge. He tells us that upon leaving Cambridge he undertook to read history from the beginning in the order of time. His antiprelatical tracts refer directly and indirectly to historians he had read by 1641, and this information is supplemented by entries in his *Commonplace Book*, most of them made after 1641. Finally we have the *History of Britain*, referring to particular sources and naming classical models of historical writing. We should not, however, base our idea of Milton's thinking about history chiefly on his *History of Britain*, and we should guard against a tendency to consider classical and humanist influences upon his thinking to the neglect of others less familiar or agreeable to our thinking. The fact is, Milton's first essay in the writing of history was not the *History of Britain* but *Of Reformation in England* and the succeeding tracts against prelacy, and not only the substance of the account there given of the history of the English reformation but the point of view come straight out of John Foxe's *Actes and Monuments*. That is to say, the view of history which governs Milton's thinking about the events in his own time is exactly in line with the view of history advanced by propaganda in support of the national settlement in church and state under Elizabeth, kept going by the increasing reaction against the policies of her successors, and revived with great effect by the puritan opposition to anglican prelacy in the Long Parliament.

Not everything that went to form the young Milton's mind came directly out of books, certainly not out of books agreeable to modern literary taste and religious prepossessions. Growing up in a protestant household within earshot of a dozen puritan pulpits in protestant London, Milton was exposed from childhood to the English protestant case against the claim of the Roman church to an authority derived from the church's founder and transmitted through an apostolic priesthood. The protestant answer to this claim was in essence an appeal to historical records which had been made more and more available both to the learned and to the general public by the advance of scholarship, translation and printing since Erasmus. But we must bear in mind that from the protestant point of view the historical record of unique authority was the scriptures. By that alone the validity of every other record and of every tradition was to be judged; anything contrary was to be rejected as corrupt; nothing additional was to be accepted as essential. The uniqueness of scriptural authority lay in the fact that in the scriptures as nowhere else history was authenticated by prophecy and prophecy was confirmed by history. Nothing had happened which had not been foretold; nothing had been foretold which had not come to pass or could not be expected to do so. History and prophecy taken together were the sum of revelation. It followed that the business of the historian was to discern and make known the providentially ordered process of events in time revealed for man's instruction in the record of things done and the promise of things to come. It was in a word to justify God's ways to man.

For the life of mankind was held to be governed by the same law as the life of every individual, and the history of mankind in general falls into the same pattern as the history of man in particular. Mankind begins by obeying God in innocence of heart. It falls to corruption, disobedience, and death. From death there would be no escape did not God in his own time and at his own choosing call some one man, some one family, some one company of men, some one nation, to be regenerated in spirit, to obey God, resist temptation, and live again, though always at the risk of falling again to corruption, disobedience, and death. But time in the Christian view of things, revived with special force in protestant thinking, does not as in classical tradition go on for ever repeating itself. Though the history of mankind like the history of every man is a story of recurring lapses and recoveries, the story is bound to come to an end. History moves through successive stages toward a foreseeable climax always impending as long as life endures. As it began with one original fall, containing within it every fall still to come, so it will end in a final advent, the summation of all the reentries of God's grace into the life of mankind since the beginning.

Holding to this view of history, Milton of course held to the belief that the form of church government as instituted by the apostles is set down for all to follow in the New Testament. But the question then arose, how and why did the church fall away from its original purity? This question dominated all Milton's thinking about history from this point on as it did that of all protestant reformers and historians, and it led him as it did others to attempt the critical testing of historical evidence, always subject to the primacy of scriptural authority. In his account of the history of the church, therefore, strange as it may seem from the point of view of the modern critical historian, he follows John Foxe, who was still for Englishmen with protestant convictions the standard authority on the subject. According to this view of the matter, the church's age of innocence had been brought to ruin by priests, prelates, and popes betraying their spiritual ministry in order to seek wealth and power in this world for themselves. To that end they either conspired with princes and emperors or usurped their authority. They promoted ignorance and superstition among the people, enthroned antichrist in the chair of Peter, and drove the true church out into the wilderness. Thus the war of Christ and antichrist which went on in the breast of every sinner went on also in the church and filled all history. It was however destined to come to an end. The Lord in his own good time would rouse up his saints for one last bout with Satan which would conclude in the final restoration of the true church. The pattern of this struggle was believed to be typified and forecast in the struggles of the chosen people of the Old Testament. Its course and outcome were foretold by the prophets and by John in his apocalyptical vision. And all this was confirmed by the known course of events in church and state from the beginning. The grand redemptive climax toward which all history moves was believed by protestants everywhere to have begun with the Reformation. English protestants at least since the time of Elizabeth were quite certain that the Reformation began in England with Wyclif, and it followed that in England it would be brought to its inevitable conclusion.

The English version of the protestant version of history was exploited endlessly by historians, pamphleteers, poets, and preachers in the reign of Elizabeth to make the English people understand the meaning of the national struggle with the catholic powers, and the victory over the Armada was hailed as its certain confirmation. But after the Armada the expected climax had not come off, not at any rate to the satisfaction of all those whose discontent had been more and more exacerbated by the policies pursued by Elizabeth's successors. Hence with the sudden collapse of royal authority puritan preachers, led by Milton's Smectymnuan associates, at once invoked the old familiar legend. In England antichrist was destined to meet his final doom. In England therefore he could be expected to put up his fiercest fight. But if parliament heeded the call voiced by the preachers, the long process of history could now be expected to come to an end with the final reformation of the church.

So we hear no more from Milton concerning a heroic poem about Arthur or some other legendary hero. The poet's imagination was filled with the expectation of the great new age now to be had for the achieving. But all speculation and discussion concerning the coming age still revolved about the scriptural theme and fable of the fall, representing the plight from which mankind was to be redeemed, and the visionary second coming and final triumph of the redeemer, expressing

the certainty of the redemption believed to be at hand. Instead
of an Arthuriad Milton planned a neoclassical tragedy on Adam
Unparadised along with a series of such works on subjects
drawn mostly from the Old Testament. Meanwhile we have
Milton in his role of pamphleteer declaring that, if the Lord
will only let his enemies come again to battle in England and
be broken, a poet will 'perhaps take up a Harp, and sing thee an
elaborate Song to Generations.'

In the meantime, however, parliament had to be made to
understand that the will of God, revealed in scripture and
history, was still directing events to their appointed end.
Divine purpose, having come thus far, was moving to its perfect
fulfilment in England, and the people of England, who had so
often before been chosen to be its instruments, were called to
be the agents of its next advance. After many dark ages, parliament was told, the Reformation had 'struck through the black
and settled night of ignorance and antichristian tyranny,' and
England had been appointed to 'set up a standard for the recovery of lost truth and blow the evangelic trumpet to the
nations.' All succeeding reformers had lit their tapers at the
light of Wyclif's kindling. Popes, prelates, and foreign tyrants
had done their utmost to stifle the light, but in Elizabeth's
time God had made a covenant with England, freed her from
bondage, built up this Britannic empire with all her daughter
islands about her, and scattered her enemy over the northern
ocean even to the frozen Thule. With all the world to choose
from, God 'hath yet ever had this island under the special
indulgent eye of his providence.' England was appointed by
heaven 'to give out reformation to the world.' Let her not
forget 'her precedence of teaching nations how to live.' It is
her people's glory and wonted prerogative to be 'the first
asserters of every great vindication.' 'Lords and commons of
England, consider what nation whereof ye are and whereof ye
are the governors.' Ancient philosophers, 'the school of
Pythagoras and the Persian wisdom took beginning from the
old philosophy of this island.' The emperor Agricola preferred
the native wits of the British to the laboured studies of the
French. Transylvanians come from the borders of Russia to
learn the English language and English theologic arts. And
now that God is once more decreeing 'some new and great

period in his church, . . . what does he then but reveal himself to his Englishmen; I say as his manner is, first to us.'

Thus Milton learned from his English protestant tradition that the English were a chosen people, elect above the rest. But we must not mistake what was meant by election. Only God, to be sure, could determine who was or was not to be saved, but it did not follow that those who believed themselves to be among the saved could rest in the assurance of grace. The saints were called to obey, and to obey meant to act, for only by acting or the readiness to act could the saints have or give assurance of their state of grace. A man having ability to write a poem or plead a cause must not hold back. A nation possessing power and opportunity to act against the enemies of Christ was required to do so, to accomplish the deeds preachers and pamphleteers were called upon to inspire, poets to celebrate, historians to record. This was the talent which was death to hide. The gift was vocation and vocation was command. But that was not all. The purpose of the command represented by the calling imposed and the gift entrusted could not possibly come to nought, whatever men and nations might or might not do. What God had covenanted with his saints to do was not in any circumstances to let them down. He would be faithful to his purpose. Let them be faithful too, and they could count on the co-operation of the inevitable.

If the final reformation of the church had been consummated according to Milton's expectation, the result would have been not simply the replacement of episcopalian by presbyterian government in the national church. Rather, church and state would have been fused into a holy community under the tutelage of the learned and the rule of the worthy. Those who ruled would maintain the freedom of those who taught. The teachers would ask nothing for themselves but freedom to learn and teach. The result would have been such 'a knowing people,' such 'a nation of prophets, of sages and of worthies,' as he urged upon parliament. The Virgilian phoenix-state would have been transfigured by the puritan New Jerusalem, while the New Jerusalem would have been humanized by Milton's ideal of the classical republic. If such a dream could have been brought to reality by the triumph of the puritan saints, he might have achieved the poem he promised to write at the height of his apocalyptical enthusiasm, a poem centred not on the tragic beginning but on the happy ending of history. But this was not to be. History does not usually turn out as intended. Revolutions have a way of moving faster and going farther in the wrong direction than their initiators anticipate, and Milton was nothing if not a man in a hurry. 'Certainly we ought to hie us from evil like a torrent, and rid ourselves of corrupt discipline as we would shake fire out of our bosoms.' He kept pressing loftier and loftier ideals to more and more impractical conclusions from which less extreme revolutionaries drew back in greater and greater trepidation while he condemned them as laggards and betrayers. The presbyterians, parliament, the chiefs of the army and the commonwealth, Cromwell himself, one after the other fell short. The revolution collapsed and counter-revolution succeeded. The people welcomed their tyrants back and re-embraced slavery. Thus antichrist did not meet his doom on English ground. God's Englishmen did not keep covenant with God.

Hence we have no epic of England trumpeting reformation to the nations or celebrating their triumph over the enemies of Christ. The poet does not question eternal providence, but his mind is now taken up with the terrible and mysterious fact of failure, with the agonizing problem of understanding how and why, seeing what men have it in them to conceive and be, they are what they are and do the things they do. The apocalyptic image of Christ's casting of antichrist out of heaven still holds the central place in his imagination, but in the poem on which he now lavishes his powers, he puts the war in heaven at the beginning of history not the end. It is the image not of the final interposition of grace in the life of mankind but of the fall from grace which sets the pattern for all that is to follow. And when it has served this purpose in Milton's version of man's external history, he makes it serve also as the image of his internal domestic tragedy. That is, man's first disobedience and its consequences now weighed more heavily upon Milton's imagination than Christ's ultimate victory. Adam, to be sure, gets assurance that the victory is certain to come some day, but the most moving and memorable scene at the conclusion of the poem is not that of the crushing of the serpent by the promised second Adam with wounds of head and heel but that of the actual Adam and his wife leaving their lost innocence behind them and entering upon the tragic process of human history.

Thus in *Paradise Lost* it is not Christ but Satan, not redemption but the fall, which most fully evokes Milton's powers as a poet, and this is still the case when in *Paradise Regained* he returns to the apocalyptical theme of Satan's overthrow. He sees in the temptation in the wilderness the image of the last judgment, and our response to his stark poem is what it is because, though we shrink from seeing ourselves in Satan, we cannot see ourselves in Milton's Christ. For what the poem does is to confront us with the implacable judgment of reason and conscience upon us all, who having been made to see and hear and know, have failed to heed. Christ in his role as judge gets the better of the argument, but we are not now lifted up in spirit to exultant anticipation of the far-off divine event.

The mood of *Paradise Lost* and *Paradise Regained* is still controversial and defensive. It is too soon after the defeat. He has not yet shaken off the pamphleteer. This is far less true of *Samson Agonistes*. There the pamphleteer has given over to the poet, and the poet sets forth not the substance of his case against the opposition but the essence of his own experience as actor and witness in the spiritual struggle of his age. The subject is still man's fall from grace, his betrayal of his vocation in the face of eternal providence commanding obedience. But the presentation of this theme is completely transposed to human and dramatic terms, and the emphasis is now upon recovery from defeat, triumph after fall. Eternal providence is asserted, God's ways are justified, as the fit outcome of a man's struggle to come to terms with the laws of his being, not as the conclusion of a debate between disputants contending for victory over his judgment. Samson is a hero in both the classic and the puritan sense. He is a mighty prince fallen from high estate through his defiance of necessity, but the necessity he had defied is the command laid upon him in his gift of strength. He is a Nazarite unto the Lord, called to smite the Lord's enemies and deliver his people from bondage. He has failed, and his tragedy lies in his own realization of his failure and the reason for it.

> Promise was that I
> Should Israel from Philistian yoke deliver;
> Ask for this great deliverer now, and find him
> Eyeless in Gaza at the mill with slaves,
> Himself in bonds under Philistian yoke.

For he knows that the cause of his own undoing is not anything outside himself. It was not Dalila, though her presence in the story does not fail to provoke the poet to another outcry against that particular aspect of the mystery of iniquity represented by woman in the life of mankind. In spite of all that she is and that she has done,

> She was not the prime cause, but I myself
> Who, vanquished with a peal of words (O weakness!)
> Gave up my fort of silence to a woman.

Nor does Samson's remorse arise from the fact that Israel is still enslaved; Israel's fate is Israel's doing and its redemption its own affair. Every man and every nation is the author of its own fall, and he himself, the elect of God, entrusted with power to fulfil divine intention, has profaned the mystery of his calling and in betraying his gift has betrayed himself.

> I God's counsel have not kept, his holy secret
> Presumptuously have published, impiously,
> Weakly at least, and shamefully.

Thus in Samson's fall Milton expresses his feeling concerning the human experience he had been a part of, the self-defeat of God's Englishman. Yet he has now risen above the mood of defeat. The irrepressible, tough, resilient arrogance of spirit which so often repels us in Milton the revolutionary pamphleteer here comes to full poetic expression. The fall of the hero is the spring of the action; defeat is the condition of recovery and triumph. The gift was nothing in itself:

> God when he gave me strength, to show withal
> How slight the gift was, hung it in my hair.

The intention behind the gift is all that matters, and any action which makes toward the achievement of that intention is already victory. Hence, having learned to sink his own will in the divine will, he recovers his strength to perform the act which God is in covenant not to let fail of its intent.

Samson seems a far different sort of hero from the Arthur who engaged Milton's imagination thirty years before. Nevertheless in *Samson Agonistes* Milton may surely be said to have accomplished something like the ambition he announced to Manso at Naples, to write a heroic poem for his fellow-countrymen on a heroic theme drawn from their own history. The fable came to be sure from the scriptures, but it was a fable which came closer home to the Englishmen of his time than anything he might have drawn from Geoffrey of Monmouth or the chronicles. And having written the poem he intended to write, he went back to pamphleteering against the old enemy in the old vein. Good men, he says, in the last work which so far as we know came from his pen, rejoice 'that God hath giv'n a heart to the people to remember still their great and happy deliverance from Popish thraldom, and to esteem so highly the precious benefit of his gospel.' And since others have begun once more to contend against the encroachments of the adversary, 'I thought it no less than a common duty to lend my hand, how unable soever, to so good a purpose.'

HERBERT DAVIS

The Augustan Conception of History

ERNST CASSIRER has maintained in *The Philosophy of the Enlightenment* that 'the common opinion that the eighteenth century was an "unhistorical" century, is not and cannot be historically justified.' For, he continues 'it was the eighteenth century which raised the central philosophical problem in this field of knowledge. It inquires concerning the "conditions of the possibility" of history, just as it inquires concerning the conditions of the possibility of natural science.' And he goes on to point out that all great historical works of the eighteenth century in France and in England were written under the influence of Voltaire's philosophical achievement, in formulating 'an original and independent conception, a new methodological plan, for which he paves the way in his *Essay on Manners.*'[1] But though in France the beginnings of this movement can be traced back into the seventeenth century—at least to the work of Bayle, who planned his *Critical Dictionary* in 1690—yet in England, in spite of the work of the antiquaries and the writers of memoirs, Hume could say in 1753 'that there is no post of honour in the English Parnassus more vacant than that of history.' This remark is justified by Godfrey Davies in an essay on Hume,[2] which begins by quoting a number of examples of

[1] *The Philosophy of the Enlightenment* (Princeton, Princeton Univ. Press, 1951), pp. 197, 200.

[2] *Elizabethan and Jacobean Studies, presented to F. P. Wilson* (Oxford, Clarendon Press, 1959), pp. 231–34.

the contemptuous comments made on English historians by Augustan critics and satirists. And it would not be difficult to add to the number.

Nevertheless I hope to show that these very remarks of the critics and satirists indicate a real concern with the matter of writing history, and that we may find plenty of other material in the works of the Augustans to reveal to us their conception of its character and purpose. And I should claim that their constant preoccupation with the function of history, their study of classical and French and Italian historians, their ability to appeal to an audience who would understand their references to persons and events in classical history as parallels to guide their judgments in current political controversies—all this contributed more than is generally realized to the achievement of the great historians of the second half of the century.

Hume was not the first to notice the empty place in the English Parnassus. From early in the seventeenth century the unworthiness and deficiencies of English history had been commented on, by Bacon, Hayward, and Raleigh,[1] and the standards by which such criticisms were made had remained pretty well the same from the sixteenth to the eighteenth century. What men looked for was the kind of history they were familiar with in their reading of Greek and Latin authors; they were waiting for an English Plutarch or Thucydides, a Livy or a Tacitus. Under the Tudors and the Stuarts however it was still dangerous to write history, as men like Hayward and Raleigh were well aware: 'who-so-ever in writing a moderne Historie, shall follow truth too neare the heeles, it may haply strike out his teeth.' But after the Revolution of 1688, and after the removal of restrictions on the press, it must have seemed that the time was ripe for an English historian to appear. Yet we still find Sir William Temple, in 1695, lamenting 'that so ancient and noble a Nation as ours . . . so adorned by excellent Writers in other Kinds, should not yet have produced one good or approved general History of England.'[2]

To encourage some worthy spirit to undertake this task

---

[1] See D. Nichol Smith, *Characters of the Seventeenth Century* (Oxford, Clarendon Press, 1918), pp. xi–xv.

[2] *An Introduction to the History of England* (London, 1695), Preface, A2.

Temple published in that year *An Introduction to the History of England*, which breaks off abruptly at the end of the first Norman reign. Eight years later, after he had finished editing Temple's *Miscellanies*, Swift set to work to continue the history; but he soon abandoned it for more exciting tasks, as he explains in a letter to the Count de Gyllenborg, dated November 2, 1719:

It is now about sixteen years since I first entertained the design of writing a History of England, from the beginning of William Rufus to the end of Queen Elizabeth; such a History, I mean, as appears to be most wanted by foreigners, and gentlemen of our own country; not a voluminous work, nor properly an abridgment, but an exact relation of the most important affairs and events, without any regard to the rest. . . .

I was diverted from pursuing this History, partly by the extreme difficulty, but chiefly by the indignation I conceived at the proceedings of a faction, which then prevailed. . . . I publish them now . . . for an encouragement to those who have more youth, and leisure, and good temper than I, towards pursuing the work as far as it was intended by me, or as much further as they please.[1]

When Temple speaks of the nation not having produced an approved account of its history, and when Swift speaks his intention to supply what 'appears to be most wanted by foreigners, and gentlemen of our own country,' it is evident that their conception of history is somewhat narrow and traditional. It is very different from that of Bayle, who demands that the historian should be

like Melchizedech, without father, without mother, and without genealogy. If he is asked; 'Whence art thou?' he must reply: 'I am neither a Frenchman nor a German, neither an Englishman nor a Spaniard, etc.; I am a citizen of the world; I am not in the service of the Emperor, nor in that of the King of France, but only in the service of Truth. She is my queen; to her alone have I sworn the oath of obedience.'[2]

---

[1] *The Prose Works of Jonathan Swift*, ed. by Temple Scott (London, 1902), X, 195.

[2] Quoted by Cassirer, p. 209.

Swift, as we know, would have had no compunction about accepting the office of Historiographer Royal, in which he would have implicitly sworn an oath of obedience to Queen Anne. His attitude at that time is abundantly clear from the words he used in presenting to the Lord Treasurer his *Proposal for correcting, improving and ascertaining the English Tongue*:

[it] would very much contribute to the Glory of her Majesty's reign; which ought to be recorded in Words more durable than Brass, and such as our Posterity may read a thousand Years hence, with Pleasure as well as Admiration.[1]

Indeed the main argument for his project is that the memories of princes and their chief ministers can only be preserved 'by the pens of able and faithful historians'; and yet, even if one appeared with a genius for history, equal to the best of the ancients, what likelihood would there be of his taking up the task, when he considered that in an age or two he would hardly be understood without an interpreter.

Even those who can find no evidence in Swift's work that he had any genius for history must admit that he was very much preoccupied with the subject, had carefully studied both classical and modern historians, and had made great efforts to leave behind a record of the last years of the Queen's reign. And when he had finished that task, he claims that he 'had no other bias than my own opinion of persons and affairs' and that he had been under no obligation to the Crown or any of the Ministers. In the opening paragraph of his *History* he states what he believes the function of the historian to be.

Although in an Age like ours I can expect very few impartial Readers; yet I shall strictly follow Truth, or what reasonably appeared to me to be such, after the most impartial Inquiries I could make, and the best Opportunityes of being informed by those who were the principal Actors or Advisers. Neither shall I mingle Panegyrick or Satire with an History intended to inform Posterity, as well as to instruct those of the present Age, who may be Ignorant or Misled: Since Facts truly related are the best Applauses, or most lasting Reproaches.[2]

[1] *The Prose Writings of Jonathan Swift*, ed. by Herbert Davis (Blackwell, Oxford), IV, 17.

[2] *Ibid.*, VII, 1–2.

Here is the appeal to truth, in so far as it may be revealed to the individual judgment; and the declaration of a double purpose so characteristic of the Augustan Age—to bring the light of reason to those who sit in darkness, and to leave a record for the enlightenment of posterity.

The conception of history as a study of the utmost importance for all those who might be in any way concerned with public affairs, and as a literary art of which many noble examples had been left by the Greeks and the Romans, was firmly established in England before the close of the sixteenth century. It was Sir Henry Savile who had written in 1591, in the preface to his translation of Tacitus, that 'there is no learning so proper for the direction of the life of man as Historie.'[1] And from his time there had been established in England as well as in France and Italy a tradition of historical studies. The Camden Readership in Ancient History, for instance, was founded in Oxford in 1622, and the first incumbent, Degory Whear, published his lectures, *De Ratione et Methodo legendi Historias dissertatio*, in 1623. These were enlarged and reached a fifth edition in 1684, and after that there were three further editions in an English translation, with the title *The Method and Order of Reading History*, before the end of the century.

In a work which appeared in 1695, the theory and practice of the ancients, and particularly the Latin historians, the natural mentors of the Augustans, were described by the French Jesuit Pierre LeMoine under the title *Of the Art Both of Writing and Judging of History, with Reflections upon Ancient as well as Modern Historians, Shewing through what Defects there are so few Good, and that it is impossible there should be any so much as Tolerable*. Here we may find conveniently brought together many of the classical common-places which were the foundation of the Augustan conception of history; and we may perhaps detect in some of the expressions introduced into the English translation their transformation into the very manner and accent of the Augustans: 'History, according to Cicero, is the Director of Manners, and the Mistress of Life . . .'; or, 'History is a kind of Civil Philosophy, and her proper Office is to instruct the *present* by the *past.*' But it has also another function, according

[1] Quoted by D. Nichol Smith (p. xx), who also drew my attention to the lectures of Degory Whear.

to Tacitus, 'of shewing the Rod to Tyrants, and advertising them of the Punishment she prepares. . . . Their future Fame keeps them more in awe than their Conscience.'[1] From this it follows that the historian must be capable of judgment. He need not be a minister of state or a great commander, but he must be a 'man of wit,' with proper standards of truth and virtue.

If we examine some of the statements in which this duty of judging is discussed, we shall find that the distinction between the historian and the wit or satirist, who exercises his judgment in commenting on the contemporary scene, tends to become blurred. Such a passage as this, for example, would surely have been accepted by Pope and Swift as indicating their function as critics of society and justifying their satirical portraits of their enemies:

Judgment follows the Narration of things . . . and this, though the least in *Mass*, ought not to be the least in *Wit*. 'Tis here the knowledge of Good and Evil must be unfolded; the Politick and Moral have their Place; that Virtue is crown'd and Vice punished; that the Historian (hardly otherwise more than a *Tale-teller*) becomes a *Statesman* and a *Soldier*; makes himself *Judge* of *Princes* and their Ministers; and Arbitrator of their good and evil Actions: 'Tis here he gives Instructions and Counsels, Degrees of Honour and Infamy, establishes a School for the time to come, and a Tribunal for the past.[2]

And again, they would certainly have approved the claim, alike for the historian and the satirist, that it is his duty

to be as free in declaring the Vices as Virtues of great Persons: He is Judge, and Judgment reaches the Bad as well as the Good: His Function is a publick Witness, and 'tis the part of a Witness to conceal nothing. And in fine, 'Tis the publick Interest, that great Men and Princes to whom the *Laws* are but *Cobwebs*, should have some Bridle to stop them. And to a People that take *Religion* for a *Fantasm*, and *Hell* for a *Bugbear* to frighten Children, we cannot propose any thing stronger, than the *Eternal Infamy* is prepared for them in *History*.[3]

[1] Pierre LeMoine, *Of the Art of History* (Eng. trans., London, 1695), pp. 28, 32.

[2] *Ibid.*, p. 117.

[3] *Ibid.*, p. 110.

In this sense Swift could claim that he was fulfilling the most important duty of a historian in what are generally regarded as his Tory tracts for the times. For in his role as Examiner he assumes this very function as a public witness against those political leaders, whose crimes were exempt from any other punishment:

whereby those whom neither Religion, nor natural Virtue, nor fear of Punishment, were able to keep within the Bounds of their Duty, might be with-held by the Shame of having their Crimes exposed to open View in the strongest Colours, and themselves rendered odious to Mankind.[1]

And so it is quite natural in prosecuting his case for him to carry his appeal further, and to summon his victim not merely to appear before a tribunal of his peers, but to convict him before the bar of history by transforming him, so that the English Duke is changed into the likeness of a Roman Emperor (as in his Letter to Crassus); or by himself assuming the mantle of Cicero and attacking the Earl of Wharton in the very terms of condemnation borrowed from the impeachment of Verres.[2] And even when he impatiently throws off his borrowed robes and confesses that the show had not been worth the pains he took over it, Swift still appeals to history when he maintains that he can find nothing to his purpose in Roman history or oratory, since 'modern Corruptions are not to be paralleled by ancient Examples.'

Pope expresses the other side of this—the possibility of an appeal from the judgment of one's own generation to the ulti-mate verdict of posterity, and the responsibility of the historian as a witness—in his letters to Atterbury: 'I congratulate not you only, but Posterity, on this Noble Defence. I already see in what Lustre that Innocence is to appear to other Ages.' And in his farewell letter he points out that Atterbury has now an opportunity, like Tully and Bacon and Clarendon, to achieve his greatest triumph in this latter, disgraced part of his life:

At this time, when you are cut off from a little society and made a citizen of the world at large, you should bend your talents not to serve a Party, or a few, but all Mankind. . . . Remember it

[1] *Swift*, ed. by Davis, III, 141.
[2] *Ibid.*, pp. 83–85, 27–29.

was at such a time, that the greatest lights of antiquity dazled and blazed the most; in their retreat, in their exile, or in their death: . . . it was then that they did good, and they gave light, and that they became Guides to mankind.[1]

Pope and Swift would have been less ready to accept some of the restrictions which LeMoine wished the historian to observe, though he also refers to the example of such Latin historians as Sallust, Livy, and Tacitus, who when writing of the vices of men 'seem to blush for Human Kind, and their Words as a Veil cover their Shame as much as possible.' LeMoine recommends Christian writers to imitate their tact and discretion, and adds further warnings to the historian against prying into things that are better left hidden, and forgetting the distinction between what is private and what is public.

If the Church herself to whom the Son of God committed the Keys, assumes not the Authority of opening what is shut, and judging of hidden things, much less ought it to be allowed History. Since the Perfection of a Civil Life is the end where his Labours tend, he must expose nothing to the publick View that has not regard to it, must therefore abstain from all sorts of Scandalous Relations, as are those that serve but to make People lose the Respect they owe their Prelates and Princes, the Hierarchy, Church and publick Government; and gives way to Heresies, Revolts and Schisms, both in Church and State.[2]

His remarks upon the style suitable for history are borrowed from Aristotle and Cicero, though he adds arguments of his own justifying the grand manner because of the dignity of the subject and the audience for whom the historian writes:

She is designed to instruct the Great; and the Governour of a Prince ought to be otherwise cloathed than a Petty School-master: . . . If a man can but crawl upon the Earth, and work in little, let him leave to others History . . . and satisfie himself as much as he pleases with writing *Chronicles* and *Legends*.

The style of the historian must be pure; there must be no mixture of various styles. It must be clear; the words must be all intelligible and placed in proper order. It must be concise;

---

[1] *Correspondence of Pope*, ed. by George Sherburn (Oxford, Clarendon Press, 1956), II, 169–70.

[2] LeMoine, p. 114.

there must be no unnecessary verbiage, for 'History is a Structure, she demands Order and Connexion.'[1]

LeMoine would have condemned Burnet for his style alone, as Swift did in his comments on the *History of his Own Time*, with its 'silly coffee-house chatter' and 'pretty jumping periods.' It lacked the dignity and propriety required for the writing of history: 'His style is rough, full of improprieties, in expressions often Scotch, and often such as are used by the meanest people.'[2]

But he would have found all the dignity and splendour, all the qualities of style he demanded—except perhaps brevity—in that great book, which was first published in 1704 and must have found its way into every library throughout the land as it continued to be reprinted, Clarendon's *History of the Rebellion*. And he would also have found a structure with order and connexion, the work of a mind enriched by a wide experience of men and affairs and ready to give judgment upon them; an example of a tradition recognized by Pope when he brings together so naturally in a phrase the names of Tully and Bacon and Clarendon. The adornments of the three tall folio volumes, 'printed at the Theater in Oxford,' engravings of classical and mythological figures symbolizing truth and justice, fame and inspiration, and the magnificent frontispiece showing the author in his high dignity as the late Lord High Chancellor of England, lend splendour to the work. There is no attempt to hide the author's place in the events he describes, his loyalty to the crown, his natural desire to vindicate the royal cause. The reader is warned in the Preface that he will meet with many passages that

may disoblige the Posterity of even well-meaning Men in those Days; much more then of such as were crafty, cunning, and wicked enough to design the mischiefs that ensued: But he shall meet with none of Malice, nor any but such as the Author, upon his best information, took to be Impartially true. He could not be ignorant of the Rules of a good Historian (which, Cicero says, *are such foundations, that they are known to every body*) That he should not dare to speak any Falsehood; and should dare to speak any Truth. . . . and we hope that the

---

[1] *Ibid.*, p. 202.
[2] *Swift*, ed. by Temple Scott, X, 327.

representing the Truth . . . will be received rather as an Instruction to the present Age, than a Reproach upon the last.[1]

In the opening sentence of his history the author likewise proclaims in Ciceronian periods his intention and his purpose:

That Posterity may not be Deceived by the prosperous Wickedness of those times of which I write, into an Opinion that nothing less than a general Combination, and universal Apostacy in the whole Nation from their Religion and Allegiance, could, in so short a Time, have produced such a total and prodigious Alteration, and Confusion over the whole Kingdom; And, that the Memory of those, who, out of Duty and Conscience, have opposed that Torrent, which did overwhelm them, may not lose the recompense due to their Virtue, but, having undergone the injuries and reproaches of This, may find a vindication in a better age:[2]

Above all else, he wishes to contribute somewhat to the blessed end of binding up the wounds left by those divisions 'to make the future Peace not less pleasant and durable.' And therefore he promises to preserve himself 'from the least sharpness that may proceed from private provocation, and in the whole, observe the rules that a man should, who deserves to be believed.'

He does not claim the impartiality of the judge, much less the impersonality of the scientific historian. He is the vindicator of a cause, the pleader for the defence. His appeal is to the judgment of posterity. But he does claim to give a fair account; and he quotes largely from documents and speeches, so that the chief characters of the drama may condemn or justify themselves out of their own mouths. He could have reminded us that he did not begin to write his history until his own public career had ended in failure and exile, when he must have felt some resentment against the royal master he had served so well and some bitterness against those at the court who had helped to bring about his fall. But his misfortunes seem rather to have led him to idealize the memories of youth, especially those twelve years of Charles I's reign, before the Long Parliament, when

this Kingdom . . . enjoy'd the greatest Calm, and the fullest

[1] Clarendon, *History of the Rebellion* (Oxford, 1704), I, iii.
[2] *Ibid.*, p. 3.

measure of Felicity, that any People in any Age, for so long time together, have been bless'd with; to the wonder, and envy of all the other parts of *Christendom.* . . .

In a word, many Wise men thought it a Time, wherein those two Adjuncts, which Nerva was Deified for uniting, *Imperium & Libertas*, were as well reconciled, as is possible.[1]

Swift was also to describe this period as 'the highest period of Politeness in England,' but he could not acccept it as a time of political liberty. He underlines 'Libertas' and writes in the margin 'Nego.' Later in 1733, when writing *The Presbyterian's Plea of Merit*, he remembers this passage and explains why he did not agree that there was no thought until 1640 of making any alteration in religion or government:

I have found, by often rumaging for old Books in *Little Britain* and *Duck-Lane*, a great Number of Pamphlets printed from the Year 1630 to 1640, full of as bold and impious railing Expressions against the lawful Power of the Crown, and the Order of Bishops, as ever were uttered during the Rebellion, or the whole subsequent Tyranny of that Fanatic Anarchy.[2]

But the real glory of that felicity did not consist for Clarendon in the balancing of any adjuncts such as sovereign rule and freedom, rather in the full flowering of a rich and noble humanity. It is perhaps not too much to say that in this he saw the full tragedy of the Rebellion, that it had destroyed this felicity. He wrote his history to leave for posterity a record of the values that had been lost, and perhaps in the hope of showing the way in which they might be recovered.

It can hardly have been without deliberate intention that he placed in the centre of his great work a portrait of Lord Falkland as the symbol of that moment of felicity at this high point of English life and culture, the ideal of what the statesman, courtier, soldier, and scholar should be, whose loss early in the conflict is its tragic climax, when that fair spirit which could alone have triumphed over the angry passions of the opposing forces was destroyed. For he does not hesitate to interrupt his narrative, and to draw our attention with all the eloquence at

---

[1] *Ibid.*, pp. 58, 60.
[2] *Swift*, ed. by Davis, XII, 264.

his command, as he approaches the performance of what he regards as the highest duties of a historian:

If the celebrating the memory of eminent and extraordinary Persons, and transmitting their great Virtues, for the imitation of Posterity, be one of the principal ends and duties of History, it will not be thought impertinent, in this place, to remember a loss which no time will suffer to be forgotten, and no success or good fortune could repair.

And then he devotes himself to the task of describing the unparalleled goodness and virtue of Falkland:

A Person of such prodigious Parts of Learning and Knowledge, of that inimitable sweetness and delight in Conversation, of so flowing and obliging a humanity and goodness to Mankind, and of that primitive simplicity and integrity of Life, that if there were no other brand upon this odious and accursed Civil War, than that single loss, it must be most infamous, and execrable to all Posterity.[1]

I find it satisfying to observe that one of his most sceptical Augustan readers falls completely under his spell, and cannot read through these pages without deep emotion; for when he comes to the last sentence, Swift pencils in the margin these words: 'It moves grief to the highest Excess.'

It must be admitted that Swift is equally approving when in his rather old-fashioned manner Clarendon on another occasion describes the miserable end of the ungodly John Pym, 'who died with great Torment and Agony of a disease unusual, and therefore the more spoken of, *Morbus pediculosus*, as was reported'; for he adds this comment: 'I wish all his clan had dyed of the same disease.'[2] We are still not very far from Fuller's *Holy and Profane State*, with the virtuous characters followed by studies of their opposites; and that this remained a popular taste well into the eighteenth century is evident from the publication of a curious popularization of Clarendon's *History* by Ned Ward in 1713, in three volumes, entitled *The History of the Grand Rebellion etc. together with the Impartial Characters of the most*

[1] Clarendon, II, 270.
[2] *Ibid.*, 353.

*Famous and Infamous Persons, for and against the Monarchy.
Digested into Verse. Illustrated with about a Hundred Heads, of
the Worthy Royalists and other Principal Actors; drawn from the
Original Paintings of* Vandike, An. More, Dobson, Cor.
Johnson, *and other eminent Painters; and Engrav'd by the best
modern Artists etc.* He explains that he had first begun to collect
the portraits as illustrations for those who had purchased Clarendon's *History,*

that the World might behold a lively Representation of those
dead Worthies, whose Images ought, for their Love and
Loyalty to their King and Country, to remain imprinted, for
ever, in the Minds of Posterity; also, that the Curious might be
acquainted with the rigid Countenances of the mouldering
Incendiaries of those bleeding Times, and observe what a
Sympathy or Analogy there seems to be between their Looks
and Actions.[1]

Then he decided that it would be more useful if a 'Chain of the
History' done in verse were added, to give a very brief résumé
of Clarendon's very copious observations. The character of the
verse is not unfairly represented by the lines referring to the
above account of the death of John Pym:

> Still rushing on till Heav'n stop'd his speed,
> And with a loathsome Evil struck him dead,
> That e're he perish'd, as he lay and mourn'd,
> His Sins, his Flesh was into Vermin turn'd,
> That his best Friends could neither bear the smell
> Or sight of such an odious Spectacle.

Here is history in its most naïve form, turned to moral tales of
good and bad men, with a little tag at the end of each portrait
so that its significance cannot be overlooked:

> Therefore if Men who ruffle humane peace,
> Would call to mind such Instances as these,
> They'd stop their wicked course, no further run,
> But tremble and repent the Ills they've done.[2]

But history had always been regarded also as the source
of valuable political experience; the sermons and the political

[1] Ward, *History of the Grand Rebellion* (London, 1713), I,ii–iii.
[2] *Ibid.,* p. 169.

pamphlets of the seventeenth century had drawn on the minutest details of Old Testament history to show how God had dealt with his people, and to draw suitable conclusions for the present times. And the Augustans were but following the same method in finding parallels in the histories of Greece and Rome. Swift provides a good example of this in an early work published in 1701, *A Discourse of the Contests and Dissensions between the Nobles and the Commons in Athens and Rome; with the Consequences they had upon both those States.* He is concerned with the problem of the balance of power in all forms of government; he gives a chapter to the dissentions in Athens between the few and the many, and another to the dissentions between the Patricians and the Plebeians in Rome, and then some examples of popular impeachments. These chapters contain only a discussion of certain abstract problems of government illustrated with suitable examples. Then he continues:

Some Reflections upon the late publick Proceedings among us, and that Variety of Factions, in which we are still so intricately engaged, gave Occasion to this Discourse. I am not conscious that I have forced one Example, or put it into any other Light than it appeared to me, long before I had Thoughts of producing it. . . .

I cannot possibly see, in the common Course of Things, how the same Causes can produce different Effects and Consequences among us, from what they did in *Greece* and *Rome*.[1]

The same appeal to the details of ancient history is repeated again and again in the journal and pamphlets of the period. The historians are appealed to and are used as familiarly as the poets, whose works had become known to a wide audience through the translations of Dryden and Pope. And when the poets writing in English seemed to be vying with Virgil and Horace the question was bound to be asked—why not an English Tacitus or Livy? In a letter to Pope on February 18, 1723–24, written from France, Bolingbroke has this in mind, but though it is clear enough what kind of history he is looking for, he is quite certain that it is not yet to be found in English:

Eloquence and History are God knows, at the lowest ebb imaginable among us. The different Stiles are not fix'd, the

[1] *Swift*, ed. by Davis, I, 228, 236.

Bar and the Pulpit have no Standard, and our Historys are Gazettes ill digested, & worse writ. The case is far otherwise in France and in Italy. Eloquence has been extreamly cultivated in both Countrys, and I know not whether the Italians have not equall'd the Greeks and the Romans in writing History. Guicciardine seems to me superior to Thusidides on a Subject still more complicated than that of the Peloponesian war, and perhaps the vastness of the undertaking is the principal advantage which Livy has over Davila.[1]

He naturally considered the possibility of filling this role himself, and in his letter to Pope the following August he tells him that he is occupied not with writing his own memoirs—'the Subject is too slight to deserve to descend to Posterity in any other manner than by that occasional Mention which will be made in the History of our Age'—but with preparations for a larger project, of which he sends a sketch, afterwards published as a 'Plan for a General History of Europe.' He proposed to make the beginning of his study the great scene at the opening of the century, after a preliminary introduction which would give a summary account of the events which followed the Pyrenean Treaty, and led to the Treaty of Ryswick in 1697. From then on he felt the task would be easier:

I think I could speak . . . with some knowledge, and with as much indifference, as Polybius does of the Negociations of his Father Lycortas, even in those points where I was myself an Actor. I will even confess to you that I should not despair of performing this part, better than the former.

But for our present purpose the most interesting remark in his letter is his attempt to describe what he considers the most difficult task of the historian, which the ancients had never done well, and which he had found most successfully carried out by Machiavelli and Father Paul, among the moderns. For here he may be said to introduce a new dimension into the conception of the task of a historian—something different from the business of narration, comment, and judgment on men and events—the need for discovering and tracing a pattern, giving a shape to the course of affairs:

[1] *Correspondence of Pope*, II, 220.

There is nothing in my opinion so hard to execute as those Political Maps, if you will allow me such an Expression, and those Systems of hints rather than Relations of Events, which are necessary to connect and explain in them and which must be so concise and yet so full, so complicate and yet so clear. It is Natures Master-piece in the most difficult kind of Writing; . . .[1]

Bolingbroke's historical masterpiece was never written, but he used some of the materials he had prepared in his *Letters on the Study and Use of History*, the first of which was dated from Chantelou in Touraine, November 6, 1735, though not published until 1752, after his death. They are not marked by any great originality, they are not even influenced by what Voltaire had already written, nor do they indicate any recognition of the importance of his work; they may therefore be taken as representing ideas about history which had been current among the Augustans, and must serve here to provide the last piece of evidence.

Though careful to warn us against the danger of applying particular examples in particular cases, he is still content to quote such commonplaces as 'history is philosophy teaching by examples how to conduct ourselves in all the situations of private and public life.' He still maintains likewise that the aim of the historian must be to instruct posterity by the examples of former ages, and to reveal all the possibilities of human nature. The interest must be centred upon the deeds and the characters of men:

Man is the subject of every history; and to know him well, we must see him and consider him, as history alone can present him to us. . . . All history that descends to a sufficient detail of human actions and characters, is useful to bring us acquainted with our species, nay with ourselves.

And, further, the emphasis is laid on the moral instruction it affords:

History is a collection of the journals of those who have travelled through the same country, and been exposed to the same accidents: and their good and their ill success are equally instructive.[2]

[1] *Ibid.*, pp. 249–52.
[2] Bolingbroke, *Letters on the Study and Use of History* (London, 1752), I, 170, 172.

This rather naïve view of morals and history in the tradition of
the Roman moralists did not wholly satisfy the Augustans, if
we may judge by a remark of Pope's in a letter to Swift written
about Bolingbroke's preoccupations just at this time:

Lord B. . . . is so taken up still (in spite of the monitory Hint
given in the first line of my Essay) with particular Men, that
he neglects mankind, and is still a creature of this world, not
of the Universe: This World, which is a name we give to
Europe, to England, to Ireland, to London, to Dublin, to the
Court, to the Castle, and so diminishing, till it comes to our own
affairs, and our own persons.[1]

It was left for the poet to remind the historian that if he was
really concerned with the whole experience of mankind and the
full story of man's attempt to make himself at home on the face
of the earth, he must enlarge the Augustan idea of history, with
its emphasis on politics and morals, and be ready to make use
of the work of those who were patiently enlarging the boundaries
of human knowledge, whether as antiquaries or as natural
philosophers:

> Awake, my St. John! leave all meaner things
> To low ambition, and the pride of Kings.
>
> .   .   .   .   .
>
> Together let us beat this ample field,
> Try what the open, what the covert yield;
> The latent tracts, the giddy heights explore
> Of all who blindly creep, or sightless soar;
> Eye Nature's walks, shoot Folly as it flies,
> And catch the Manners living as they rise;
> Laugh where we must, be candid where we can;
> But vindicate the ways of God to Man.

[1] *Correspondence of Pope*, III, 445.

R. S. CRANE

The Houyhnhnms, the Yahoos, and the History of Ideas

I SHALL be concerned in this essay with two ways of using the history of ideas—or, in the case of one of them, as I shall argue, misusing it—in literary interpretation. The particular issue I have in mind is forced on one in an unusually clear-cut manner, I think, by what has been said of the 'Voyage to the Country of the Houyhnhnms' in the criticism of the past few decades; and for this reason, and also because I wish to add a theory of my own about Swift's intentions in that work to the theories now current, I shall base the discussion that follows almost exclusively on it.

I

With a very few exceptions (the latest being George Sherburn),[1] since the 1920s, and especially since the later 1930s, writers on the fourth Voyage have been mainly dominated by a single pre-occupation.[2] They have sought to correct the misunderstanding

This paper was read, in somewhat different form, at Wadham College, Oxford, in April, 1959, before the Annual Conference of Non-professorial University Teachers of English of the British Isles.

[1] See his 'Errors Concerning the Houyhnhnms,' *MP*, LVI (1958), 92–97.

[2] The list of writings that reflect this preoccupation is now a fairly long one; in the present essay I have had in view chiefly the following: Ernest

of Swift's satiric purpose in the Voyage which had vitiated, in their opinion, most earlier criticism of it and, in particular, to defend Swift from the charge of all-out misanthropy that had been levelled against him so often in the past—by Thackeray, for example, but many others also—on the strength of Gulliver's wholesale identification of men with the Yahoos and his unqualified worship of the Houyhnhnms.

It is easy to see what this task would require them to do. It would require them to show that what Gulliver is made to say about human nature in the Voyage, which is certainly misanthropic enough, and what Swift wanted his readers to believe about human nature are, in certain crucial respects at any rate, two different and incompatible things. It would require them, that is, to draw a clear line between what is both Swift and Gulliver and what is only Gulliver in a text in which Gulliver alone is allowed to speak to us.

The resulting new interpretations have differed considerably in emphasis and detail from critic to critic, but they have been generally in accord on the following propositions: The attitudes of Swift and his hero do indeed coincide up to a certain point, it being true for Swift no less than for Gulliver that men in the mass are terrifyingly close to the Yahoos in disposition and behaviour, and true for both of them also that the Houyhnhnms are in some of their qualities—their abhorrence of falsehood,

Bernbaum, 'The Significance of "Gulliver's Travels," ' in his edition of that work (New York, 1920); T. O. Wedel, 'On the Philosophical Background of *Gulliver's Travels*,' *SP*, XXIII (1926), 434–50; John F. Ross, 'The Final Comedy of Lemuel Gulliver,' in *Studies in the Comic* ('University of California Publications in English,' Vol. VIII, No. 2, 1941), pp. 175–96; Robert B. Heilman, Introduction to his edition of *Gulliver's Travels* (New York, 1950), especially pp. xii–xxii; Ernest Tuveson, 'Swift: the Dean as Satirist,' *University of Toronto Quarterly*, XXII (1953), 368–75; Roland M. Frye, 'Swift's Yahoo and the Christian Symbols for Sin,' *JHI*, XV (1954), 201–15; W. A. Murray's supplementary note to Frye, *ibid.*, pp. 596–601; Samuel H. Monk, 'The Pride of Lemuel Gulliver,' *Sewanee Review*, LXIII (1955), 48–71; Irvin Ehrenpreis, 'The Origins of *Gulliver's Travels*,' *PMLA*, LXXII (1957), 880–99 (reprinted with some revisions in his *The Personality of Jonathan Swift* [London, 1958]); Kathleen Williams, *Jonathan Swift and the Age of Compromise* (Lawrence, Kansas, 1958); Calhoun Winton, 'Conversion on the Road to Houyhnhnmland,' *Sewanee Review*, LXVIII (1960), 20–33; Martin Kallich, 'Three Ways of Looking at a Horse: Jonathan Swift's "Voyage to the Houyhnhnms" Again,' *Criticism*, II (1960), 107–24.

for instance—proper models for human emulation. That, however, is about as far as the agreement goes: it is to Gulliver alone and not to Swift that we must impute the radical pessimism of the final chapters—it is he and not Swift who reduces men literally to Yahoos; it is he and not Swift who despairs of men because they cannot or will not lead the wholly rational life of the Houyhnhnms. Gulliver, in other words, is only in part a reliable spokesman of his creator's satire; he is also, and decisively at the end, one of the targets of that satire—a character designed to convince us, through his obviously infatuated actions, of the absurdity both of any view of man's nature that denies the capacity of at least some men for rational and virtuous conduct, however limited this capacity may be, and of any view of the best existence for man that makes it consist in taking 'reason alone' as a guide. What, in short, Swift offers us, as the ultimate moral of the Voyage, is a compromise between these extremist opinions of Gulliver: human nature, he is saying, is bad enough, but it is not altogether hopeless; reason is a good thing, but a life of pure reason is no desirable end for man.

Now it is evident that however appealing this interpretation may be to those who want to think well of Swift and to rescue him from his nineteenth-century maligners, it is not a merely obvious exegesis of the 'Voyage to the Houyhnhnms,' or one that most common readers, past or present, have spontaneously arrived at. It is not an exegesis, either, that goes at all comfortably with that famous letter of Swift's in 1725 in which he told Pope that his chief aim was 'to vex the world rather than divert it' and that he never would have peace of mind until 'all honest men' were of his opinion. For there is nothing particularly vexing in the at least partly reassuring moral now being attributed to the Voyage or anything which 'honest men' in 1726 would have had much hesitation in accepting. And again, though we must surely agree that there is a significant difference between Gulliver and Swift, why must we suppose that the difference has to be one of basic doctrine? Why could it not be simply the difference between a person who has just discovered a deeply disturbing truth about man and is consequently, like Socrates' prisoner in the myth of the cave, more than a little upset and one who, like Socrates himself, has known this truth

233

all along and can therefore write of his hero's discovery of it calmly and with humour ?

I introduce these points here not as decisive objections to the new interpretation but rather as signs that it is not the kind of interpretation which (in Johnson's phrase), upon its first production, must be acknowledged to be just. Confirmatory arguments are plainly needed; and a consideration of the arguments that have in fact been offered in support of it will bring us rather quickly to the special problem I wish to discuss.

A good deal has been made, to begin with, of what are thought to be clear indications in the Voyage itself that Swift wanted his readers to take a much more critical view than Gulliver does of 'the virtues and ideas of those exalted Houyhnhnms' and a much less negative view of human possibilities. If he had designed the Houyhnhnms to be for us what they are for Gulliver, namely the 'perfection of nature' and hence an acceptable standard for judging of man, he would surely, it is argued, have endowed them with more humanly engaging qualities than they have; he would surely not have created them as the 'remote, unsympathetic, and in the end profoundly unsatisfying' creatures so many of his readers nowadays find them to be. We must therefore see in Gulliver's worship of the rational horses a plain evidence of the extremist error into which he has fallen. And similarly, if Swift had expected us to go the whole way with Gulliver in his identification of men with the Yahoos, he would hardly have depicted the human characters in his story—especially the admirable Portuguese captain, Don Pedro de Mendez, and his crew—in the conspicuously favourable light in which they appear to us. They are bound to strike us as notable exceptions to the despairing estimate of 'human kind' to which Gulliver has been led by his Houyhnhnm master; and we can only conclude that Gulliver's failure to look upon them as other than Yahoos, whom at best he can only 'tolerate,' is meant as still another sign to us of the false extremism of his attitude.

All this looks at first sight rather convincing—until, that is, we begin to think of other possible intentions that Swift might have had in the Voyage with which these signs would be equally compatible. Suppose that his primary purpose was indeed to 'vex the world' by administering as severe a shock as he could to the cherished belief that man is par excellence a 'rational creature,' and suppose that he chose to do this, in part at least, by forcing his readers to dwell on the unbridgeable gap between what is involved in being a truly 'rational creature' and what not only the worse but also the better sort of men actually are. It is plain what he would have had to do in working out such a design. He would have had to give to his wholly rational beings precisely those 'unhuman' characteristics that have been noted, to their disadvantage, in the Houyhnhnms; to have made them creatures such as we would normally like or sympathize with would have been to destroy their value as a transcendent standard of comparison. And it would have been no less essential to introduce characters, like Don Pedro, who, in terms of ordinary human judgments, would impress us as unmistakably good; otherwise he would have exempted too many of his readers from the shock to their pride in being men which, on this hypothesis, he was trying to produce. He would have had to do, in short, all those things in the Voyage that have been taken as indications of a purpose very different from the one I am now supposing, and much less misanthropic. Clearly, then, some other kind of proof is needed than these ambiguous internal signs before the current view of Swift's meaning can be thought of as more than one possibility among other competing ones.

A good many defenders of this view, especially during the past decade, have attempted to supply such proof by relating the Voyage to its presumed background in the intellectual and religious concerns of Swift and his age; and it is their manner of doing this—of using hypotheses based on the history of ideas in the determination of their author's meaning—that I want to examine in what immediately follows.

They have been fairly well agreed on these three points: in the first place, that Swift's main design in the Voyage was to uphold what they describe as the traditional and orthodox conception of human nature, classical and Christian alike, that 'recognizes in man an inseparable complex of good and evil,' reason and passion, spiritual soul and animal body; secondly, that he conceived the Houyhnhnms and the Yahoos, primarily at least, as allegorical embodiments of these two parts of man's constitution taken in abstraction the one from the other; and thirdly, that he developed his defence of the orthodox view by directing his satire against those contemporary doctrines, on the one hand, that tended to exalt the Houyhnhnm side of man in forgetfulness of how Yahoo-like man really is, and those doctrines, on the other hand, that tended to see man only as a Yahoo in forgetfulness of his Houyhnhnm possibilities, limited though these are. All this has been more or less common doctrine among critics of the Voyage since Ernest Bernbaum in 1920; there has been rather less agreement on the identity of the contemporary movements of ideas which Swift had in view as objects of attack. It was usual in the earlier phases of the discussion to say simply, as Bernbaum does, that he was thinking, at the one extreme, of the 'sentimental optimism' of writers like Shaftesbury and, at the other, of the pessimism or cynicism of writers like Hobbes and Mandeville. Since then, though, other identifications have been added to the list, as relevant especially to his conception of the Houyhnhnms; we have been told, thus, that he 'obviously' intended to embody in the principles and mode of life of these creatures, along with certain admittedly admirable qualities, the rationalistic errors of the neo-Stoics, the Cartesians, and the Deists—some or all of these, depending on the critic.

Now if we could feel sure that what was in Swift's mind when he conceived the fourth Voyage is even approximately represented by these statements, we should have little reason for not going along with the interpretation of his design they have been used to support. For if he was indeed engaged in vindicating the 'Christian humanist' view of human nature against those contemporary extremists who made either too much or too little of man's capacity for reason and virtue, then the current view of Gulliver as partly a vehicle and partly an object of the satire is surely correct. Everything depends, therefore, on how much relevance to what he was trying to do in the Voyage this particular historical hypothesis can be shown to have.

Its proponents have offered it as relevant beyond reasonable doubt; which suggests to me that some special assumptions about the application of intellectual history to the exegesis of literary works must be involved here. For they would find it difficult, I think, to justify their confidence in terms merely of the ordinary canons of proof in this as well as other historical fields.

They can indeed show that the hypothesis is a possible one, in the sense that it is consistent with some of the things we know about Swift apart from the Voyage. We know thus that he was a humanistically educated Anglican divine, with traditionalist inclinations in many matters; that he looked upon man's nature as deeply corrupted by the Fall but thought that self-love and the passions could be made, with the help of religion, to yield a positive though limited kind of virtue; that he held reason in high esteem as a God-given possession of man but distrusted any exclusive reliance on it in practice or belief, and ridiculed the Stoics and Cartesians and made war on the Deists; and that he tended, especially in his political writings, to find the useful truth in a medium between extremes. A man of whom these things can be said might very well have conceived the 'Voyage to the Houyhnhnms' in the terms in which, on the present theory, Swift is supposed to have conceived it. And beyond this, it is possible to point to various characteristics in the Voyage itself which, *if* the hypothesis is correct, can be interpreted as likely consequences of it. *If* Swift had in fact intended to symbolize, in the sustained opposition of Houyhnhnms and Yahoos, the deep division and conflict within man between his rational and his animal natures, he would undoubtedly have depicted these two sets of creatures, in essentials at least, much as they are depicted in the text (though this would hardly account for his choice of horses as symbols of rationality). So too with the supposition that we were meant to see in the Houyhnhnms, among other things, a powerful reminder of how inadequate and dangerous, for weak and sinful human nature, is any such one-sided exaltation of reason as was being inculcated at the time by the Deists, the neo-Stoics, and the Cartesians: it would not be surprising, if that were actually Swift's intention, to find Gulliver saying of 'those exalted quadrupeds,' as he does, that they consider 'reason alone sufficient to govern a rational creature,' that they neither affirm nor deny anything of which they are not certain, and that they keep their passions under firm control, practise 'universal friendship and benevolence,' and remain indifferent to human fear of death and human grief for the death of others.

Now all this is to the good, to the extent at least that without such considerations as these about both Swift and the fourth Voyage there would be no reason for entertaining the hypothesis at all. But can we say anything more than this— so long, that is, as we judge the question by the ordinary standards of historical criticism? In other words, do the considerations I have just summarized tend in any decisive way to establish the hypothesis as fact? The answer must surely be that they do not, and for the simple reason that they are all merely positive and favouring considerations, such as can almost always be adduced in support of almost any hypothesis in scholarship or common life, however irrelevant or false it may turn out to be. It is a basic maxim of scholarly criticism, therefore, that the probability of a given hypothesis is proportionate not to our ability to substantiate it by confirmatory evidence (though there obviously must be confirmatory evidence) but to our inability—after serious trial—to rule it out in favour of some other hypothesis that would explain more completely and simply the particulars it is concerned with. We have to start, in short, with the assumption that our hypothesis may very well be false and then permit ourselves to look upon it as fact only when, having impartially considered all the counter-possibilities we can think of, we find disbelief in it more difficult to maintain than belief. This is a rule which few of us consistently live up to (otherwise we would not publish as much as we do); but there are varying degrees of departure from it; and I can see few signs that its requirements are even approximated to in the current historical discussions of the fourth Voyage. It would be a different matter if these critics had been able to show statements by Swift himself about *Gulliver's Travels* that defy reasonable interpretation except as references to the particular issues and doctrines which the hypothesis supposes were in his mind when he wrote the Voyage. But they have not succeeded in doing this; and they have given no attention at all to the possibility that there were other traditions of thought about human nature in Swift's time (I can think of one such, as will appear later) which he can be shown to have been familiar with and which they ought to have considered and then, if possible, excluded as irrelevant before their hypothesis can be said—again on ordinary scholarly grounds—to be confirmed.

What are, then, the special assumptions about interpretative method in the history of ideas on which, in view of all this, their confidence must be presumed to rest? Their problem has naturally led them, as it would any historian, to make propositions about Swift's thought apart from *Gulliver* and about the thought of Swift's age: what is distinctive is the character of these propositions and the use they are put to in the interpretation of the Voyage. In the eyes of the ordinary historian of ideas inquiring into the intellectual antecedents and causes of this work, the thought of Swift as expressed in his other writings is simply an aggregate of particular statements and arguments, some of which may well turn out to be relevant to an understanding of its meaning; for any of them, however, this is merely a possibility to be tested, not a presumption to be argued from. It is the same, too, with the thought of Swift's age: this, again, in the eyes of the ordinary historian, is nothing more determinate than the sum of things that were being written in the later seventeenth and early eighteenth centuries, from varying points of view and in varying traditions of analysis, on the general theme of human nature; some of these, once more, may well be relevant to the argument developed in the Voyage, but the historian can know what they are only after an unprejudiced inquiry that presupposes no prior limitation on the ideas Swift might have been influenced by or have felt impelled to attack in constructing it. For the ordinary historian, in short, the fact that the 'Voyage to the Houyhnhnms' was written by Swift at a particular moment in the general history of thought about man has only this methodological significance: that it defines the region in which he may most hopefully look for the intellectual stimuli and materials that helped to shape the Voyage; it gives him, so to speak, his working reading-list; it can never tell him—only an independent analysis of the Voyage can do that— how to use the list.

That the critics we are concerned with have taken a different view of the matter from this is suggested by the title of the book in which the current historical theory of Swift's intentions in the Voyage is argued most fully and ingeniously—Kathleen Williams's *Jonathan Swift and the Age of Compromise*. For to think of a period in intellectual history in this way—as the age *of* something or other, where the something or other is designated by an abstract term like 'compromise'—is obviously no longer to consider it as an indefinite aggregate of happenings; it is to consider it rather as a definite system of happenings; something like the plot of a novel in which a great many diverse characters and episodes are unified, more or less completely, by a principal action or theme. It is to assume, moreover, not only that the historian can determine what was the central problem, the basic conflict or tension, the dominant world-view of a century or generation, either in general or in some particular department of thought, but that he can legitimately use his formula for this as a confirmatory premise in arguing the meanings and causes of individual works produced in that age. It is to suppose that there is a kind of probative force in his preferred formula for the period which can confer, a priori, if not a unique at least a privileged relevance on one particular hypothesis about a given work of that period as against other hypotheses that are less easily brought under the terms of the formula, so that little more is required by way of further proof than a demonstration, which is never hard to give, that the work makes sense when it is 'read' as the hypothesis dictates.

These are, I think, the basic assumptions which underly most of the recent historical discussions of the fourth Voyage and which go far toward explaining the confidence their authors have felt in the correctness of their conclusions. It would be hard, otherwise, to understand why they should think it important to introduce propositions about what was central and unifying in the moral thought of Swift's age; the reason must be that they have hoped, by so doing, to establish some kind of antecedent limitation on the intentions he could be expected to have had in writing the Voyage. And that, indeed, is the almost unavoidable effect of the argument for any reader who closes his mind, momentarily, to the nature of the presuppositions on which it rests. For suppose we agree with these critics that the dominant and most significant issue in the moral speculation of the later seventeenth and early eighteenth centuries was a conflict between the three fundamentally different views of man's nature represented by the orthodox 'classical-Christian' dualism in the middle and, at opposite extremes to this, by the newer doctrines of the rationalists and benevolists on the one side and of the materialists and cynics on the

other. Since this is presented as an exhaustive scheme of classification, it will be easy for us to believe that the view of man
asserted in the Voyage must have been one of these three. And
then suppose we agree to think of Swift as a character in this
three-cornered plot, who was predisposed by his humanist
education and his convictions as an Anglican divine to adhere to
the traditional and compromising view as against either of the
modern extremisms. It will be difficult for us now to avoid
believing that the 'Voyage to the Houyhnhnms' was therefore
more probably than not an assertion of this middle view against
its contemporary enemies, and it will be harder than it would be
without such an argument from the age to the author to the
work, to resist any interpretations of its details that may be
necessary to make them accord with that theory of Swift's
intentions.

This is likely to be our reaction, at any rate, until we reflect
on the peculiar character of the argument we have been persuaded to go along with. There are many arguments like it in
the writings of modern critics and historians of ideas in other
fields (those who have interpreted Shakespeare in the light of
'the Elizabethan world-picture,' for instance); but they all
betray, I think, a fundamental confusion in method. The objection is not that they rest on a false conception of historical
periods. There is nothing intrinsically illegitimate in the mode
of historical writing that organizes the intellectual happenings
of different ages in terms of their controlling 'climates of
opinion,' dominant tendencies, or ruling oppositions of attitude
or belief; and the results of such synthesizing efforts are sometimes—as in A. O. Lovejoy, for example—illuminating in a very
high degree. The objection is rather to the further assumption,
clearly implicit in these arguments, that the unifying principles
of histories of this type have something like the force of
empirically established universal laws, and can therefore be
used as guarantees of the probable correctness of any interpretations of individual writings that bring the writings into harmony with their requirements. That this is sheer illusion can be
easily seen if we consider what these principles really amount
to. Some of them amount simply to assertions that there was a
tendency among the writers of a particular time to concentrate
on such and such problems and to solve them in such and such

ways; there is no implication here that this trend affected all writers or any individual writer at all times; whether a given work of the age did or did not conform to the trend remains therefore an open question, to be answered only by independent inquiry unbiased by the merely statistical probabilities affirmed in the historian's generalization. But there are also principles of a rather different sort, among which we must include, I think, the formula of Swift's critics for the dominant conflict about human nature in his time. These are best described as dialectical constructs, since they organize the doctrinal facts they refer to by imposing on them abstract schemes of logical relationships among ideas which may or may not be identical with any of the various classifications of doctrines influential at the time. Thus the characterization of Swift's age and of Swift himself as a part of that age in our critics derives its apparent exhaustiveness from a pattern of general terms—the concept of 'Christian humanism' and the two contraries of this—which these critics clearly owe to the ethical and historical speculations of Irving Babbitt and his school. Now it may be that this scheme represents accurately enough the distinctions Swift had in mind when he conceived the fourth Voyage; but that would be something of a coincidence, and it is just as reasonable to suppose that he may have been thinking quite outside the particular framework of notions which this retrospective scheme provides. We must conclude, then, that this whole way of using the history of ideas in literary interpretation is a snare and a delusion. From the generalizations and schematisms of the synthesizing historians we can very often get suggestions for new working hypotheses with which to approach the exegesis of individual works. What we cannot get from them is any assurance whatever that any of these hypotheses are more likely to be correct than any others that we have hit upon without their aid.

I should now like to invite the reader's criticism, in the light of what I have been saying, on another view of the intellectual background and import of the fourth Voyage (or a considerable part of it at least) which I have attempted to argue on the basis merely of ordinary historical evidence, independently of any general postulates about Swift or his age.

II

Whatever else may be true of the Voyage, it will doubtless be agreed that one question is kept uppermost in it from the beginning, for both Gulliver and the reader. This is the question of what sort of animal man, as a species, really is; and the point of departure in the argument is the answer to this question which Gulliver brings with him into Houyhnhnmland and which is also, we are reminded more than once, the answer which men in general tend, complacently, to give to it. Neither he nor they have any doubt that only man, among 'sensitive' creatures, can be properly called 'rational'; all the rest—whether wild or tame, detestable or, like that 'most comely and generous' animal, the horse, the reverse of that—being merely 'brutes,' not 'endued with reason.' The central issue, in other words, is primarily one of definition: is man, or is he not, correctly defined as a 'rational creature'? It is significant that Gulliver's misanthropy at the end is not the result of any increase in his knowledge of human beings in the concrete over what he has had before; it is he after all who expounds to his Houyhnhnm master all those melancholy facts about men's 'actions and passions' that play so large a part in their conversations; he has known these facts all along, and has still been able to call himself a 'lover of mankind.' The thing that changes his love into antipathy is the recognition that is now forced upon him that these facts are wholly incompatible with the formula for man's nature which he has hitherto taken for granted—are compatible, indeed, only with a formula, infinitely more humiliating to human pride, which pushes man nearly if not quite over to the opposite pole of the animal world.

What brings about the recognition is, in the first place, the deeply disturbing spectacle of the Houyhnhnms and the Yahoos. I can find nothing in the text that forces us to look on these two sets of strange creatures in any other light than that in which Gulliver sees them—not, that is, as personified abstractions, but simply as two concrete species of animals: existent species for Gulliver, hypothetical species for us. The contrast he draws between them involves the same pair of antithetical terms (the one positive, the other privative) that he has been accustomed to use in contrasting men and the other animals.

The essential character of the Houyhnhnms, he tells us, is that they are creatures 'wholly governed by reason'; the essential character of the Yahoos is that 'they are the most unteachable of brutes,' without 'the least tincture of reason.' The world of animals in Houyhnhnmland, in other words, is divided by the same basic differences as the world of animals in Europe. Only, of course—and it is the shock of this that prepares Gulliver for his ultimate abandonment of the definition of man he has started with—it is a world in which the normal distribution of species between 'rational creatures' and irrational 'brutes' is sharply inverted, with horses, whom he can't help admiring, in the natural place of men, and man-like creatures, whom he can't help abhorring, in the natural place of horses.

This is enough in itself to cause Gulliver to view his original formula for his own species, as he says, 'in a very different light.' But he is pushed much farther in the same misanthropic direction by the questions and comments of his Houyhnhnm master, acting as a kind of Socrates. What thus develops is partly a reduction to absurdity of man's 'pretensions to the character of a rational creature' and partly a demonstration of the complete parity in essential nature between men and the Houyhnhnmland Yahoos. There is of course one striking difference—unlike the Yahoos, men are after all possessed of at least a 'small proportion,' a 'small pittance' of reason, some in greater degree than others. But I can see no clear signs in the text that this qualification is intended to set men apart as a third, or intermediate, species for either Gulliver or the reader. For what is basic in the new definition of man as a merely more 'civilized' variety of Yahoo is the fundamentally irrational 'disposition' which motivates his habitual behaviour; and in relation to that his 'capacity for reason' is only an acquired attribute which he is always in danger of losing and of which, as Gulliver says, he makes no other use, generally speaking, than 'to improve and multiply those vices' whereof his 'brethren [in Houyhnhnmland] had only the share that nature allotted them.'

It is clear what a satisfactory historical explanation of this line of argument in the Voyage would have to do. It would have to account for Swift's very patent assumption that there would be a high degree of satirical force, for readers in 1726, in a fable which began with the notion that man is pre-eminently a 'rational creature' and then proceeded to turn this notion violently upside down, and which, in doing so, based itself on a division of animal species into the extremes of 'rational creatures' and irrational 'brutes' and on the paradoxical identification of the former with horses and of the latter with beings closely resembling men. Was there perhaps a body of teaching, not so far brought into the discussion of the Voyage but widely familiar at the time, that could have supplied Swift with the particular scheme of ideas he was exploiting here? I suggest that there was, and also that there is nothing strange in the fact that it has been hitherto overlooked by Swift's critics. For one principal medium through which these ideas could have come to Swift and his readers—the only one, in fact, I know of that could have given him all of them—was a body of writings, mainly in Latin, which students of literature in our day quite naturally shy away from reading: namely, the old-fashioned textbooks in logic that still dominated the teaching of that subject in British universities during the later seventeenth and early eighteenth centuries.[1]

It is impossible not to be impressed, in the first place, by the prominence in these textbooks of the particular definition of man which the Voyage sought to discredit. *Homo est animal rationale*: no one could study elementary logic anywhere in the British Isles in the generation before *Gulliver* without encountering this formula or variations of it (e.g., *Nullus homo est irrationalis*) in his manuals and the lectures he heard. It appears as the standard example of essential definition in the great majority of logics in use during these years at Oxford, Cambridge, and Dublin; and in most of those in which it occurs, it is given without comment or explanation as the obviously correct formula for man's distinctive nature, as if no one would ever question that man is, uniquely and above all, a rational creature. It is frequently brought in many times over, in various contexts, in individual textbooks: I have counted a dozen or so occurrences of it in Milton's *Art of Logic*, and many times that number in the *Institutionum logicarum . . . libri duo* of

---

[1] There are useful descriptions of many, though by no means all, of these in Wilbur Samuel Howell, *Logic and Rhetoric in England, 1500–1700* (Princeton, 1956).

Franco Burgersdijck (or Burgersdicius), which was one of the most widely used, and also one of the longest lived, of all these writings—it appeared in 1626 and was still prescribed at Dublin when Edmund Burke went there as a Junior Freshman in 1744.[1] I shall have some more to say of Burgersdicius, or 'Burgy' as Burke called him, presently; but it is worth noting that he provides us, in one passage, with the very question on which much of the fourth Voyage was to turn, with the answer Swift was *not* to give to it: 'Quærenti enim, Quale animal est homo? apposité respondetur, Rationale.'

Not only, however, was the definition omnipresent in these books, but there is some evidence that it was thought of, in Swift's time, as the special property of the academic logicians. Locke, for instance, calls it in his *Essay* 'the ordinary Definition of the Schools,' the 'sacred Definition of *Animal Rationale*' of 'the learned Divine and Lawyer'; it goes, he implies, with 'this whole *Mystery* of *Genera* and *Species*, which make such a noise in the Schools, and are, with Justice, so little regarded out of them' (iii.iii.10; vi.26; iii.9). And there are other later testimonies to the same effect; among them these opening lines of an anonymous poem of the period after *Gulliver*, once ascribed to Swift—'The Logicians Refuted':

> Logicians have but ill defin'd
> As rational, the human kind;
> Reason, they say, belongs to man,
> But let them prove it if they can.
> Wise Aristotle and Smiglesius,
> By ratiocinations specious,
> Have strove to prove with great precision,
> With definition and division,
> *Homo est ratione preditum*;
> But for my soul I cannot credit 'em.[2]

But the logicians had more to offer Swift than the great authority which they undoubtedly conferred on the definition

---

[1] *The Correspondence of Edmund Burke*, ed. by Thomas W. Copeland, I (Cambridge and Chicago, 1958), 4, 7–9, 21, 28.

[2] *The Busy Body*, No. 5, October 18, 1759. Both the ascription to Swift, which occurs in a note prefixed to this first known printing of the poem, and the later ascription to Goldsmith seem to me highly dubious.

'rational animal.' They could have suggested to him also the basic principle on which the inverted animal world of Houyhnhnmland was constructed, and consequently the disjunction that operated as major premise in his argument about man. Whoever it was, among the Greeks, that first divided the genus 'animal' by the differentiae 'rational' and 'irrational,' there is much evidence that this antithesis had become a commonplace in the Greco-Roman schools long before it was taken up by the writer who did more than any one else to determine the context in which the definition *animal rationale* was chiefly familiar to Englishmen of Swift's time. This writer was the Neoplatonist Porphyry of the third century A.D., whose little treatise, the *Isagoge*, or introduction to the categories of Aristotle, became, as is well known, one of the great sources of logical theorizing and teaching from the time of Boethius until well beyond the end of the seventeenth century. There is no point in going into the details of Porphyry's doctrine: what is important for our purpose here is the new sanction he gave to the older division of animal species through his incorporation of it into the general scheme of differentiae for the category of substance which was later known as the *arbor porphyriana* or Porphyry's tree, especially in the diagrams of it that became a regular feature of the more elementary textbooks. Here it is, set forth discursively, in the crabbed prose of Burgersdicius (I quote the English version of 1697, but the Latin is no better). In seeking the definition of man, he writes, we must first observe that

Man is a Substance; but because an Angel is also a Substance; *That it may appear how Man differs from an Angel,* Substance ought to be divided into Corporeal and Incorporeal. A Man is a *Body,* an Angel *without a Body:* But a Stone also is a *Body*: That therefore a Man may be distinguished from a Stone, divide Bodily or Corporeal Substance into Animate and Inanimate, that is, *with or without a Soul.* Man is a Corporeal Substance Animate, Stone Inanimate. But Plants are also *Animate*: Let us divide therefore again Corporeal Substance Animate into *Feeling and void of Feeling.* Man feels, a Plant not: But a Horse *also feels,* and likewise other Beasts. Divide we therefore Animate Corporeal Feeling Substance into Rational and Irrational. Here therefore *are we to stand*, since it appears that every, and only Man *is Rational*.[1]

And there was, finally, one other thing in these logics that could have helped to shape Swift's invention in the fourth Voyage. In opposing man as the only species of 'rational animal' to the brutes, Porphyry obviously needed a specific instance, parallel to man, of an 'irrational' creature; and the instance he chose—there were earlier precedents for the choice[2]—was the horse. The proportion 'rational' is to 'irrational' as man is to horse occurs more than once in the *Isagoge*; and the juxtaposition, in the same context, of *homo* and *equus* was a frequently recurring cliché in his seventeenth-century followers, as in the passage in Burgersdicius just quoted: other species of brutes were occasionally mentioned, but none of them nearly so often. And any one who studied these books could hardly fail to remember a further point—that the distinguishing 'property' of this favourite brute was invariably given as whinnying (*facultas hinniendi*); *equus*, it was said again and again, *est animal hinnibile*.

To most Englishmen of Swift's time who had read logic in their youth—and this would include nearly all generally educated men—these commonplaces of Porphyry's tree, as I may call them for short, were as familiar as the Freudian commonplaces are to generally educated people today, and they were accepted, for the most part, in an even less questioning spirit, so that it might well have occurred to a clever satirist then that he could produce a fine shock to his readers' complacency as human beings by inventing a world in which horses appeared where the logicians had put men and men where they had put horses, and by elaborating, through this, an argument designed to shift the position of man as a species from the *animal rationale* branch of the tree, where he had always been proudly placed, as far as possible over toward the *animal irrationale* branch, with its enormously less flattering connotations. But have we any

[1] *Monitio Logica: or, An Abstract and Translation of Burgersdicius his Logick* (London, 1697), pp. 13–14 (second pagination).

[2] E.g., Quintilian, *Institutio oratoria*, VII.iii.3, 24. For the contrast of man and horse in Porphyry see especially Migne, *PL*, LXIV, col. 128 (Boethius' translation): 'Differentia est quod est aptum natum dividere ea quæ sub eodem genere sunt: rationale enim et irrationale, hominem et equum quæ sub eodem genere sunt animali dividunt.'

warrant for thinking that this, or something like it, was what Swift actually had in mind? It is clearly possible to describe the Voyage as, in considerable part at least, an anti-Porphyrian satire in the genre of the poem I quoted from earlier, 'The Logicians Refuted.' But is there any evidence that Swift planned it as such?

That the Porphyrian commonplaces had been known to him in their full extent from his days at Trinity College in the early 1680s we can hardly doubt in view of the kind of education in logic he was exposed to there. Among the books which all Junior Freshmen at Dublin in those years were required to study or hear lectures on, we know of three in which the Porphyrian apparatus and examples had a prominent place: the *Isagoge* itself (which was prescribed by the statutes of the College to be read twice over during the year), the older logic of Burgersdicius, and the newer *Institutio logicae* of Narcissus Marsh. It is true that Swift, according to his own later statement, detested this part of the curriculum, and it is true that on one examination in his last year his mark in Philosophy was *Male* (he had a *Bene* in Greek and Latin). But this was an examination in the more advanced branches of the Aristotelian system, and it is likely that he had fared better in the earlier examination in logic, since he had evidently been allowed to proceed with his class. It is possible, moreover, to infer from his occasional use of logical terms in his later writings that, abhorrent as the subject was to him, the time he had been compelled to spend on it as a Junior Freshman was not a total loss. He at least remembered enough of it to allude familiarly in different places to such things as a 'long sorites,' 'the first proposition of a hypothetical syllogism,' and the fallacy of two middle terms in a single syllogism;[1] and if this was possible, there is good reason to suppose that he had not forgotten the much simpler Porphyrian points about genera, species, and definition, 'rational' versus 'irrational' animals, men and horses which he had been introduced to at the same time.

The crucial question, however, is whether he had these notions of the logicians at all actively in mind when, in the

[1] See John M. Bullitt, *Jonathan Swift and the Anatomy of Satire* (Cambridge, Mass., 1953), p. 73. Cf. also Swift, 'A Preface to the B——p of S——m's Introduction,' in *Works*, ed. by Temple Scott, III, 150.

1720s, he conceived and wrote the 'Voyage to the Houyhnhnms.' And here it will be well to take a fresh look at the two much-quoted letters about *Gulliver's Travels* which he sent to Pope in 1725, just after that work was completed. In the first of these, that of September 29, after having told Pope that his chief aim is 'to vex the world rather than divert it' and that he hates and detests 'that animal called man,' he goes on to remark: 'I have got materials towards a treatise proving the falsity of that definition *animal rationale*, and to show it should be only *rationis capax*. Upon this great foundation of misanthropy, though not in Timon's manner, the whole building of my Travels is erected; and I never will have peace of mind till all honest men are of my opinion.' In the second letter, that of November 26, he desires that Pope and 'all my friends' will 'take a special care that my disaffection to the world may not be imputed to my age, for I have credible witnesses . . . that it has never varied from the twenty-first to the f———ty-eighth year of my life.' He then adds a passage which has been read as a retraction of the judgment on humanity expressed in the first letter, though the final sentence makes clear, I think, that it was not so intended: 'I tell you after all, that I do not hate mankind; it is *vous autres* [i.e., Pope and Bolingbroke] who hate them, because you would have them reasonable animals, and are angry for being disappointed. I have always rejected that definition, and made another of my own. I am no more angry with ——— than I am with the kite that last week flew away with one of my chickens; and yet I was glad when one of my servants shot him two days after.'

The casual references in both letters to 'that definition'— '*animal rationale*' and 'reasonable animals'—which Swift tells Pope he has 'always rejected' have usually been interpreted by modern critics as allusions to such contemporary philosophical or theological heresies (from Swift's point of view) as the 'optimism' of Shaftesbury or the 'rationalism' of Descartes and the Deists. It is surely, however, a much less far-fetched conjecture, especially in view of the familiar textbook Latin of the first letter, to see in 'that definition' nothing other or more than the 'sacred definition' of the logicians which he had had inflicted on him, by thoroughly orthodox tutors, in his undergraduate days at Dublin.

I find this explanation, at any rate, much harder to disbelieve than any other that has been proposed; and all the more so because of another passage in the first letter which is almost certainly reminiscent of the Trinity logic course in the early 1680s. It is the famous sentence—just before the allusion to 'that definition *animal rationale*' and leading on to it—in which Swift says: 'But principally I hate and detest that animal called man, although I heartily love John, Peter, Thomas, and so forth.' Now to any one at all widely read in the logic textbooks of Swift's time two things about this sentence are immediately evident: first, that the distinction it turns on is the distinction to be found in nearly all these books between a species of animals and individual members of that species; and second, that the names 'John, Peter, Thomas, and so forth' are wholly in line with one of the two main traditions of names for individuals of the species man that had persisted side by side in innumerable manuals of logic since the Middle Ages: not, of course, the older tradition of classical names—Socrates, Plato, Alexander, Caesar—but the newer tradition (which I have noted first in Occam, though it doubtless antedates him) that drew upon the list of apostles—Peter, John, Paul, James, Thomas, in roughly that descending order of preference. (Other non-classical names, like Stephen, Catharine, Charles, Richard, also appear, but much less frequently.)

We can go farther than this, however. For although all three of Swift's names occur separately in divers texts (Thomas least often), the combination 'John, Peter, Thomas, and so forth' was an extremely unusual one. I have met with it, in fact, in only one book before 1725; and I have examined nearly all the logics, both Latin and English, down to that date for which I can find any evidence that they had even a minor circulation in Great Britain. The exception, however, is a book which Swift could hardly have escaped knowing as an undergraduate, since it was composed expressly for the use of Trinity College students by the then Provost and had just recently come 'on the course' when he entered the College in 1682—namely, the *Institutio logicae*, already referred to, of Narcissus Marsh (Dublin, 1679: reissued Dublin, 1681). Early in the book Marsh gives a full-page diagram of Porphyry's tree, with its inevitable opposition of *animal–rationale–homo* and *animal–irrationale–brutum*; and here, as *individua* under *homo*, we find 'Joannes, Petrus, Thomas, &c.' And a little later in the book the same names are repeated in the same order as individual specimens of *homo* in Marsh's analytical table for the category *substantia*.

Was this combination of names, then, Marsh's invention? There is one further circumstance which suggests that it may well have been. We know from his own testimony,[1] as well as from internal evidence, that the source on which he based the greater part of his Dublin logic of 1679 was his own revision, published at Oxford in 1678, of the *Manuductio ad logicam* of the early seventeenth-century Jesuit logician Philippe Du Trieu. Now of the two passages in the Dublin book that contain Swift's three names, the first—the diagram of Porphyry's tree—has no counterpart in the Oxford book of 1678, though it has in Du Trieu's original text, where the names are 'Petrus' and 'Joannes.' It would seem likely, then, that Marsh first thought of the combination 'John, Peter, Thomas, and so forth' when he revised his earlier revision of Du Trieu for his Trinity students in 1679; and this is borne out by what he did at the same time with the other passage—the table of substance. This he retained almost exactly as it had been in Du Trieu except for the names under *homo*: here, where in 1678 he had reprinted Du Trieu's 'Stephanus, Johannes, Catharina, &c.', he now wrote 'Johannes, Petrus, Thomas, &c.' Which would seem to imply a certain sense of private property in these particular names in this particular combination.

It is somewhat hard, then, not to conclude that Swift was remembering Marsh's logic as he composed the sentence, in his letter to Pope, about 'John, Peter, Thomas, and so forth.' But if that is true, can there be much doubt, in view of the

---

[1] See his preface 'Ad lectorem' in the 1681 issue (it is missing from some copies but can be found in the Cambridge University Library copy and in that belonging to Archbishop Marsh's Library, Dublin); also the entry for December 20, 1690, in his manuscript diary. I owe this latter reference to Miss Mary Pollard, of Archbishop Marsh's Library. For the rather complicated bibliographical history of Marsh's *Institutio logicae* (the title was altered to *Institutiones logicae* in the reissue of 1681), see her article, 'The Printing of the Provost's Logic and the Supply of Text-books in the late Seventeenth Century,' in *Friends of the Library of Trinity College, Dublin: Annual Bulletin*, 1959–61.

Porphyrian context in which these names appear in Marsh, as to what tradition of ideas was in his mind when he went on to remark, immediately afterwards, that 'the great foundation of misanthropy' on which 'the whole building' of his *Travels* rested was his proof—against Marsh and the other logicians he had been made to study at Trinity—of 'the falsity of that definition *animal rationale*'?[1]

[1] Since this essay went to press I have discussed some further aspects of the subject in a brief article, 'The Rationale of the Fourth Voyage,' in *Gulliver's Travels: An Annotated Text with Critical Essays*, ed. by Robert A. Greenberg (New York, 1961), pp. 300–7, and in a review of two recent papers on Swift and the Deists, in *PQ*, XL (1961), 427–30.

ERNEST TUVESON

Locke and Sterne

T HAT Laurence Sterne should have admired John Locke's *Essay concerning the Human Understanding* seems at first as odd as anything in *Tristram Shandy*. Yet Sterne himself gave unmistakable testimony that Locke's great treatise had a most important influence on his own life and work. He ranked the *Essay* with the Bible as the books that had affected him most. Allusions to Locke, Lockian terminology, even exhortations to read—really read—the master, abound in *Tristram Shandy*. 'It was his glory,' Tristram exclaims, 'to free the world from the lumber of a thousand vulgar errors.' Wilbur Cross remarked that 'the famous Essay became Sterne's companion to the end of life and coloured much of his own thinking.'[1] But this statement leaves the most interesting questions to be answered. What does the apparently, dry, proper, commonsense mind of Locke have in common with that of the mercurial Yorick? First, of course, the literary artist, whose subject is the human personality, was impressed by the fact that it was Locke who had finally written 'a history-book . . . of what passes in a man's own mind.' But what really was Sterne's attitude towards the history-book of the understanding? Did Locke merely give Sterne the idea for a superb joke, the ludicrous possibilities of association of ideas, around which the vast learning and rich comedy of *Tristram* are put together, rather as the Pavilion at

[1] *The Life and Times of Laurence Sterne* (New Haven, 1909), p. 33.

Brighton was built around the Oriental room the Prince Regent happened to acquire? It has been said that Sterne makes out of Locke something that is not Locke. Is Sterne, perhaps, satirizing the new way of ideas? Even though accepting the Lockian account as inescapably true in general, is he entering a humanistic protest against what new psychology made of human dignity? And what about many fundamental attitudes of Sterne—his faith in sentiment, for example—for which there seems to be no parallel in Locke?[1] Without attempting to treat exhaustively this problem, which indeed reaches to the very heart of Sterne's significance, and without presuming in an essay of this length to document every point fully, I shall attempt to indicate a new line of enquiry. I suggest, to put it briefly, that, in order to understand what Locke meant for Sterne, we should stand off at a greater distance. Instead of being preoccupied with the many detailed 'sources,' we should try to see what was Locke's ultimate purpose in studying the human mind. Then, perhaps, we can perceive a similarity between that purpose and Sterne's.

To begin with, it is essential to recognize *why* Locke became interested in re-examining the ways of the mind and what he proposed in the *Essay* to accomplish. He was not a 'researcher,' in a modern sense of the word, investigating for the sake of truth pure. Nor was he a true systematic philosopher, concerned to bring all aspects of thought under the heads of a consistent structure; after all, he called his book by the modest name of 'essay,' rather than 'treatise' or 'theory.' Hence, perhaps, some of the loose ends and ambiguities of his work, which, indeed, may have increased its appeal to the great imaginative writer who was so keenly aware of the loose ends and ambiguities in human nature. I shall not repeat here what I said before about the general significance of Locke's study for the literary artist.[2] The essential thing, it seems to me, is that he was not

---

[1] Among studies dealing in whole or in part with this subject, I may list the following: Kenneth MacLean, *John Locke and English Literature of the Eighteenth Century* (New Haven, 1936); Theodore Baird, 'The Time-Scheme of *Tristram Shandy* and a Source,' *PMLA*, 51 (1936), 803 ff.; John Traugott, *Tristram Shandy's World* (Berkeley and Los Angeles, 1954); and Ian Watt, *The Rise of the Novel* (Berkeley and Los Angeles, 1957).

[2] *The Imagination as a Means of Grace: Locke and the Aesthetics of Romanticism* (Berkeley and Los Angeles, 1960).

primarily either scientist or philosopher, but reformer. In *The Conduct of the Understanding*, a kind of manifesto he wrote at the end of his life, he sets forth what had motivated him far more fully than he could in the more formal writings. It becomes clear that his essays on the social contract, on civil right, on education, and on the mind all are branches of one tree. They grow out of a desire to further a radical reform, so sweeping that it would reach into every aspect of culture. I say 'further,' since, to appreciate Locke and what he represents, we must look beyond him, and realize that he is only one figure, although a central one, in a great movement of Western thought. It was with that movement, not merely with one writer, that Sterne was connected; it was not merely Locke the original observer of the mind, but Locke the centre of a liberating force that appealed so strongly to Sterne.

The source of the movement (at least according to most of its participants in the earlier stages) was Bacon; and Locke justifies his study of the mind by the 'great lord Verulam's authority' (*The Conduct*, sec. 1). There was a growing conviction that Western Europe was being smothered by an intellectual heritage which, like a heavy layer of smog, prevented men from seeing nature as it really is. Sterne's images present with great exactitude the intellectual world of his time. He asks the question that incited this revolution:

Tell me, ye learned, shall we for ever be adding so much to the *bulk*—so little to the *stock*— . . . Are we for ever to be twisting, and untwisting the same rope? for ever in the same track—for ever at the same pace?

(*Tristram Shandy*, Vol. V, chap. 1)

Is Man, he asks, the image of God, the ray of divinity, etc., 'to go sneaking on at this pitiful—pimping—pettifogging rate?' A whole new departure was necessary, Bacon had proclaimed, if man was not to suffer for ever, a pitiable creature: pitiable not because of necessity but because of his own folly and ignorance in binding himself in chains of his own forging. An essential part of the reform would be the examination of our own minds, to learn why we had got so far off the course God had intended for us; hence the 'idols' of the tribe and of the cave. Locke's investigation is an extended and detailed carrying out of such hints, rather inspirations, as these following; and, as we shall see, Sterne's work is an extended imaginative embodiment of these germinal ideas:

For it is a false assertion that the sense of man is the measure of things. On the contrary, all perceptions as well of the sense as of the mind are according to the measure of the individual and not according to the measure of the universe. And the human understanding is like a false mirror, which, receiving rays irregularly, distorts and discolours the nature of things by mingling its own nature with it.

(Novum Organum, Book i, Aphorism xli)

For every one (besides the errors common to human nature in general) has a cave or den of his own, which refracts and discolours the light of nature; owing either to his own proper and peculiar nature; or to his education and conversation with others; or to the reading of books, and the authority of those whom he esteems and admires; or to the differences of impressions, accordingly as they take place in a mind preoccupied and predisposed or in a mind indifferent and settled; . . .

(Ibid., Aphorism xlii)

Locke cites the *Novum Organum* as the authority of his work: 'That it is absolutely necessary, that a better and perfecter use and employment of the mind and understanding should be introduced.' The Royal Society, dedicated to carrying on the Baconian mission, condemned the 'old talkative arts' as Sprat, in the *History* of the Society, called them. He associated the Restoration with the new enterprise, and his words could be the motto of the Enlightenment that was beginning: '. . . as it began in that time, when our Country was freed from confusion, and slavery; So it may, in its progress, redeem the minds of Men, from obscurity, uncertainty, and bondage.'[1] Part of the essence of Locke's *Essay* is in Sprat, including the proposal for a reform of language and the call for a straight, honest look at the two natures: the nature without; and the human nature within, to be observed by honest, unbiased introspection.

---

[1] Thomas Sprat, *History of the Royal Society* (London, 1667), p. 58.

Europe possessed what Sterne called the 'lumber-rooms of learning,' of elaborate and 'fantastical' ideas, for which 'metaphysical' became the contemptuous term. To get rid of them was necessary if nature was to be reconquered; but to attack them one by one was to cut off the Hydra's heads. We must find their source, in the mind itself. Knowing what it is, we can be on the alert—against ourselves; and we can judge ourselves and our lives as they really are.

Locke carried this most basic investigation into details as Bacon had not done, and did so in a different spirit from that of Hobbes. It is unnecessary to give anything like a full account of Locke's famous theory. We need only recall here that knowledge is in no way innate; thus no philosophy could clothe itself in an imprescriptible authority, for nothing is above the test of experience. The test, moreover, of common experience, and of the common, but alert mind. But most people's minds are like Uncle Toby's picture of the 'smoak-jack;—the funnel unswept, and the ideas whirling round and round about in it, all obfuscated and darkened over with fuliginous matter!' To clear the understanding, to let light into it—for Locke imaged activity as 'seeing'—is the desideratum. We must realize, moreover, that when we perceive, and even when we think most profoundly, we do not participate in ultimate reality. We perceive not reality but the sense impressions that something— we can never know just what—causes. Locke's constant effort to reduce the intellectual pride in which dogmatism grows emphasizes Bacon's point that perceptions are 'according to the measure of the individual and not according to the measure of the universe.' But, one may ask, is not all this the ultimate in pessimism? Why did Bacon, and Locke, with their hopes for the future of the race, seem to beat us out of all certainty about our knowledge? The answer is their confidence that we *can* know our inner selves; and by knowing what we are, we can find our true relation to reality. Locke, the good pedagogue, had no desire to abase the mind; he hastens to assure us that we are able to deal quite adequately, in a utilitarian way, with the real world. What we must not do is to exaggerate what we can comprehend: we must not proudly assume that our minds can soar to grasp the final causes, or penetrate into the heart of the universe. But we can be certain that the mind, as part of what we should now call its biological endowment, has the power to arrange the simple ideas, the impressions, in patterns that enable the animal man to cope with the environment. So much God has granted us, and no more.

Locke attacks the traditional view that the mind is an independent, incorporeal, self-contained being, inhabiting its tenement of clay for a term, engaged in a constant struggle to maintain its dominance over a partner to which it is intrinsically and infinitely superior. Maybe a certain quantity of matter is endowed with the powers of receiving impressions and of 'reflecting' on its own operations. In any case, the mind is in, not outside and above nature. In a suggestive section of *The Conduct of the Understanding*, he compares that power itself to a physical organ; thus the mind is like a 'sinew,' which must be gradually strengthened (sec. 28). 'Knowing is seeing,' he says elsewhere. Knowledge is perceiving, by an 'internal sense,' the agreement or disagreement of the simple ideas. (See the *Essay*, ii.i, 4; iv.i.) The fact of intellection is physical; and a corollary is that sense impressions, emotional drives, and reflection are all not separate operations of a soul and a body, but ultimately components of an organic process. All this, of course, is quite alien to the traditional complete separation of body and mind. The problem is not to attempt to find, as Cartesians had attempted to do, some point of contact between alien entities, but to realize that the *body thinks*.

The issue, I believe, was of the greatest importance for Sterne. Mr. Shandy's ludicrous speculations about 'so noble, so refined, so immaterial, and so exalted a being as the *Anima*, or even the *Animus*, taking up her residence, and sitting dabbling, like a tadpole, all day long, both summer and winter, in a puddle,—'present the issue, the burlesque language exactly hitting the centre of the problem. Body and mind, Tristram speculates, are 'exactly like a jerkin, and a jerkin's lining;—rumple the one—you rumple the other' (Vol. III, chap. 4). Body and mind appear as integral parts of one garment. A reason for Sterne's 'indecencies' may be here. Swift and Pope and many others had satirized the 'stoic pride' of those who imagine they can transcend the physical impulses. Man loves to talk about himself as if he were a celestial being, but, since he is not, he constantly falls into prudishness and hypocrisy. The debate between the Shandys and Slop exposes asceticism in religion. In *A Sentimental Journey*, Yorick asks, 'What trespass is it that man should have [passions]? or how his spirit stands answerable to the Father of spirits but for his conduct under them. If Nature has so wove her web of kindness that some threads of love and desire are entangled with the piece—must the whole web be rent in drawing them out?' By showing us how mind and body are one nature, how words and gestures, for example, bring to all minds associations supposed to be lower than the spirit, he uses an old satirical method to make his point. Bodily impulses help the spirit realize man's natural, therefore divinely purposed end, for those impulses are themselves part of the spiritual being. Swift's scatology seems intended to warn us to be on our guard constantly against the physical side, and not to preen ourselves with a false confidence that we have ever conquered it. Sterne, however, calls for a co-operation of the two; let us, he urges, be 'natural.' But opinion has given us a fictitious impression that the two are enemies, and thus the 'natural' man has been divided against himself. 'REASON is, half of it, SENSE; and the measure of heaven itself is but the measure of our present appetites and concoctions—' (Vol. VII, chap. 13). 'Soul and body are joint-sharers in every thing they get . . .' (Vol. IX, chap. 13).

Sterne remained with Locke, and, despite his keen interest in psychology, showed no sign of going along with the more 'up-to-date' post-Lockians of the Hartley school. Certainly Locke's own attitude towards the mind was more acceptable to Sterne than the mechanical system envisaged by the pure associationists. Sterne could never think of mental activity as the mere setting up of connections in a neural machine. Locke thought that, even if the mind be matter, still at the centre was a living, sensitive something, capable of self-awareness. He solved the vexed problem of personal identity (to his own satisfaction, if not to that of others) with the statement that '*Self* is that conscious thinking thing,—whatever substance made up of (whether spiritual or material, simple or compounded, it matters not)—which is sensible or conscious of pleasure and pain, capable of happiness or misery, and so is concerned for itself, as far as that consciousness extends' (*Essay*, II.xxvii.17).

The 'self' of Locke is transformed into the 'sensibility' of Sterne, which Yorick apostrophizes in *A Sentimental Journey* as 'source inexhausted of all that's precious in our joys, or costly in our sorrows! thou chainest thy martyr down upon his bed of straw—and 'tis thou who lift'st him up to HEAVEN—Eternal fountain of our feelings!—'tis here I trace thee—and this is thy "divinity which stirs within me." ' New values have been added to the 'self': it is now also the agency of aesthetic and ethical experience. We exist to feel. The more the chords of our senses, external and internal, are touched, the more we become spiritual beings in the true sense of the word. The idea that the mind is a physical organ finally could lead to opposite kinds of response. One would make everything mechanical; the spiritual is eliminated, as in the young Godwin. On the other hand, the physical could be absorbed into the spiritual, as in Romanticism generally. Emotion, impulse, raw sensation, could take on values previously reserved exclusively to the soul. Purely physical experience takes on spiritual excellence, and, in Carlyle's phrase, nature is 'supernaturalised.' The sensibility, the divinity within us, must be exercised, as the mind must be strengthened. When we feel compassion for another, as often as we are in love, even when we suffer, we resemble the 'great SENSORIUM of the world! which vibrates, if a hair of our heads but falls upon the ground, in the remotest desert of thy creation—.' The capacity for intense feeling for others as well as self is the prerogative that man and God share. Illusory opinion, however, by cutting off as unworthy many sources of stimulus for the sensibility, has withered many souls. The end of life is not the contemplation of the Aristotelian tradition, but an exquisite awareness.

Locke, as I have indicated, assumed that there is a direct, unmediated intuitus of truth when the understanding sees the ideas arranged in proper order. Thus he condemned the operations of formal logic as usually unnecessary and often misleading. The inference is that the more elaborately reasoned a theory is, the more we should suspect it. Sterne illustrates the point in common and simplified imagery, in Volume III, chapter 40 of *Tristram Shandy*. Locke believed that the common man can see the truth at least as clearly as the specialist. The idea, of course, is essential to the whole Enlightenment; the Royal Society, as

Sprat reported, preferred the language of artisans to the terms of art. Uncle Toby, the least philosophical and most uncomplicated person in *Tristram Shandy*, at once accounts for the sense of duration in the same manner as Locke—"'Tis owing, entirely, . . .' to the 'succession of our ideas'—although, he says, he understands the 'theory of that affair' no more than his horse. By simply observing his own mind without preconceptions as to what he would discover, he solved the puzzle that had baffled the philosophers.

In the eighteenth century there was growing a reliance on the immediate response to experience—a reliance that to be sure went beyond what Locke himself would have approved.[1] If the understanding has operated so inefficiently, if the faults of thinking are so deeply imbedded in the mind, may not the intuitive, even instinctive response to a situation—before ratiocination—be the most trustworthy? Shaftesbury and Thomas Burnet suggested and Hutcheson developed the theory of an 'inner sense,' corresponding to the outer ones, that reacts with pleasure or displeasure to situations as reflected in the mind's eye; it perceives good and bad as the outer sense perceives, or seems to perceive colour. There is a movement in Sterne from the sermon in Volume II of *Tristram Shandy*, with its definition of 'conscience' as a sort of monitor or judge in the mind, recalling Adam Smith's 'third person' who views our conduct from without, to the unqualified emphasis on immediate sensibility in *A Sentimental Journey*. The development is typical of the times.

The opinions of the understanding, unfortunately, can break the circuits nature has set up, which should operate as naturally and instantly as the reflexes. Theological dogmas are among the worst offenders. In *A Sentimental Journey*, Yorick, influenced by his acquired prejudices, rejects the poor monk, whom he sees as an abstraction created by generations of preaching and propaganda. The reality, the pitiable human being, has been replaced by an artificial entity. But, a moment later, as the figure crowds back into his imagination, his natural reactions reassert themselves, and he responds in the right, the

[1] The 'moral sense' theory owed much, as it seems to me, to Lockian psychology, even though Locke himself was dubious about the idea. See my article 'The Origins of the "Moral Sense,"' *HLQ*, 11 (1948), 241.

natural manner, with sympathy. This is an example of the
sentimental education we all need, and it demonstrates the part
the imagination can play in restoring us to ourselves. Yorick's
sermon on 'Vindication of Human Nature' gives another instance
of opinion destroying the harmonious operation of natural
benevolence. There are selfish and unscrupulous persons in the
world, to be sure; and logic, universalizing instead of looking
into the heart, has produced the doctrine that human nature is
innately evil. What is the consequence?

... to involve the whole race without mercy under such detested characters, is a conclusion as false, as it is pernicious; and
was it in general to gain credit, could serve no end, but the
rooting out of our nature all that is generous, and planting in
the stead of it such an aversion to each other, as must untie the
bands of society, and rob us of one of the greatest pleasures of
it, the mutual communications of kind offices; and by poisoning
the fountain, rendering every thing suspected that flows through
it.[1]

The title *The Life and Opinions of Tristram Shandy, Gentleman* hints strongly at the relation of this book to Locke's reform.
The epigraph of Volumes I and II, from Epictetus, is translated:
'It is not actions but opinions concerning actions, which disturb
men.'[2] For, as Locke says in the following eloquent passage,
opinions are the most dynamic things in our lives.

Temples have their sacred images, and we see what influence
they have always had over a great part of mankind. But, in
truth, the ideas and images in men's minds are the invisible
powers, that constantly govern them; and to these they all
universally pay a ready submission. It is, therefore, of the
highest concernment, that great care should be taken of the
understanding, to conduct it right, in the search of knowledge,
and in the judgments it makes.

(*The Conduct of Understanding*, sec. 1)

Sterne, employing the comic and satirical imagination, shows
us how opinions rise; by taking us into other minds, and

[1] *The Sermons of Mr. Yoricke* (Oxford and Boston, 1927), I, 83.
[2] I have used, for *Tristram Shandy*, the indispensable edition of James
A. Work (Odyssey Press), whose translation this is.

primarily into his own, for that is what he can know best, he gives concrete reality to what Locke had discussed. Sterne, like most satirists, aims at pride. In the sermon 'Job's Account of Life,' he asks:

Does not an impartial survey of man—the holding up this glass to shew him his defects and natural infirmities, naturally tend to cure his pride and cloath him with humility, which is a dress that best becomes a short-lived, wretched creature?

But the pride satirized is not that which Swift or Pope had attacked. The glass most satirists hold up reflects the deviations from a 'norm' and contrasts its objects with the ideal of the reasonable man. Sterne's mirror reflects the mind in its hidden operations, underneath the appearance of reason on which we all pride ourselves. He seeks to correct our smug assumption that all within our heads is neat and orderly, and that the mad and even the eccentric are different in *kind* from ourselves.

Tristram Shandy frequently is classified as a novel and fitted, although not without awkwardness, into the history of that form. To be sure, Sterne's influence on the techniques of such modern novelists as Virginia Woolf is not to be denied; but, I should suggest, neither the evocation of the atmosphere of the mind nor the presentation of character in the round a primary intention for him. Sterne connected his work with those of Rabelais, Cervantes, and Swift. The first named, as Erich Auerbach has pointed out, had a serious purpose underneath the jest: 'a fruitful irony which confuses the customary aspects and proportions of things, which makes the real appear in the super-real, wisdom in folly, rebellion in a cheerful and flavorful acceptance of life.'[1] Rabelais and Swift and Sterne, for all their differences, had in common the fact that they lived in times of great change and they were aware of the need for shaking up sacrosanct and ossified opinions; they used satirical comedy, in their respective ways, as a kind of solvent to break up the crystallizations of thought. To change the figure, Sterne, with Locke, saw the need for letting air and light into the stuffy world of Europe, represented by the little world of the

[1] 'The World in Pantagruel's Mouth,' in *Mimesis: The Representation of Reality in Western Literature*, transl. Willard Trask.

Shandys. Rabelais tells us that the drug within the box is more valuable than the outside promises and that the subjects treated are not so foolish as the title suggests. The wise reader will search for the deeper meaning as a dog breaks open a bone to get at the marrow. Perhaps with the precedent in mind, Sterne said that he wrote a 'careless kind of a civil, nonsensical, good-humored *Shandean* book, which will do all your hearts good—. And all your heads, too,—provided you understand it.' He assumed the role of the jester, whose cap and bells license him to tell home truths to his exalted audience. For the epigraph to Volumes III and IV, he expanded the *Policraticus* of John of Salisbury: 'in quibus fuit proposti semper, a jocis ad seria, a seriis vicissum ad jocos transire.' What wisdom do we learn? It is that we are beholding the human family; we look into the glass the author holds up and we behold—our own minds. So comprehensive a scope called for a different, a more 'civil' satire. Sterne could write the more biting kind, also; but his purpose, it may be, called for the persona of Yorick, the most attractive of Shakespeare's jesters, or for that of the ill-fated but romantic Tristram. In disagreeing with Locke's condemnation of wit, however, Sterne associated himself with the tradition of Rabelais and Swift rather than with the new, more and more biteless, 'good-humored' comedy with which he was to be identified in the years after his death.

Finding the reasons for the prevalent 'obscurity and confusion' of thought was, as I have remarked, the first cause of Locke's investigation. Mr. Shandy, that universal philosopher, identified some obvious ones—'dull organs,' 'slight and transient impressions made by objects,' 'a memory like unto a sieve' (Vol. II, chap. 2). We may add to these the dominance of passion over reason. That is to say, the usual explanation for human error and folly was in terms of physical defects or ethical fault. Locke's contribution was to identify other sources of error, which are indigenous to the mind. One is the tendency, without any reason of self-interest or passion, to construct towering, well organized theories giving every appearance of being true:— but, unfortunately, false, because, like the webs constructed by the Spider in Swift's *Battle of the Books*, they are spun from the mind and not based on the facts of nature. Man loves to spin these gossamers: a harmless enough amusement, if only they were not often accepted as true. 'Who knows not what odd notions many men's heads are filled with, and what strange ideas all men's brains are capable of?' (*Essay*, iv.v.7). It could well be the epigraph of *Tristram Shandy*. The vast extent of human thought, philosophy, religion, science, literature, medicine, is seen as a hothouse of grotesque and fantastic growths. Sterne's purpose is to make us see these growths as they are, exposing them to raillery by setting forth parodies of them. The prodigious Slawkenbergius is akin to the heroic Scriblerus. But Slawkenbergius is much closer to ourselves. Hence, perhaps, we feel an affection for the German Gothic marvel greater than we feel for the pedants of earlier satirists.

Mr. Shandy is the ordinary man touched by this kind of folly. He emulates, at a humble distance, the eminent philosophers who have imposed their fancies on the world. Swift regarded system-makers and conquerors as the great scourges of the human race. Sterne in fact took a dark view of them also, but he shows us humour under what seems to be a different and kindlier light. Mr. Shandy constructs his wondrous hypotheses for the sheer joy of hypothesizing. He is constantly trapped in odd dilemmas that exist only within his own brain, and he recalls Locke's warning that 'The eagerness and strong bent of the mind after knowledge, if not warily regulated, is often an hindrance to it.' (*The Conduct*, sec. 25.) He is one of those who, as Locke again says, 'stick at every useless nicety, and expect mysteries of science in every trivial question or scruple.' Amusing as he is, he still represents a class that Sterne's age especially feared. He 'was systematical, and like all systematick reasoners, he would move both heaven and earth, and twist and torture every thing in nature to support his hypothesis' (Vol. I, chap. 19). The difficulty is that we are all system-makers, at least in potentia, and so we are easily dazzled and misled by theories which attract us more than does the plain face of truth. Madame du Chatelet expressed the attitude of her time when she wrote: 'Les hipothèses deviennent le poison de la philosophie quand on les veut passer pour la vérité.'[1]

Mr. Shandy takes on a further meaning, however, when we remember that the age was in its way as paradoxical as a

[1] Quoted by Ira O. Wade, in *Voltaire and Candide* (Princeton, 1959). See his clear summary of the problem of hypotheses in this time.

Shandean hypothesis. On one side was the bugaboo of the system, and everyone was glad that the world was progressing beyond the darkness of scholasticism. Yet no century, not even the thirteenth, was fonder of constructing systems; only this period could have produced the tribe of Whiston and his many successors, who explained the whole geological history of the earth from Creation to Judgment on the basis of one idea. Titles of systems published in this age, of both moral and natural philosophy, would fill a volume. What, then, impels people, against their own principles, into this extravagance? Most of Mr. Shandy's theories, Tristram says, 'I verily believe, at first enter'd upon the footing of mere whims, and of a vive la Bagatelle'; and he warns the reader, as Locke had done, 'against the indiscreet reception of such guests, who, after a free and undisturbed entrance, for some years, into our brains,—at length claim a kind of settlement there' (Vol. I, chap. 19).

Tristram Shandy rides along on what Locke had identified as the 'association of ideas,' and it has the distinction of being the first literary work to exploit thoroughly this discovery. Sterne continued to use the phrase in Locke's meaning, disregarding later psychological theorists who described all mental activity as fortuitous combinings of impressions; therefore, the term means for Sterne the combinations which by chance form outside the reflective activity of the understanding. Simple ideas enter into associations (and there is the feeling that they do indeed act independently, motivated by forces beyond and sometimes unknown to the understanding) which do not correspond to anything in nature. These combinations, once formed, 'always keep in company, and the one no sooner at any time comes into the understanding, but its associate appears with it; and if they are more than two which are thus united, the whole gang, always inseparable, show themselves together' (*Essay*, ii.xxxiii.5). Today we are so constantly bombarded by these gangs that it is hard for us to realize the shocking effect of Locke's chapter. It inaugurated a Copernican revolution in psychology, even though its full implications for advertising and propaganda did not begin to be realized until the nineteenth century. To Sterne it was not merely a novelty, the source of another and promising kind of humour. He was, for example, one of the first to realize what manipulated associations—consciously created by new magicians of the mind—could achieve. The contrast between Mr. Shandy's and Trim's respective orations on death leads to an important although seemingly off-hand observation. Mr. Shandy is a natural rhetorician, of the old school, 'proceeding from period to period, by metaphor and allusion, and striking the fancy as he went along' (phrases, by the way, adapted from Locke's severe criticism of rhetorical arts); but Trim, by a simple, perfectly managed gesture, dropping his hat, created an immediate, unreasoned association of impressions, producing a much greater effect on the heart than did Mr. Shandy's rhetorical philosophizing (Vol. V, chap. 7). Then Sterne is moved to recommend Trim's hat to 'Ye who govern this mighty world and its mighty concerns with the engines of eloquence.' They were slow to wake up to the possibilities of this wonderful device, but of what they have done with it since, we are only too sadly aware. Locke did distrust appeals to fancy in metaphors and analogies, but how would he have regarded this new and more powerful method of enchaining the mind?

Locke, then, described in detail the idols of the tribe and of the cave. Some are intrinsic to the psyche itself; and we are at the mercy of forces within our own minds which seem to carry on their own life and which, Locke went so far as to say, may be irresistible. We can only understand them and try to avoid the situations, especially in childhood, that liberate them. He first identified what we should call obsession, and showed how ubiquitous it is. We recall Mr. Shandy when we read this passage:

we may find that the understanding, when it has a while employed itself upon a subject which either chance, or some slight accident, offered to it, without the interest or recommendation of any passion; works itself into a warmth, and by degrees gets into a career wherein, like a bowl down a hill, it increases its motion by going, and will not be stopped or diverted. . . . (*The Conduct*, sec. 45)

Behind this interesting phenomenon is a 'troublesome intrusion of some frisking ideas which thus importune the understanding, and hinder it from being better employed.' What a suggestion

the antics of the 'frisking ideas' might have provided for
Sterne! 'Strange combination of ideas,' he explains, 'the
sagacious *Locke*, who certainly understood the nature of these
things better than most men, affirms to have produced more
wry actions than all other sources of prejudice whatsoever'
(Vol. i, chap. 5). Having emphasized the point so strongly,
Locke, we might expect, would proceed to show how great
superstitions, wars, and persecutions have come out of the
waywardness of the mind. But there is none of the porten-
tousness we expect from Freudian studies of abnormality.
Sterne, with his genius for language, uses Locke's own word to
describe the illustrations Locke gives—'wry.' They are
congenial to the spirit of Sterne, sometimes even in language
as well as in substance. Comic-grotesque, most of them are
taken from commonplace episodes of life. Sterne, of course,
recalls the statement of the general principle of association,
but Locke's concrete suggestions may well have had their
influence also. Some people, Locke recounts, see in the dark 'a
great variety of faces, most commonly very odd ones, that
appear to them in a train one after another.' There was a lady
'of excellent parts,' who had got to be past thirty without
having had such an experience, and doubted its possibility;
but, sure enough, 'some time after drinking a large dose
of dilute tea,' she did see exactly such a variety of faces'
(*The Conduct*, sec. 45). There is the strange case of the young
gentleman

who having learnt to dance, and that to great perfection, there
happened to stand an old trunk in the room where he learnt. The
idea of this remarkable piece of household stuff had so mixed
itself with the turns and steps of all his dances, that though in
that chamber he could dance excellently well, yet it was only
whilst that trunk was there; nor could he perform well in any
other place, unless that or some other trunk had its due
position in the room.   (*Essay*, ii.xxxiii.16)

People may be oblivious to the company, so that 'when by any
strong application to them they are roused a little, they are like
men brought to themselves from some remote region; whereas
in truth they come no farther than their secret cabinet within,
where they have been wholly taken up with the puppet, which

is for that time appointed for their entertainment.' Here are sketches for Shandean portraits.

How Sterne probed dogmas may be shown by the Shandys' discussion of duration and time, in volumes II and III. Time, we hardly need to be reminded, has always been a puzzle, but the eighteenth century found itself in one of its oddest dilemmas with regard to the problem. It found itself confronted by two quite contradictory but seemingly irrefutable conclusions. The pillars of the Newtonian universe were the conceptions of absolute space and absolute time. As Miss Nicolson has shown in *Mountain Gloom and Mountain Glory*, the space in which the planets move came to be identified with infinity and to be considered a divine attribute. Absolute time in like manner came to be identified with eternity and also to form an attribute of deity. Must not our experience, logically, share in this majestic and invariable march which carries everything in the universe? How, if nature forms a great and harmonious system, could any part go its own eccentric way, or exist in its own private time?

But, Locke had demonstrated from introspection, our sense of 'duration,' which gives rise to the complex idea of time, is purely subjective—owing, as Uncle Toby notes, 'entirely to the succession of our ideas.' As we observe the ideas pass before our inner eye, reflected as it were on the screen of consciousness, we form the idea of duration, from the intervals between the impressions. But how uncertain, how completely subjective this is! Time may be 'long' or it may be 'short'; we lose time entirely, Locke tells us, when we are asleep, for without consciousness it does not exist for us. If Adam and Eve, when they were alone in the world, 'instead of their ordinary sleep, had passed the whole twenty-four hours in one continued sleep, the duration of that twenty-four hours had been irrecoverably lost to them, and been for ever left out of their account of time' (*Essay*, ii.xiv.5). If this wholly subjective sense of duration is, as Locke believed, the foundation for the idea of time, on what a shaky foundation must be based our apprehension of the cosmos! The confidence of the whole Enlightenment that the two histories—of the inner life, and of nature—must harmoniously fit within one ordered universe could be challenged at this point. Sterne saw the dilemma more clearly than did the philosophers, for even Hume felt that the question of time, although not answered satisfactorily by Locke, could be quite nicely solved.

Sterne used the old debate about the interpretation of Aristotle's observations on 'unity of time' in the drama as the vehicle for his presentation of the paradox. Our inner experience, as we observe the succession of ideas—itself subject to moods and passion—is what we really know. The critics who demanded that the chronological time of the action of a play must correspond exactly with the measured time elapsed in presenting it had got this inner experience hopelessly confused with the march of the universe. But it is with the inner life that the literary artist, whether dramatist or narrator, is concerned. If he is successful, he governs the consciousness of the spectator, causing the ideas to pass before it, slowly or rapidly as the mood he creates may dictate. 'The train and succession of our ideas,' Sterne assures his readers, 'is the true scholastic pendulum,—and by which, as a scholar, I will be tried in this matter,—abjuring and detesting the jurisdiction of all other pendulums whatever' (Vol. II, chap. 8).

Yet, as Theodore Baird has shown in a perceptive article cited above, Sterne does not abandon 'all other pendulums whatever.' Behind the apparent ramblings and inconsequences of the book is a carefully worked out plot which has a consistent time sequence, fixed not only by Shandy family history but also by references to important events of Europe in the reigns of William and Mary and of Anne. That is, the characters do have both external and internal histories. Sterne avoids the dangers lurking in the 'stream of consciousness' technique, which may give the reader a feeling of remaining stationary as impressions float aimlessly by. Enclosed and self-contained as the Shandean world is, we are reminded of its existence in the greater one, as Uncle Toby's fortifications reflect the great campaigns of Louis XIV and the allies. So we never lose the feeling that the significance of the whole work transcends the story of one small group of humour figures.

Obviously, the book does not exist for the sake of the plot. As in many learned satires, the story serves partly as convenience, a scaffolding that supports the material in which the author is primarily interested. It wins and delights the reader, so that he will follow the author's 'digressions' into the various realms of the mind. Here I can try to point out only one of the manifold functions of the plot of *Tristram Shandy*. The plot gives the author the opportunity to do something no one had ever deliberately done in this way before, because the key had not been available before the new psychology: to show how the mind works in reconstructing a story out of memory. He anticipates, he recalls associations, a simple event calls forth reflections and associated stories; his whole personality, with its interests and special character, becomes involved and gradually emerges. A formally organized, logical plot delights the understanding, and Tristram keeps lamenting that he cannot tell his story in that way. At the end of Volume VI, he draws a series of kinky lines illustrating the advance of the action, which he contrasts with an absolutely straight line drawn, in significant symbolism, with the aid of a 'writing-master's ruler (borrowed for that purpose).' Artificiality, in the emblem of the writing-master and his ruler, contrasts with the natural movement of the mind. But Sterne warns us, as he does elsewhere, that this is not to be taken too literally: 'In a word, my work is digressive, and it is progressive, too,—and at the same time' (Vol. I, chap. 22). Neither is the work, like a 'stream of consciousness' novel, a look into the mind in undress. It is, indeed, a 'conversation.' The affectation of whimsy covers a development of effects. We come to know the Shandy family, as we come to know most families, not in a systematic way, but bit by bit, puzzling pieces of information gradually coming to fit into a pattern, and a unique atmosphere coming to be sensed. To understand people, with all their oddities and eccentricities which really constitute personality, we should discover them naturally, as we do in the disorganized but revealing course of ordinary experience. Again, however, although we observe people and events from within Tristram's consciousness, we are not imprisoned in that subjective world. As we have the history of Europe establishing points of reference for the divagations of the Shandy family, so we observe Tristram himself from the outside—in the person of his alter ego, Yorick. We have an objective description and estimate of his appearance and his character as they are after he had become a man, and we return to Tristram with a new insight.

Those two curious but very important phenomena of the mind, fantastical opinionizing, and association of ideas, are for Sterne as for Locke central problems of life. But Sterne's evaluation of them differs from that of Locke himself. The moral of *Tristram Shandy*, if so formal a word can be applied to such a creation, is the danger of Opinion itself. The impulse to erect theories on every subject, to elaborate, distinguish, force everything into an artificial order, constantly threatens to narrow and distort the psyche. The over-busy intellect intrudes upon and threatens to dominate the direct reactions to impression. Many instances are scattered throughout *Tristram Shandy*. Ernulphus' anathema is representative. The hatred engendered by squabbling over logical but essentially unreal theological opinions leads to this glorious but terrible exercise of the imagination. The wonderfully elaborate condemnation of fellow human beings to all kinds of frightful punishments, for nothing but a disagreement in logic, shows how the chords of sympathy can be severed.

A supreme irony in this book is the demonstration of how Locke's own attack on false and obscure reasoning can be perverted to produce exactly what he tried to eliminate. Mr. Shandy prides himself on his deep reading of the *Essay*, but his educational programme is one ideally designed to produce in the child exactly what Locke most deplored. One of Locke's most cherished points was that words must have precise and concrete meanings. A word corresponds to a simple idea. Even an abstract word may designate one simple quality—e.g., whiteness— isolated from many different groups of simple ideas. The substitution of words for things had been one of the most fruitful sources of error. However, the gradual but accurate process of stocking the mind with ideas derived only from experience is too slow for Mr. Shandy. Ordinarily, he explains, a single word represents an idea, and, 'when the mind has done that with it— there is an end,—the mind and the idea are at rest,—until a second idea enters;—and so on' (Vol. V, chap. 42). How much better to multiply ideas without waiting for the experience! Hence his astounding scheme for using the 'auxiliaries'—'to set the soul a going by herself upon the materials as they are brought her; and by the versatility of this great engine, round which they are twisted, to open new tracks of enquiry, and make every idea engender millions.' And so back to opinion-spinning.

In contrast, there are Uncle Toby's inveterate association of every idea with his military game, and his inability to follow learned discourse. Instinctively kind and benevolent, he is a secular saint, but he seems to be hopelessly impractical in this world. Thus we tend to see him, with Mr. Shandy's eyes, as both lovable and irritating. Again, however, the deeper meaning is not what appears on the surface. One of Yorick's functions is to expose these prejudiced judgments. Thus when Trim, who shares much of Toby's character, repeats the ten command-ments (having to begin with the first, since they form a train of ideas and go together), he inspires one of Mr. Shandy's typical orations. It is all rote learning, he says, believing he is applying Locke's principle that words are substituted for things, and that we must know truth by experience. He will lay out Aunt Dinah's legacy in 'charitable uses (of which, by the bye, my father had no high opinion) if the corporal has any one deter-minate idea annexed to any one word he has repeated.' Where-upon the corporal replies that the words mean he allowed his parents, when old, 'three halfpence a day out of my pay'; and Yorick exclaims 'thou art the best commentator upon that part of the Decalogue; and I honour thee more for it, corporal *Trim*, than if thou hadst had a hand in the *Talmud* itself' (Vol. V, chap. 32). A chapter could be written on the many signifi-cances of this episode. It can only be noted here that the story points up the meaning of Locke in a way that, we may be sure, would have delighted him. The comparison of Trim's answer and the Talmud suggests that concrete meaning, represented by action, is vastly superior to the multiplication of elaborate but abstract interpretations and allegories. The story has implica-tions also for benevolism, an emotion which, as was to become clear, could easily be merely a self-indulging luxury.

The truth about Uncle Toby is rather different from what we at first expect. He epitomizes the immediate, forthright, response to experience, and can hardly be the absurd but saintly fool we at first take him for. He it is who discovers, without reading, the explanation of duration. He defends his taking up the profession of arms with a real eloquence that contrasts with the pompous rhetoric of Mr. Shandy. He teaches

Tristram the lesson about compassion, in the episode of the fly, with an instinct for truly effective pedagogy. His compassion for Le Fever—based, by the way, on old military comradeship as well as on the general sense of sympathy—produces the great act of *practical* benevolence in the book. An important sign post to his real nature is the contrast between his and Mr. Shandy's respective humours. Tristram informs us that Mr. Shandy gave himself up to his great 'TRISTRA-*poedia*,' or institute for the boy's education, 'with as much devotion as ever my uncle *Toby* had done to his doctrine of projectils.—the difference between them was, that my uncle *Toby* drew his whole knowledge of projectils from *Nicholas Tartaglia*—My father spun his, every thread of it, out of his own brain,—or reeled and cross-twisted what all other spinners and spinsters had spun before him, that 'twas pretty near the same torture to him' (Vol. V, chap. 16). Thus the one derives his information from a factual authority, even if an old one, while the other is a web-spinner of theories.

But what are we to say of his comic obsession with curtins and horn works? Here Sterne, I should suggest, makes a departure from Locke. As we read the latter's examples of the involuntary association of ideas, we may wonder, a little, whether they are so unfortunate after all. They provide spectators with innocent amusement, and most of them are quite harmless; they may even provide the victim himself with a kind of pleasing and consoling illusion. Sterne shared the common faith of his generation that the system of the universe reflects the benevolence of its Creator. Are the strange obsessions and curious quirks of the mind nothing but pointless oddities or nuisances? May they not ease our way through this life, which Sterne, beneath his gaiety, felt so deeply to be troubled and sad? May they not compensate for sorrows and disappointments, enabling us to 'Shandy it' through this mortal life with a fair share of the joy we should all have? The erratic fortune of the Shandys has robbed Uncle Toby of his profession and his ideal. He is not really a perennial ineffectual, for he has mastered a difficult and hard profession and has served bravely in war. Is not his hobby-horse a kindly provision in the scheme of things, filling up the void in his life? And, indeed, as Sterne asks, why should we begrudge each other our hobby-horses if we ride peaceably down the King's highway, and if we do not attempt to force our humours on others?

Alas, however, we do not tolerate one another. Our opinions become sacred truths, above the test of experience. Mr. Shandy's hypotheses are backed only by his impetuous and domineering personality, but those of others, just as odd and illusory in their ways, have acquired the support of powerful institutions and turned into instruments of repression. We try to understand what we cannot understand, and, trying to peer into the empyrean, we lose our way in this world.

I might summarize all this by comparing, once again, Rabelais and Sterne. To the former the new learning of the Renaissance provided a lever by which he could move the mass of dead ideas and institutions that lay like a heavy weight on the human spirit in his time. For Sterne, it seems to me, Locke's *Essay concerning the Human Understanding* performed a somewhat comparable function. It was not that Locke and Sterne agreed in everything, but that Locke had, so to speak, wiped clean the window of the soul from the false ideas that had hitherto obscured it. Now we are in a position to look into ourselves, and, armed with that knowledge, begin to regain our place in the great system. Sterne, in a passage of *Tristram Shandy* about 'Nature,' that true deity of the age, expressed the meaning of his own work and much of the significance of Locke's as well:

She, dear Goddess, by an instantaneous impulse, in all *provoking cases*, determines us into a sally of this or that member—or else she thrusts us into this or that place, or posture of body, we know not why—But mark, madam, we live amongst riddles and mysteries—the most obvious things, which come in our way, have dark sides, which the quickest sight cannot penetrate into; . . . so that this, like a thousand other things, falls out for us in a way, which tho' we cannot reason upon it,—yet we find the good of it, may it please your reverences and your worships —and that's enough for us. (Vol. IV, chap. 17)

Literary Criticism and Artistic
Interpretation

Eighteenth-Century English Illustrations of The Seasons

RALPH COHEN

A R T historians have made clear that paintings not only can be, but need to be interpreted to be understood. Such works are assumed to be nonverbal communications, and they belong to a significant realm of human behaviour. Psychologists have pointed out that 'art both codifies and interprets. . . . Symbolic representation in art is more than merely a code; it also contains a comment, an interpretation, and a suggestion of how to understand its symbols.'[1] When illustrations or paintings are exemplifications of specific passages or parts of a poem, they are governed by principles of interpretation, and they constitute nonverbal criticisms. It is possible for an interpretation—whether verbal or nonverbal—to be irrelevant to the poem, but such irrelevance is discoverable only upon analysis.

The fact that poetry or painting or sculpture could serve as interpretation or explanation of each other was recognized in the eighteenth century; Addison declared that 'poetry being in some respects an art of designing as well as painting or sculpture,

[1] Jurgen Ruesch, *Nonverbal Communication* (Berkeley and Los Angeles, 1956), pp. 30–31.

they may serve as comments upon each other.'[1] Lord
Roscommon had earlier noted that looking at painting and looking at drama involved common visual terms. Charles Lamotte
wrote that art gives subjects to poetry as poetry gives subjects
to art.[2] Joseph Spence in *Polymetis* used poetry to explain the
iconography of ancient sculpture;[3] the development of the very
word 'illustration' is an example of this interpretive function.
The original meaning of 'illustration' was 'explanation' or
'spiritual enlightenment.' Bullokar in 1676 defined 'to illustrate'
as 'to make famous, or noble, to unfold or explain.' 'Illustration,' 'illustrious,' 'lustre' continued to be applied in 1713 by
Henry Felton to spiritual illumination in literature or life. By
the end of the eighteenth century, however, the term had come
to be identified with engravings, and the meaning was extended
to 'embellishment' as well as 'explanation.'[4] The reason for this
was that illustrations or nonverbal explanations had become, as

[1] Joseph Addison, *Dialogues upon the Usefulness of Ancient Medals, in
Works*, ed. by Thomas Tickell (London, 1804), V, 20–21; Robert Wolseley,
'Preface to Rochester's *Valentinian* (1685),' *Critical Essays of the Seventeenth Century*, ed. by J. E. Spingarn (Bloomington, Ind., 1957), III,
16–17; John Dryden, *Essays*, ed. by W. P. Ker (Oxford, 1900), II,
130–131; Richard Blackmore, *The Lay Monastery*, 31 (Jan. 25, 1713),
quoted in Nathan Drake, *The Gleaner* (London, 1811), I, 33–35.

[2] Lord Roscommon, 'Notes to Horace of the Art of Poetry,' *Poems*
(London, 1717), p. 278. For a discussion of the interpretative significance
of stage setting, paintings, and book illustration upon Shakespeare criticism, see W. Moelywyn Merchant, *Shakespeare and the Artist* (London,
Oxford, 1959). For an extensive review of classical and later writers who
accepted this interchange, see Charles Lamotte, *An Essay upon Poetry and
Painting* (Dublin, 1745), pp. 41–49.

[3] Joseph Spence, *Polymetis* (London, 1755), 2d ed., p. 291. See also,
John Scott, *Critical Essays* (London, 1785), p. 205n, who proposed an
interpretive illustration for 11. 49–52 of Gray's 'Elegy.' For study of
interrelation of the arts in emblem literature see Henri Stegemeier,
'Problems of Emblem Literature,' *JEGP*, XLV (1946), 26–37; for bibliography see Robert J. Clements, 'Iconography on the Nature and Inspiration of Poetry in Renaissance Emblem Literature,' *PMLA*, LXX (1955),
781–804.

[4] [John Bullokar] *An English Expositour* (Cambridge, 1676). Henry
Felton, *A Dissertation on Reading the Classics* (London, 1713), pp. 7,
225, 'lustre'; p. 7, 'illustrious'; pp. 95, 120, 'illustrations.' For a study of
the term 'ornament' see Ruth Wallerstein, *Studies in Seventeenth-Century
Poetry* (Wisconsin, 1950), pp. 13–15, and John Bray, *A History of English
Critical Terms* (Boston, 1898), pp. 212–214.

a result of increased production and lowering of artistic standards, merely decoration. Solomon Gessner wrote that the 'warmth of imagination, without which there can be no invention, is either enfeebled or totally lost,' by constantly engraving works of others.[1] The explanatory basis of illustration, therefore, tended to be minimized and its decorative function exploited; the defenders of book illustration at the beginning of the nineteenth century sought to win it status as an independent art or brought in 'explanation' as a subsidiary function. In 1824, for example, Richard Plowman defined 'illustration' as 'nothing more than the exemplification of works of literature by works of art,'[2] but he urged that it could also be an incentive to topographical and biographical (portrait) study as well as an incentive to interpretation by causing the reader to reflect on the words and the seen (scene).

Illustration plays an extremely important part in the criticism of *The Seasons* because for more than one hundred and fifty years it was the most illustrated poem in the English language. By examining the verbal criticism in the light of nonverbal criticism, the range of literary inquiry can be determined. For there were subjects, tones, insights which this inquiry could have undertaken, but neglected or resisted. And it is equally possible to specify the range of the illustrations. Literary criticism, for example, neglected the emotive unity of each season which William Kent illustrated in 1730, and did not develop explanations for it until John Aikin in 1777. Moreover the critics neglected until the nineteenth century the mythological and natural interrelations so that the processes of nature were not seen as recurrent forces which man had in all seasons to accept. Even Thomson's concern with diverse social and economic classes was neglected by critics until John Wilson stressed it in 1831.

---

[1] Solomon Gessner, 'Letter on Landscape Painting,' *New Idylles*, trans. by W. Hooper (London, 1776), p. 99; *Eighteenth-Century Book Illustration*, ed. by Philip Hofer (Los Angeles, 1956), p. iii.

[2] Richard Plowman, *An Essay on the Illustration of Books* (London, 1824), p. 9; William Gilpin, *An Essay on Prints* (1768; London, 1802), 5th ed., pp. 1–30; Carl P. Moritz, *Travels of Carl Phillipp Moritz in England in 1782* (reprint of English trans. of 1795), intro. by P. E. Matheson, (London, 1924), p. 9; 'Address,' *The Poetical Works of James Thomson* (London, C. Cooke, 1800), pp. v–vi.

The literary critics, however, recognized the independence of Thomson's nature descriptions, and in 1756 Joseph Warton even singled out a number of scenes for painting, but landscape illustrations in which the figures were insignificant began at the very end of the eighteenth century and only became characteristic in the mid-nineteenth century. Literary critics obviously dealt with a great many subjects, such as diction, imagery, comparisons between different works which illustrations could not depict, but even within the range of eighteenth-century illustration there was a frequent disregard for the moving passages such as the walk in *Spring* or the falling of the snow in *Winter*.

The resistance of literary critics to Thomson's burlesque passages—Lord Lyttelton removed the fox-hunt from the 1751 edition of Thomson's works—is revealed by their offence at such passages; illustrations, however, present caricature as an element of the poem. Wordsworth's comment (1815) that in 'any well-used copy of the Seasons the book generally opens of itself with the rhapsody on love, or with one of the stories (perhaps Damon and Musidora)'[1] reflected the prudish critical fears, whereas the tradition of the nude led artists to illustrate the passage, some even recognizing the ironic tone of the description.

If illustration can function as nonverbal criticism, it can also function as an independent work of art, but it cannot function as both simultaneously. Thomas Pennant praised Thomson as a naturalist and sprigs of flowers serve as end pieces in some editions. This function of decorative illustration began as early as 1730 in B. Picart's engravings of the statues of the seasons at Versailles, which had no relevance to Thomson's mythology. Illustrations sometimes show no actual knowledge of the poem, as Raymond Picart has remarked of Racine's eighteenth-century illustrators: 'engravers who think out for themselves the problem of illustrating, by re-reading the text they have to illustrate are very few.'[2] But most of Thomson's eighteenth-century illustrators did read the text, and William Kent, for example, revised his depiction of Musidora in the *Summer*

[1] William Wordsworth, *Works* (London, 1909), p. 871.
[2] 'Racine and Chauveau,' *Journal of the Warburg and Courtauld Institutes*, XIV (1951), 260.

illustration (1744) to accord with Thomson's revision of the Musidora passage.

Thomson's *Seasons* provided the text and perhaps even the incentive for many of Turner's and Constable's paintings. 'How I pity the unfeeling landscape painter, whom the sublime pictures of Tomson [*sic*] cannot inspire,' wrote Solomon Gessner.[1] But the inspiration of one art by another must not be confused with the interpretation of one art by another. This confusion of function has steered discussions of two arts, especially in *The Seasons*, into blind alleys. Thomas Twining remarked in 1789 that Greek poetry 'had no Thomsons because, they had no Claudes'; Sir Harris Nicolas wrote in 1830 that 'his pictures of scenery and of rural life are the productions of a master, and render him the Claude of Poets,' and the 1855 editor of Thomson remarked that 'no other poet combined to an equal extent the glow of Claude and the gloom of Salvator.'[2] Such remarks are statements about the causes of poetry or the similarity (or identity) of subject matter or effects in two arts. Neither Elizabeth Manwaring nor any other critic has provided information demonstrating that Thomson was familiar with Claude or Rosa in 1730, the publication date of the first edition of the poem. Ralph Williams has argued that *Summer* (1727) included many more 'prospect' scenes than *Winter* (1726) because Thomson was close to the poet-painter John Dyer during this period. But *Spring*, published the following year (1728), indicates no continuity of this approach and underlines the unlikeliness of Williams's explanation.[3] Although 'nature' could serve poet and painter as subject, the examination of 'effects' requires, at the least, specific works which can be examined. Passages have been compared with paintings which Thomson may or may not have seen, and 'effects' derived from

[1] Gessner, p. 102.

[2] Thomas Twining, *Aristotle's Treatise on Poetry* (London, 1789), p. 35; *The Poetical Works of James Thomson*, ed. by Sir Harris Nicolas, p. lxxxi; *The Poetical Works of Thomson, Goldsmith, and Gray* (London, 1855), p. xxvi.

[3] For discussions of poetry and painting in *The Seasons* see Elizabeth Manwaring, *Italian Landscape in Eighteenth Century England* (New York, 1925), pp. 100–108; Jean Hagstrum, *The Sister Arts* (Chicago, 1958), pp. 243–267; Alan D. McKillop, *The Background of Thomson's Seasons* (Minnesota, 1942), p. 71.

similarities in subject matter rather than from an analysis of
artistic qualities. Such approaches overlook the fact that the
poets themselves were aware of classical and renaissance traditions governing 'poetical pictures.' John Hughes, for example,
traced descriptions of morning in poets from Homer to Otway,
indicating the consistency of pictorial imagery:

'In some of these Poetical Pictures which I have here set before
the Reader, the Heavens only are shewn, and the first Springing
of Light there. In others the Earth is taken into the Prospect,
with her Flowers wet with Dew, and her rising Vapours. And
sometimes the Occupations of living Creatures, proper to the
Season, are represented and afford a yet greater Diversity of
amusing Images.'[1]

What this essay does, therefore, to avoid the vagueness of
such discussions, is to locate specific interrelations of the arts;
these occur in the illustrations to specific passages in the poem
and in the interpretation of these passages. The illustrations
need to be 'read' with the text, and in this respect they partake
of Hogarth's concept of narrative painting. Early eighteenth-
century definitions of 'read' meant not only 'to read a book'
(peruse) but (Bailey) 'to guess, divine or foretell,' and Johnson
included 'to discover by character or marks; to learn by observation.' To consider illustrations as needing to be read is not
inconsistent with these definitions, and the illustrations from
1730 to 1800 are governed by diverse reading premises.

The significance of illustrations for theory of criticism is
irrefutable: they supported, supplemented, or contradicted
verbal criticisms, but above all they tested theories of assumed
relations between descriptive poetry and painting. This test
concept was clearly and forcefully expressed in 1807:

I have often thought that there is no better way to prove the
defects or excellences of a poet, in respect to his descriptive
powers or knowledge of nature, than by making a composition
for a picture from the images which he raises, and from his own
description of his characters and their actions. You by these
means put him on trial; you will detect every deviation from
nature; and when his performance is brought to this strict

---

[1] *Poems on Several Occasions* (London, 1735), II, 334.

examination, it will sometimes happen, that what in words might seem like a true representation of nature to the poet, to the painter may appear much like a false witness in the court of justice, and he will soon be convinced that the admired work is no more than an ingenious falsehood.[1]

One critical theory that was 'put on trial' by the illustrations was that 'words . . . are but Pictures of the Thought.'[2] The illustrations constituted a refutation of this doctrine by making explicit that pictures always involved more than the words, or a selection of the words; that the same words created different pictures; that some words led not to specific pictures but to imaginative associations expressed in pictures. John Landseer, in 1807, even though he admitted that the arts could not always achieve similar effects, explained that an image such as 'the breezy call of incense-breathing morn' could be engraved—was indeed in the *Aurora* of Count Goudt—but that those 'who have not enjoyed this early freshness, in a romantic country, cannot forcibly enjoy this print, because it operates—like all the higher efforts in art, by stimulating the imagination to more than is exhibited.'[3]

Illustrations also tested the critics' use of painting vocabulary by actual illustrations, supposedly examples of this vocabulary. Robert Shiels wrote of Thomson that 'the object he paints stands full before the eye, we admire it in all its lustre.'[4] But the English illustrations to *The Seasons* up to 1753 did not display close views of objects, so that the kind of 'painting' Shiels described was independent of the available examples to the poem and prescriptive of other types. And in 1852 James R. Boyd pointed out that eighteenth-century literary critics tended to use 'picturesque' in contexts quite different from artists.[5]

Another kind of criticism directly tested by illustrations was the naming of passages that were excellent 'paintings.' Joseph Warton, for example, referred to a summer scene (11. 485–489) as 'worthy the pencil of Giocomo da Bassano, and so minutely

---

[1] *The Artist*, IX (May 9, 1807), 3–4.
[2] Abraham Cowley, 'To the Royal Society' (1667), 1. 69.
[3] *Lectures on the Art of Engraving* (London, 1807), p. 174.
[4] 'The Life of James Thomson,' in *The Lives of the Poets*, ed. by T. Cibber (London, 1753), V, 202.
[5] *The Seasons*, ed. by James R. Boyd (New York, 1852), p. 156.

delineated, that he might have worked from this sketch.'[1] The 'various groups' of herds and flocks had been included in Kent's design for summer (Fig. 1) and were a small part of the plenitude of the summer landscape, not a minutely delineated painting. When in 1793 Thomas Stothard drew the 'group' as a single illustration (Fig. 2), the illustrative concept had changed from a picture of the unity of the season to a fragmented detail of the emotive coherence of man and animal, as seen in the shape of the shepherd and the sheep. The two designs revealed quite different interpretations despite the fact that they used the same scene as subject.

The very first illustration (1730) implied that poetic as well as artistic vision was selective and emotive, but although the art critic Jonathan Richardson recognized this, literary critics developed a theory of imagined use of reality only in the second half of the century. Kent's emotive or associative view of unity rather than the dramatic view described by some literary critics came to be taken for granted, although not as a result of his illustrations. Percival Stockdale, for example, wrote in 1793: 'To excite that eager and anxious curiosity, suspense and expectation, which it is incumbent on the writer of a novel or of a drama to raise, did not enter into the plan of the Seasons.'[2] By the last decade of the century, some literary criticism stressed the need for heightened selectivity or perspectives as a basis for criticizing the poem, and the illustrations which abounded in the presentation of a variety of specific scenes supported this view. They also attacked theories of literal accuracy, for each illustration served to refute the literalness of the poem.

In the pathetic of *The Seasons*, the illustrators of the 1790's supplemented criticism by interpreting benevolence and 'goodness' in terms of the human family; with regard to the sublime of *The Seasons*—what Robert Shiels had in 1753 called Thomson's finest quality—they presented sufficiently varied instances to question the concept for criticism. The illustrations seized upon certain characteristics of the poem, and these were reshuffled in importance, depending upon the interpretation.

[1] *An Essay on the Genius and Writings of Pope* (1756; London, 1782), I, 46.

[2] Quoted in Stockdale's own *Lectures on the Truly Eminent English Poets* (London, 1807), II, 114.

The choice among the total possibilities within the four seasons tended to be restricted, but even within these limits certain scenes—such as fishing (*Spring*, 11. 379–442), Musidora, Celadon and Amelia (*Summer*, 11. 1171–1222), the man dying in the snow (*Winter*, 11. 275–321), boys skating (*Winter*, 11. 760–771)—were frequently redone, whereas the lonely mariner (*Summer*, 11. 939–950), Stothard's bare winter scene, or the drowning sailor (*Summer*, 11. 992–1000) were undertaken only once in the eighteenth century. Such repetition not only served to clarify individual interpretations, but provided examples of the robustness, vigour and broad social range of *The Seasons* (in 'Haying,' *Summer*, 11. 352–360, and in 'Sheep-shearing,' *Summer*, 11. 394–411) deliberately rejected by literary critics for moral or social reasons.[1]

The illustrations, moreover, provided an iconography which suggested the interchangeability of certain images and actions in the poem, such as the lonely wayfaring stranger (*Winter*, 11. 179–180) and the shepherd who himself becomes a lonely stranger in the storm (*Winter*, 11. 277–283). And especially in illustrations which were reworked and reinterpreted, such as the education of the young or the meeting of Palemon and Lavinia, it was possible to recognize the legitimate range of interpretation, that is, the provision of foreground, background, and expressive behaviour which the poet omitted and the illustrator required. The difference, therefore, between William Hamilton's parents teaching the young at the table (1797) and Henry Singleton's parents observing the children at their prayers, the books still lying open, specified an increased morality and sentimentality of interpretation.

The interpretative shifts from the Kent illustrations to those of the last two decades of the eighteenth century revealed, in the multiple scene illustrations, a considerable reduction in detail and scenes; unity became more representative and less encyclopædic. The variations of detail applied to one activity rather than a multiplicity of activities—ploughing and planting, for example, became representative of spring. The narrowed selection supported the verbal arguments of critics like Patrick Murdoch and James Beattie who sought to identify in the poem what the former called Thomson's 'distinguishing qualities of

[1] See John Scott, *Critical Essays* (London, 1785), pp. 322–325.

mind and *heart*.'¹ These illustrations sought to capture the characteristic elements of the seasons with reference to their expressiveness, whereas Kent sought the characteristic elements with reference to conventions of a genre.

Simultaneous with continued interpretations of unity were single scenes of representative moments. These scenes fragmented the poem far more than Kent's illustrations but, by their selection, they insisted that some passages were more typical than others. Single scenes rather than multiple scenes predominated, but within these there existed a diversity of interpretative comments far more related to current literary criticism than to the earlier comments of Thomson or his contemporaries.

There was an obvious increase in the number of scenes depicted so that the concept of 'typical' was called into question by the varied attempt to picture typicality. But despite the increase, the areas of the typical were limited to the sublime, the pathetic, and the picturesque. The high frequency of domestic scenes supported verbal statements by critics like John Aikin, Percival Stockdale, and James Beattie, who found Thomson's benevolence and piety throughout the poem. 'The rural character,' wrote Aikin, 'as delineated in his feelings, contains all the softness, purity and simplicity that are feigned of the golden age.'²

This view was not, however, unanimous among the illustrators. Thomas Stothard selected scenes depicting the gentleness and piety of man and nature, but Charles Ansell (*Spring*, 11. 690–694) and Charles Catton (the terrified sailor) and Richard Corbould (the lonely mariner, *Summer*, 11. 939–950) selected highly expressive scenes of human nastiness, terror, and loneliness. These direct expressive statements sought to capture a view of nature different from that of Kent or Stothard. They sought the immense, uncontrollable processes of nature overcoming man, or the archetypal moments of human experience. The individual and the family, the contrasting views of isolation and sociability were seen resolved in the varied powers

¹ Patrick Murdoch, 'An Account of the Life and Writings of Mr. James Thomson,' in *The Works of James Thomson* (London, 1762), I, xix.
² 'An Essay on the Plan and Character of Thomson's Seasons' (1778), reprinted in *The Seasons* (London, 1802), p. lxii.

Fig. 1. William Kent–Nicolas Tardieu, *Summer*

Fig. 2. Thomas Stothard, *Sleeping Shepherd*

Fig. 3. B. Picart, *Winter*

Fig. 4. William Kent–Nicolas Tardieu, *Spring*

Fig. 5. George Wright–E. Malpas, *Spring*

Fig. 6. William Hamilton, *Palemon and Lavinia*

Fig. 7. David Allen–James Caldwell, *Autumn*

Fig. 8. William Hamilton, Headpiece to *Spring*

Fig. 9b. Charles Ansell–A. Birrell,
Winter

Fig. 10. William Hamilton, *Skating*

Fig. 11. Charles Catton–Francis Chesham, *Summer*

Fig. 12. William Hamilton–F. Bartolozzi, *Caledon and Amelia*

of nature, and such resolutions supplanted the contrasts of status fused in the great chain of being.

II

In 1730 two sets of engravings were published, one for the octavo edition and another for the quarto. The octavo edition, issued twice in 1730, contained engravings for each season (B. Picart, designer; J. Clark, engraver), based on 'marble statues in the Garden of Versailles 7 foot high.' There were also tailpieces which had no relation to the poem (*Summer* and *Autumn* both showed a knight on horseback slaying a dragon), but the headpiece to *Summer* showed one man assisting another in sowing, and *Autumn* displayed a man in an attitude of contemplation with a book in his hand, sitting near a tree, a scene that at the end of the century became a clue to the lonely poet.

In the quarto edition of 1730 were published the Kent-Tardieu engravings, containing a frontispiece for each season. The Picart-Clark illustrations (Fig. 3) were reprinted only once again, in 1735, but the Kent designs were twice reengraved for smaller editions by Pierre Fourdrinier during Thomson's lifetime, and by Neist, Ridge, Donaldson and others after his death. There exist no comments by Thomson on these engravings, but it appears likely that the continuation of this set and the discontinuance of Picart's was in itself an expression of preference, perhaps also a judgment. Moreover, Thomson's respect for Kent as a landscaper was written into *The Seasons* in his praise of Esher Park (*Summer*, 11. 1431–1432): 'Enchanting vale! beyond whate'er the Muse / Has of Achaia or Hesperia sung!'[1]

Jean Hagstrum has suggested that the Kent illustrations suffered from badly drawn allegorical figures (see Fig. 4), and Edgar Breitenbach has objected to the allegorical figures because they are 'hollow, worn-out metaphorical imagery.'[2] But it should be stated that there exist different criteria for the

---

[1] *The Poetical Works of James Thomson*, ed. by J. Logie Robertson (London, 1951). All quotations from *The Seasons* are taken from this edition. The critical edition of *The Seasons*, including all revisions, is Otto Zippel, ed., *Thomson's Seasons, Palaestra*, LXVI (Berlin, 1908).

[2] Hagstrum, p. 263. Edgar Breitenbach, 'The Bibliography of Illustrated books,' *The Library Association Record* (May, 1935), II, 179.

illustration as interpretation and the illustration as an independent work of art, for a 'bad' engraving may be a valuable commentary upon artistic tradition or the text.

The engravings to *The Seasons* were marked, from the very beginning, by conflicting allegorical and naturalistic tendencies. Just as the poem addressed 'gentle Spring' and personified it (*Spring*, 1. 1), so, too, the illustrations in 1730 sought to convey this allegorical and naturalistic view of spring. In his designs Kent attempted to create a representative picture of the unity of each season, governed by the great chain of being leading in a series of inclined planes from natural to allegorical figures, and including earth, water, clouds, and animals, man and heavenly figures. However, the analogical unity suggested by the engravings was not that of the subject matter of each season, but the relation between the distant past and the immediate present—the movement from rural immediacy to the vague mountains in the background.

Margaret Jourdain has written that Kent's designs for *The Seasons* show Italian influences, and Bertrand Bronson has called the lower halves of the engravings 'faintly Claudian,'[1] but a comparison between Claude's *An Autumnal Evening* and Kent's *Autumn* reveals that only the use of trees as a framing device and the faint mountains in the background suggest a similarity, for the management of movement and the handling of planes are considerably different. Kent's designs were representations of types of unity in *The Seasons*, designed with a close knowledge of the particular poem, and they differed from the single-scene designs he created for *The Faerie Queene* and Gay's *Fables*. The artistic landscape tradition was absorbed and altered by the literary text.

Early illustrations for *The Seasons* show the concentration on unity rather than particularity of each season that Warton was to recommend in 1756. At least for the designer in 1730, the unity of the poem did not represent an issue, just as the letter to the London *Journal* in 1726 praised Thomson for the manner in which he connected reflections with descriptions.[2] Swift objected

---

[1] Jourdain, *The Work of William Kent* (London, 1948), p. 73; Bronson, *Printing as an Index of Taste in Eighteenth Century England* (New York, The New York Public Library, 1958), p. 35.

[2] London *Journal* (1726), as quoted in McKillop, p. 175.

to the lack of unity of action in *The Seasons*, declaring (1732) that the seasons 'are all description, and nothing is doing; whereas Milton engages me in actions of the highest importance,'[1] but Kent's illustrations implied a unity of feeling and moral value.

The unity which Kent created involved a spatial view of the supernatural and natural worlds. The upper half of each design represented the personified allegorical introduction to the season, and the bottom half several naturalistic scenes from the poem. Each of the four plates was seen from a direct and central point of view from which the countryside ascended, either to the right or the left. In the central background each plate had a mountain, faintly drawn. The engraving moved to the background in a series of inclined planes, each of which grew fainter as one looked out on the mountain. Clouds separated these planes from the allegorical figures which presided over the entire scene.

Since each season included men, women, animals, and supernatural beings, Kent was able to convey a relation between the orders of nature, beast, man, and the heavens that Thomson himself accepted. In *Spring* (11. 860–866) Thomson wrote:

> The informing Author in his works appears :
> Chief, lovely Spring, in thee and thy soft scenes
> The smiling God is seen–while water, earth,
> And air attest his bounty, which exalts
> The brute-creation to this finer thought
> And annual melts their undesigning hearts
> Profusely thus in tenderness and joy.

This attempt to convey in design the relation between heaven and earth which Thomson's *Spring* included, involved, for Kent, a careful selection of scenes (see Fig. 4). The whole top half of the design was devoted to the first allegorical lines of the poem, and those dealing with surly winter and the 'bright bull' of the zodiac, although these passages occupied a very small part of the season.

---

[1] Jonathan Swift, Letter to Charles Wogan (August 2, 1732), in *The Correspondence of Jonathan Swift*, ed. by F. Elrington Ball (London, 1913), IV, 330.

Come, gentle Spring, etherial mildness, come,
And from the bosom of yon dropping cloud,
While music wakes around, veiled in a shower
Of shadowing roses, on our plains descend.

(11. 1–4)

In addition to the area occupied, it was connected to the earth by the rainbow, a description indicated in the poem (lines 203–212). As for the naturalistic scenes, the engraving included the poet as a swain playing to the Countess of Hertford (11. 5–10), the shepherd pointing to the rainbow (11.212–217), the ducks and swans in the pond (11. 776–782), the cooing dove in amorous chase (11. 786–788), the shepherd on the mountain brow with his sportive lambs (11. 832–838), a hall (the home of one of the lovers?), a lover and his beloved (11. 962–979). Kent omitted all scenes involving violence or sorrow—the robbing of the nightingale's nest, the violent love-making of the bulls (11. 792–808), the lover's dream of death (11. 1052–1073); what he included were specific scenes representing the benevolent variety of the universe.

The interpretation, therefore, was not based upon mere subject matter, because the order and manner of treatment were different. It conveyed the activity of the allegorical figures who were in motion, and while the heavens were moving and acting the natural universe received their benefits. In visual terms Kent interpreted Thomson's argument to *Spring*: 'This Season is described as it affects the various parts of Nature, ascending from the lower to the higher; and mixed with digressions arising from the Subject.'[1] Spring and her train were sportively in motion, matched only by the earthly gambolling lambs. Thus the significance of the introduction to spring was the expression of those forces attributed to God:

But chief
Chief, lovely Spring, in thee and in thy soft scenes,
The smiling God is seen.

The function of the rainbow, too, was central to this interpretation of spring as a smiling season; the beauty of the heavens was reflected in the pond, and, like a smile, it was engaging and ephemeral. Thomson had the boy chasing the rainbow in the

[1] Thomson, 'Argument to Spring' (1728).

field, and it was an example of Kent's presentation of heavenly effects to create heaven's reflection in the pond. Not only did Kent analogize the relation between heaven and man, but he also created a structural relation between earth and the heavens. When, in 1744, Thomson added a poetic prospect from Hagley Hall, it was a possibility that the poetic passage was placed next to the lovers in the text not only because of the ideal love of Lyttelton and his wife, but also because of the 'hall' that already existed in the illustration (despite the fact that it was not a prospect view). For Thomson's description summarized the dusky landscape and the mountains 'like far clouds.'

> your eye excursive roams—
> Wide-stretching from the Hall, in whose kind haunt
> The hospitable Genius lingers still,
> To where the broken landscape, by degrees
> Ascending, roughens into rigid hills
> O'er which the Cambrian mountains, like far clouds
> That skirt the blue horizon, dusky rise.
>
> (*Spring*, 11. 956–962)

The mountains, compared to 'far clouds,' were marked by the arc-like quality of the clouds supporting and surrounding spring. Thus the rising hills were the earthly counterparts of the beclouded heaven; by establishing a relation between foreground and background (mountains) which was analogous to that between earth and heaven (top and bottom of the design) Kent created a visual unity between the hill and dales, reflective of that benevolence to be found in the allegorical heavens.

The use of inclined planes conveyed a series of incidents in the poem. But, despite the fact that Shaftesbury and later Lessing argued that a painting revealed instantaneous time, it was not possible to see all the incidents simultaneously. Moreover, the diverse scenes implied a succession of some type, whether circular or random, all appropriate to spring, and in that sense implied a period—a season—of time rather than simultaneous occurrences. Kent's illustration could be properly understood only if read within the context of specific passages. Perception was not a matter of mere instantaneous response; Dryden earlier had noted this, despite the assumption that the action, passions, and manners in a picture were theoretically to be discerned 'in the twinkling of an eye.' For, as he remarked in the discussion of Poussin's painting of 'the *Institution of the Blessed Sacrament*,' there was 'but one indivisible point of time observed; but one action performed by so many persons, in one room, and at the same table; yet the eye cannot comprehend at once the whole object, nor the mind follow it so fast; 'tis considered at leisure and seen by intervals.'[1]

The variety of incident in the poem, involving shifts in place and time, was incorporated in the engraving through artistic concepts of place and time. By the use of heavy and light shading, the mountain in the distance appeared faint and the immediate foreground very dark. But the relation between them was such that the different actions—the swain playing to the lady and the faint shepherd on the brow of the mountain—which had been seen precisely and closely in the poem were seen at receding distances in the engraving. Yet, although the shepherd grew fainter, he also grew closer to heaven. And the manner in which simultaneous and similar actions in the foreground and on the mountain could be both vivid and faint gave to the illustration a meaning independent of distance.

The poem and the illustration expressed common views of nature and man, Kent's interpretation of the poem being the smiling reflection on earth of the heavenly benevolence in *Spring*, of the astonishing power and ferocity of nature in *Winter*. This was, of course, a highly selective view of Thomson's *Spring*, but it was one view that Thomson developed. There were, too, other methods by which Kent interpreted the poem: he developed a series of correspondences between physical shapes on earth and heaven, just as Thomson compared the Cambrian mountains to 'far clouds'—

> To where the broken landscape, by degrees
> Ascending, roughens into rigid hills
> O'er which the Cambrian mountains, like far clouds
> That skirt the blue horizon, dusky rise.
>
> (*Spring*, 11. 959–962)

—and the mountains of snow to 'an atmosphere of clouds':

> And icy mountains high on mountains piled
> Seem to the shivering sailor from afar
> Shapeless and white, an atmosphere of clouds.
>
> (*Winter*, 11. 906–908)

[1] Dryden, *Essays*, II, 132.

Kent used particular scenes from the poem in his design, but the significance of these incidents was not identical with that in the poem. Neither the order nor the emphasis was the same. He used the introduction to *Spring*, the rainbow, the passion of the groves, and others, but the subjects and their role in the poem became materials to be converted into a different kind of entity in the engraving. The incidents served to establish an identification for the illustration, but the basis for the comparison was in the attitude which the artist had toward his materials, the manner in which he joined the incidents together. Thus, the introduction to *Spring*, which functioned in the poem as a formal device to create aesthetic distance, became in the illustration the central allegorical force presiding over all the events and, because of its role in the design, formed a basis for correspondence between the heavens and earth. The framing or formal device was accomplished by the marginal trees within which the whole scene was viewed.

Kent's illustration supported the proposition voiced by Addison and others that in the arts the same effects could be achieved by different means. But the second interpretative implication was that 'unity' involved selective elements and that 'wholeness' in the poem was not synonymous with wholeness of interpretation. The illustration depended upon a variety of detail both of incident and nature, so that the lambs in the foreground and on the mountain's brow, the shepherd piping to his lady and the man making love to the woman, the classical structure and the cluster of farm houses, served to convey the contrasting views of simplicity and refinement. But the illustration lacked the sensuousness, the awareness of natural processes characteristic of Thomson's description, for example, of spring flowers:

> And in yon mingled wilderness of flowers,
> Fair-handed Spring unbosoms every grace—
> Throws out the snow-drop and the crocus first,
> The daisy, primrose, violet darkly blue,
> And polyanthus of unnumbered dyes.

(11. 528–532)

III

For approximately fifty years (1730–80) the illustrations which dominated *The Seasons* were those by William Kent.

These illustrations or reengravings of them appeared in English editions of 1736, 1738, 1744, 1746, 1750, 1752, 1756, 1757, 1758, 1761, 1762, 1763, 1764, 1766, 1767, 1768, 1773, 1774, 1778, 1782. In the 1770's, however, there appeared two sets of illustrations—those by George Wright engraved by E. Malpas, (1770?) and those by David Allan, and William Hamilton engraved by [James?] Caldwell, 1778—which, while continuing some aspects of Kent's work, moved in different directions. It was not, however, until 1793, when reworkings of the Kent plates were reprinted for the last time—Daniel Dodd, designer, Thomas Cook, engraver—that Kent's direct influence disappeared from illustrations of *The Seasons*. In 1770 George Wright, while still presenting several scenes from the poem in a single plate (Fig. 5), was nevertheless intent upon a purely naturalistic unity, and the 1778 Hamilton-Caldwell illustrations separated the allegorical sculptures for each season from plates presenting single, naturalistic scenes from the poem (Fig. 6). Both sets of illustrations, however, were at one in moralizing the poem by eliminating or isolating the classical personifications. The poem was studded with reworkings of the *Georgics*, and Kent's illustration had conveyed the relation between classical and Christian concepts by means of artistic conventions. But Wright's and subsequent illustrations began to disengage the classical from the Christian view.

Wright's designs, inept as they were, had significance because they were the first which completely naturalized the poem, creating a complete separation between rural and other natural environments that was unsupported by Thomson's own words.

The notes Wright appended to the illustrated edition are directed to a new audience, and they mark the beginning of his self-imposed task of moral anthologist. In 1782, his anthology *Dear Variety, Suited to all Ages and Conditions of Life* contained the following advertisement: 'The ensuing compilation may be justly stiled *Variety*, as it consists of a *Variety* of extracts from *various* authors, upon *various* subjects; a *variety* of sentiments from *various* publications, collected at *various* times, and will doubtless be perused by *various* readers.'[1] And in *Gentleman's Miscellany* (1797) he quoted in the preface a *Monthly Reviewer* of 1788 on a previous collection, *Pleasing Reflections*

[1] George Wright, *Dear Variety*, 1782.

on Life and Manners: 'Miscellaneous collections of this kind are become very numerous; but as they generally consist of *moral* pieces, they are, to say the least of them, innocent as well as entertaining. The multiplication, therefore, of such compliments, is of no disservice to society.'[1]

Wright's illustrations, therefore, were directed to the same class which purchased the anthologies, and his badly designed frontpiece was based on the poet who retreated into the 'mid-wood shade.'

> Hence let me haste into the mid-wood shade,
> Where scarce a sunbeam wanders through the gloom,
> And on the dark-green grass, beside the brink
> Of haunted stream, that by the roots of oak
> Rolls o'er the rocky channel, lie at large
> And sing the glories of the circling year.
>
> (*Summer*, 11. 9–14)

The subject he chose to illustrate was one which, after 1790, became a commonplace in Thomson illustration: the isolated poet. The poet was aware of the conflicts between critics and creators and of his own increasing isolation; Wordsworth even pointed out the need for the poet to create his own audience. But the literary critics of *The Seasons* did not consider the wandering poet-narrator a significant figure in the work, except as he framed the point of view; however, in the illustrations of Stothard, Cranmer, or Roberts, he possessed the contemplative, dreamy qualities which were to become characteristic traits.

In criticism the disengagement of classical personification from moralized nature was argued by John Aikin (1778), who identified the unity of the poem with the seasonal laws of natural science and rejected the urban passages. Aikin sought not only to limit the poem to naturalistic subjects, with religious digressions, but he was the first to declare that the poem was the beginning of a new genre—description.

The David Allan–William Hamilton illustrations to the very edition for which Aikin wrote his 'Essay on the Plan and Character of Thomson's *Seasons*' still contained pseudo-classical allegorical figures (Fig. 7) representing each of the seasons.

[1] George Wright, *Gentlemen's Miscellany*, 1797.

Thus the illustrations presented two views of the poem, one of which insisted upon the applicability of the classical heritage as represented in sculpture. Not only did these illustrations (reprinted 1779, 1792, 1796) continue a double focus on the poem, but the removal of the allegorical figures to the title page as vignettes or ornaments was further indication of the artistic reduction of their importance from the central place given them by Kent. In 1792 Charles Ansell designed and A. Birrell engraved a title-page which contained a globe surrounded in a circle by the signs of the zodiac, but the illustrations to the text were naturalistic. In 1794 Thomas Stothard engraved a title-page to *The Seasons* in which four allegorized female figures in a ring were tied to the lines from the *Hymn*:

> 'Mysterious round! What skill, what force divine,
> Deep felt, in these appear! a simple train,
> Yet so delightful mix'd with such kind art,
> Such beauty and beneficence combine,'
>
> (11. 21–24)

The allegorized seasons had become four maidens, and the personifications in *The Seasons* who were masculine and feminine were supplanted by a naturalistic and prettified view. Even William Hamilton's attempt to recombine the allegorical and the naturalistic in 1797 failed. The headpiece to *Spring* was a combination of a single allegorical balloon-like figure of Spring floating on clouds with a garland of roses in the background of which appeared the sign of the zodiac and in the foreground two farming scenes: ploughing and planting. The naturalistic scenes were separate frames quite unrelated to allegorical spring (Fig. 8). In the 1802 (also 1805) edition edited by the Reverend Mr. J. Evans, the allegorized female figures of the seasons were relegated to the ends of each season and placed as tailpieces, in emblematic poses, although Summer and Autumn were the same figures. And in the title piece to the 1818 edition from the Chiswick Press, engraved by Thompson, the four seasons were naturalistic figures, walking with representative burdens, Spring being, as Thomson created her, the only woman among the seasons. But in addition to the reduction of importance of the allegorical figures, usually females, and their incorporation into the females of the naturalistic scenes, a similar process was apparent in the transfer of emblematic attributes from cherubs—as indicative of the seasons—to children. In the Ansell-Birrell (1792) illustrations (Fig. 9), a cherub introduced each season, but the cherub was not clearly distinguishable from an infant, and in Hamilton's *Winter* the cherub had become a child skating (Fig. 10).

According to Edgar Breitenbach, Kent's personifications of Spring and her train belong to a tradition of the late Middle Ages: 'The scheme of composition is astonishingly similar to the ones of the "planet children" representations in the fifteenth century, which likewise show, under the reign of the astral rules of providence, a survey of human occupations.'[1] But whether 'planet children' or *putti*, Kent's figures were moved from an allegorical tradition to a more literal personification by Hamilton, and to naturalistic poses by Stothard and others. Of the roles of children, there existed three types: the child as representative of the season as a whole (Ansell-Birrell's *Winter*), the child within the family related to the past through adults, home, books—involving idealized relationships within the group (Hamilton's *Paternal Instruction*), and one example (Ansell-Birrell) of children as mean—nest-snatching.

The domestication of *The Seasons*, a process apparent in the illustrations of this decade, involved simultaneously its praise as a poem expressing sentiments and feelings. Regardless of the obvious attempt to sell editions by sentiment, the absence of nature as an entity, that is, without people, was especially notable. The engravings, by disengaging themselves from a single point of view, also left behind a significant artistic tradition: the allegorical imagery which had been part of a long tradition in painting.

The Kent illustrations contained no naturalistic children, not even the swain chasing the rainbow. But beginning in 1792, the illustrations for an entire decade celebrated and sentimentalized the role of the child. The passage from the poem on paternal instruction—*Spring*, 11. 1152–1156—was illustrated by Stothard (1794) as were the passages on sheep-shearing, skating, and story-telling (*Winter*, 11. 617–620). Thomson had in *Autumn* referred to the love of kindred among many values of rural life: 'The little strong embrace / Of prattling children, twin'd around

[1] Breitenbach, p. 197.

his neck' (11. 1339–1344). But in the Cruikshank-Laurie
illustrations, scenes from the poem which did not contain children
suddenly accumulated them; thus the fisherman urged 'to thy
sport repair' (*Spring*, 11. 396–442) brought his family, and
instead of the lover (Stothard, 1793) gathering nuts for his
beloved (*Autumn*, 11. 610–619), a child shook the tree and
another held the basket. Children swam and children skated,
and in the 1797 illustrations by Hamilton, five out of seventeen
illustrations to the four seasons included children, a far greater
proportion than the space devoted to them even in the last draft
of the poem.

The domestication of *The Seasons* had its complementary
development in literary criticism with John More's argument
(1777) of the moral value of the poem and the attention to
narratives and moralizing in Aikin's essay. Such comments
were, however, beginning to be seriously questioned by the
end of the century, though still repeated. John Aikin himself
pointed out that in this respect Thomson was most easily
imitated: 'excellent as the moral and sentimental part of his
work must appear to every congenial mind, it is, perhaps, that
in which he may the most easily be rivalled.'[1] 'Moral sentiment,'
wrote John Scott (1785), quoting an 'ingenious critic,' 'is the
cheapest product of the human mind.'[2] But another aspect of the
importance of childhood in Thomsonian criticism was the Earl
of Buchan's assumption—obviously dependent upon Rousseau
—that Thomson's infancy and early years were spent in the
'pastoral country of Teviotdale in Scotland, which is full of the
elements of natural beauty, wood, water, eminence and rock,
with intermixture of rich and beautiful meadow,' and there a
child will receive impressions most conducive to genius 'more
readily than in towns or villages.'[3]

The frequent editions during this period—there were thirty-
two publications, exclusive of American and foreign, from
1790 to 1799—indicated the widened appeal of *The Seasons*.
There was a widened audience for the poem, to which the

[1] John More, *Strictures Critical and Sentimental on Thomson's Seasons*
(London, 1777), p. 166; Aikin, pp. lxii–lxiii.
[2] Scott, p. 143.
[3] Earl of Buchan (David Stuart), *Essays on the Life and Writings of
Fletcher of Saltoun and the Poet Thomson* (London, 1792), p. 183.

illustrations could cater, and both Thomas Campbell and Tennyson referred to *The Seasons* as the poem which early led them to look feelingly on nature. This view was clearly put by John Landseer (1807): 'Every artist that is worthy of his appellation, desires and endeavours by his works, that the average or general feeling of the Society to which those works address themselves, shall sympathize or accord with his own.'[1]

The social illustrations presented idealized views of the family, but in so far as these views were single scenes, they served as fragmentary insights which could be representative or particular but could not be indicative of the poem's diversity. Nevertheless this fragmentation by moving social behaviour— or its opposite—to the foreground, concentrated on expressiveness, acuteness of detail, and the contrast between sharpness of human form and the encompassing vagueness of nature.

Scenes of death in *Winter* were sometimes included with scenes of domestic bliss even in the same season. The illustrations conveyed the poem's unevenness of attitude, though Stockdale and Beattie insisted on its benevolence or purity. A good example of this procedure was the 1793 edition, which contained the fishing scene populated with children uncreated by Thomson and an illustration of the terrified sailor. In the illustration, the very mouth of the fish can be seen caught on the hook, and in Catton's design of the terrified sailor (Fig. 11) the scene is pictured as though the spectator were directly in front of the open-eyed, open-mouthed mariner and his sinking ship. Thus a sense of immediacy was created by closeness, and expressiveness of the scene made possible direct sympathy from the viewer.

This view of expression provided an interpretation similar to that developed by Robert Heron in an essay on *The Seasons* in the same volume. Heron defined poetry as the operation of sentiments and images (in this order) on the imagination and feelings, and then proceeded to compare the imagery of *The Seasons* with that of other works.[2] Thomson's passage was as follows:

[1] Landseer, p. 219.
[2] Robert Heron, 'A Critical Essay on the Seasons,' in *The Seasons* (Perth, 1793), p. 4.

A faint deceitful calm,
A fluttering gale, the demon sends before,
To tempt the spreading sail. Then down at once,
Precipitant, descends a mingled mass
Of roaring winds and flame and rushing floods.
In wild amazement fixed the sailor stands.
Art is too slow: By rapid rate oppressed,
His broad-winged vessel drinks the whelming tide,
Hid in the bosom of the black abyss.

(*Summer*, 11. 992–1000)

The passage described the contrast between the 'deceitful calm' and the precipitant onslaught of the waves, the manner in which the forces of nature suddenly surrounded and 'hid' the sinking ship. The insignificance of the sailor and his fright before the powers of nature is noted by the single line 'In wild amazement fix'd the sailor stands.' But the illustrator, Catton, made the expression of the sailor central, and he interpreted the passage as the terror of man in the face of the violent forces of nature (Fig. 11). The sailor, standing with eyes popping, mouth open, jacket unbuttoned, legs set apart—in the position of terrified amazement, of immovable uncontrol—is surrounded by a cave of waves, a 'black abyss.' The open-mouthed man is about to be swallowed by the huge mouth of waves, one sailor having already been sucked from the vessel, others clutching supports of the sinking ship. Thus man and nature are seen as two forces, the expressiveness of man helplessly overcome by the dark surrounding power, the circular tide and hollow wave indicating continuous time as well as continuous action. The interpretation of the illustration, therefore, conveyed the poem's development of clashing forces, despite the fact that it did so by altering the action of conflict. The critic, however, who would have examined Thomson's imagery, would have discovered that the vessel was personified—'drinks the whelming tide, / Hid in the bosom of the black abyss' and would have discovered that the ship is seen in a suicidal image of comfort or love ('hid in the bosom of the black abyss').

The artistic interpretation was expressed through associations, and indeed, the centrality of the mariner was the result of a painting tradition. For this reason, the 'reading' of these illustrations demanded a language of gesture that was often associative rather than directly responsive to the poem. The 'reading' or 'interpretation' required for single scenes, containing frequently the pertinent passage at the foot of the illustration, was different from that applied to Kent's designs. The mariner involved a considerable alteration of emphasis as well as fact, for Thomson had made reference to 'the sailor,' not to a crew. Such changes of fact occurred in many illustrations: for example, G. Wright annotated 'steers' as 'oxen' (*Spring*, 11. 35–36) and then drew horses or donkeys as plough animals. But the difference between factual changes and interpretative changes was considerable. Expressive illustrations of the seventeen-nineties attempted to interpret not facts or literal statements, but the associative or emotive qualities of the poem. They sought to interpret language through gesture and feeling by direct proximity. The reduction of scenes, therefore, was an attempt to create immediacy rather than an artistic procedure which presupposed instantaneous response. And the amorphous shape of the background—as in William Hamilton's illustration of Caledon and Amelia (Fig. 12)—became the deliberately undefined nature in which man lived and died.

Thomson's use of nature as background can be studied in these illustrations with respect to a concept such as the 'sublime.' Illustrations of 'sublime' passages in *The Seasons* revealed that Thomson's 'sublime' language and his situations were used in diverse contexts. The poetic terms used by Thomson for the sublime included 'astonish,' 'astound,' 'admire,' 'daunt,' 'dreadful' ('dreadful motion'), 'howling' ('howling waste'), 'stiffened' ('stiffened corpse'), 'froze,' 'polished,' 'marbled.' The terms were related to death, to the final absence of mobility, to dread of death, to awe, moral and physical, though they could be used to suggest the pleasurable sublime in such a phrase as 'pleasing dread.'

The poem contained varied uses of the sublime: the cattle killed by lightning—'and stretched below / A lifeless group the blasted cattle lie' (*Summer*, 11. 452)—the sailor in 'wild amazement fixed' (*Summer*, 1. 997), the amazed swain who 'runs / To catch the falling glory' (*Spring*, 11. 214–215), the Eastern tyrants who know not love but only 'bosom-slaves, meanly possessed / Of a mere lifeless, violated form' (*Spring*, 11. 1133–1134). Caledon staring at the dead Amelia,

Pierced by severe amazement, hating life
Speechless, and fixed in all the death of woe.
So, faint resemblance! on the marble tomb,
The well-dissembled mourner stooping stands,
For ever silent and for ever sad.

(*Summer*, 11. 1218–1222)

The nude Musidora returning from her swim and discovering
the note from Damon,

With wild surprize,
As if to marble struck, devoid of sense,
A stupid moment motionless she stood.

(*Summer*, 11. 1344–1346)

The illustrations of the sailor, the swain, Caledon, and Musidora made clear that the conceptions of the sublime involved
not only situations and places, but applied to good or bad
situations, to serious or sentimental ones. Johnson's definition
of 'amazement'—'astonishment or perplexity, caused by an
unexpected object, whether good or bad—in the former case it
is mixed with admiration, in the latter with fear'—summarized
only some of the uses of the term in *The Seasons*. The critical
value of illustrations of passages identified as 'sublime' was that
they interpreted a variety of specific instances. These illustrations and John Scott's and Robert Heron's examination of
specific passages were all the consequence of a view insisting
on the critical descent to particulars. But the illustrations also
drew attention to concepts assumed to be clear in one art, but
not equally clear or traditional in another. Thus the illustrations
supported the diversity of meaning of 'sublime' by indicating
the variety of contextural characteristics.

The criticism implicit in the illustrations, governed by
artistic traditions, were not identical with literary criticisms,
even when both were interpretative. For it was self-evident that
artistic interpretation, keyed to specific passages, dealt with the
range of the poet, his attitude toward his material, his organiza-
tion or unity, and his attitude to the audience. The Kent illustrations, for example, dealt with unity in a formalized rural or
landscape view. But Stothard's illustrations (1793) domesticat-
ing the poem were directed at an audience with sentimental
attitudes toward the family and nature. That *The Seasons*

contained both these elements could be certified by an analysis of specific passages. The illustrations of Stothard and other designers who did individual scenes seemed to encourage interpreting *The Seasons* as a series of poems, what Robert Shiels in 1753 had called an 'assemblage of ideas.'[1] But the random quality of the illustrations seemed sufficient warranty against such procedure. Interpretation, in other words, had to be analysed with respect to specific concepts such as unity, the sublime, or the pathetic.

There were many critical areas to which illustrations were not relevant. Even within analysis they could not handle versification, and they could handle imagery only if language was assumed to be pictured. The tests of poetic value could be treated only if they were based on vividness, visual or imaged, and illustration could only eliminate such inadequate theories, not provide better ones. But the study of illustrations reveal that they implied solutions to literary problems (emotive unity) often before such unity was articulated, and that they pointed to a range of illustration which criticism often deliberately or for literary reasons ignored—like the nude and Thomson's burlesque. Such illustrations also demonstrated, in the last decade of the eighteenth century, that valuable interpretative practices often resulted from pressures external to the poem. In the 1790's twelve new sets of illustrations were published, exclusive of the reprints of earlier illustrations. (This flurry of interpretation continued for two more decades —seven from 1800 to 1810, five from 1810 to 1820.) Such variety of interpretation did not always do justice either to the art or the poem. But in themes of the isolated poet, or the lover's dream, the illustrations called attention to subjects completely ignored in the literary comments on the poem.

The illustrations in the eighteenth century conveyed the interpretative transitions from the hierarchical views of landscape to the expressive interrelation between man and nature. From the fusion of convention and diversity seen as inclined planes in a great chain, it moved to man as an object of nature surrounded and often engulfed by it. From illustrations of 'unified' views it moved to single fragments, representative either of 'wholes' or of significant actions. In moving from the significance of

[1] Shiels, p. 202.

background as hierarchical to the foreground as detailed and particularized, it moved from a view of eternity governed by status to eternity as connected with past and future (nature or family). And it moved finally from an interrelation of personified nature and naturalistic activity to man's representative role, both of forces which surrounded him and those which shaped him. Only Charles Catton and Henry Fuseli among the illustrators at the turn of the century saw the forces of nature, as Thomson did, in process; among the critics, such insight had to wait for William Hazlitt.

Bibliographical Afterword

ALL literary scholarship is, in one sense or another, involved with the history of ideas. But, since Arthur O. Lovejoy imposed method on this amorphous discipline, it has come to mean something special: the study of a complex of ideas in any period, or the genetic history of a complex of ideas ('an idea' has been found virtually not to exist any more). From 1923, when she first entered Lovejoy's seminar at the Johns Hopkins University, to 1962, when she retired as Chairman of the Department of English and Comparative Literature at Columbia University, Marjorie Hope Nicolson has been in the van of this intellectual movement. One demonstration of her influence upon the history of ideas is this volume, made up of contributions by her fellow-scholars and her former students; another is the list of her works with which the volume ends.

Miss Nicolson's theme, the title of a great course given first at Smith College and later at Columbia, now the title also of a collection of her shorter studies, is 'Science and Imagination.' Like twentieth-century scientists, Miss Nicolson has rearranged our views of our intellectual world. No one now would dream of teaching Donne's *Anniversary Poems* without reliance upon her studies of the new science, or the third voyage of *Gulliver's Travels* without Miss Nicolson's explanation of Swift's use of the *Philosophical Transactions of the Royal Society*, or eighteenth-century poetic imagery without connecting images of light to the influence of Newton's *Opticks*. And it would be rash to talk as in the past about the rise of Romantic interest in external Nature without recourse to her account, *Mountain Gloom and Mountain Glory*, of the change of attitude from ancient times to the nineteenth century.

Miss Nicolson's contributions to scholarship have, however, by no

307

means been limited to the impact of science upon the aesthetic imagination. In the *Conway Letters* she skilfully edited vast numbers of unpublished documents, arranging them to tell a fascinating story. In *The Breaking of the Circle* she combined literary criticism with the history of ideas to demonstrate the meaning of an idea important, both in form and content, to seventeenth-century poetry. Recently she has been at work explicating the texts of Milton's major poems. Yet in this age of long-range rockets it is significant that we honour one who has done more than any other to remind us of the long history of man's thinking about outer space. When, as now seems certain, the first intrepid human travellers land on the moon, perhaps they will carry with them Marjorie Hope Nicolson's *Voyages to the Moon*.

In the list of her works which follows, no attempt has been made to include all of Miss Nicolson's publications; they range from witty remarks on the difficulties facing women scholars to the needs of modern education. Only those publications which bear directly upon her major scholarly interests, the history of ideas and the literature of the seventeenth and eighteenth centuries, are given. That list is the only proper close to a volume made to do her honour.

J. L. C.

R. L. C.

BOOKS

1930. Conway Letters: The Correspondence of Anne, Viscountess Conway, Henry More, and their Friends, 1642–1684. New Haven: Yale University Press; London: Oxford University Press.

1935. The Microscope and English Imagination. Northampton, Mass.: Smith College. 'Studies in Modern Languages,' Vol. XVI, No. 4.

1936. A World in the Moon: A Study of the Changing Attitude toward the Moon in the Seventeenth and Eighteenth Centuries. Northampton, Mass.: Smith College. 'Studies in Modern Languages,' Vol. XVII, No. 2.

1946. Newton Demands the Muse: Newton's 'Opticks' and the Eighteenth-Century Poets. Princeton: Princeton University Press.

1948. Voyages to the Moon. New York: Macmillan. Reissued, paper, 1960.

1950. The Breaking of the Circle: Studies in the Effect of the "New Science" upon Seventeenth-Century Poetry. Evanston, Ill.: Northwestern University Press.

1956. Science and Imagination. Ithaca, New York: Cornell University Press. Reprints, with minor changes, of earlier essays.

1959. Mountain Gloom and Mountain Glory: The Development of the Aesthetics of the Infinite. Ithaca, New York: Cornell University Press.

1960. The Breaking of the Circle. Revised edition. New York: Columbia University Press; London: Oxford University Press.

1962. Milton: Major Poems and Selected Prose Works. New York: Bantam Books. A critical handbook.

Selected Shorter Studies and Articles

1925. 'The Spirit World of Milton and More,' *SP*, XXII (October), 433–52.

1926. 'Milton's "Old Damoetas," ' *MLN*, XLI (May), 293–300.
— 'Milton and Hobbes,' *SP*, XXIII (October), 405–33.

1927. 'Milton and the *Conjectura Cabbalistica*,' *PQ*, VI (January), 1–18.

1928. 'The Real Scholar Gypsy' [Francis Mercury Van Helmont] *Yale Review*, N.S. XVIII (December), 347–63.

1929. 'The Early Stage of Cartesianism in England,' *SP*, XXVI (July), 356–74.
— 'Christ's College and the Latitude-Men,' *MP*, XXVII (August) 35–53.
— 'New Material on Jeremy Taylor,' *PQ*, VIII (October), 321–34.

1930. 'George Keith and the Cambridge Platonists,' *Philosophical Review*, XXXIX (January), 36–55.

1933. George Rust, A Letter of Resolution Concerning Origen and the Chief of His Opinions. [Reproduced from the edition of 1661, with a bibliographical note by Marjorie Hope Nicolson.] New York: Columbia University Press, for the Facsimile Text Society.

1935. 'The Telescope and Imagination,' *MP*, XXXII (February), 233–60.
— 'Milton and the Telescope,' *ELH*, II (April), 1–32.
— 'The "New Astronomy" and English Literary Imagination,' *SP*, XXXII (July), 428–62.

1936. 'Thomas Paine, Edward Nares, and Mrs. Piozzi's Marginalia,' *Huntington Library Bulletin*, No. 10 (October), 103–33.

1937. 'Milton and the Bible,' in *The Bible and Its Literary Associations*, ed. by Margaret B. Crook. New York: Abingdon Press. Pages 278–308.

1937. [With Nora M. Mohler] 'The Scientific Background of Swift's "Voyage to Laputa," ' *Annals of Science*, II (July), 229–334.

— [With Nora M. Mohler] 'Swift's "Flying Island" in the "Voyage to Laputa," ' *Annals of Science*, II (October), 405–30.

1938. 'Milton's Hell and the Phelegraean Fields,' *University of Toronto Quarterly*, VII (July), 500–13.

1939. 'English Almanacs and the "New Astronomy," ' *Annals of Science*, IV (January), 1–33.

— Introduction to *Navis Aeria of B. Zamagna*, trans. by Mary B. McElwain. Northampton, Mass.: Smith College. 'Classical Studies,' No. 12. Pages 1–26.

1939–40. [With Nora M. Mohler] 'The first "Electrical" Flying Machine,' *Smith College Studies in Modern Languages*, XXI (Nos. 1–4, October-July), 143–58.

1940. 'The History of Literature and the History of Thought,' in *English Institute Annual, 1939*. New York: Columbia University Press. Pages 56–89.

— Introduction to *A Voyage to Cacklogallinia*, by Capt. Samuel Brunt [pseud.] (1727). New York: Columbia University Press, for the Facsimile Text Society.

— 'Cosmic Voyages,' *ELH*, VII (June), 83–107.

— 'Kepler, the *Somnium*, and John Donne,' *JHI*, I (June), 259–80. Reprinted 1957 in *Roots of Scientific Thought: A Cultural Perspective*, ed. by Philip P. Wiener and Aaron Noland. New York: Basic Books. Pages 306–27.

1947. 'New Philosophy Calls All in Doubt,' *Scripps College Bulletin*, XXI (No. 4), 1–21. 'Scripps College Papers,' No. 9.

1948. 'A. O. Lovejoy as Teacher,' *JHI*, IX (October), 428–38.

1951. Introduction to *The Best of Defoe's Review: An Anthology*, ed. by William L. Payne. New York: Columbia University Press. Pages ix-xxi.

1959. 'Aesthetic Implications of Newtons' *Opticks*,' in *Eighteenth-Century English Literature*, ed. by J. L. Clifford. New York: Oxford University Press, Galaxy Series. Pages 194–211. Condensed version of Chapter V of *Newton Demands the Muse*.

— 'Early Space-Travellers,' *Columbia Library Columns*, IX (November), 9–15.

— 'Many Moons,' *New York Times Magazine*, November 22, pp. 22–24.

Index

In view of the nature of this volume, some attempt has been made to provide topical headings for concepts and ideas; continued discussions of a subject have been indicated by bold type. Authors and titles mentioned in the text have for the most part been given independent entries but minor references to proper names have been excluded. Footnotes have been treated selectively, with attention to authorities cited more than once.